W9-DBL-265

CALIFORNIA
CRIMINAL LAW

Liberty without learning is always in peril; and learning without liberty is always in vain. . . . Any educated citizen who seeks to subvert the law, to suppress freedom, or to subject other human beings to acts which are less than human, degrades his heritage, ignores his learning, and betrays his obligations.

Our nation is founded on the principle that observance of the law is the eternal safeguard of liberty. . . . Even among law-abiding men, few laws are universally loved, but they are uniformly respected and not resisted. Americans are free to disagree with the law, but not to disobey it. . . .

JOHN F. KENNEDY

C.A. PANTALEONI
Rio Hondo College

JAMES C. BIGLER

CALIFORNIA CRIMINAL LAW

A GUIDE FOR POLICEMEN

Prentice-Hall, Inc., Englewood Cliffs, New Jersey

13–112565–6

Library of Congress Catalog Card Number 78–91921

Printed in the United States of America

Current printing (last digit):
10 9 8 7 6 5 4 3 2 1

Prentice-Hall International, Inc., *London*
Prentice-Hall of Australia, Pty. Ltd., *Sydney*
Prentice-Hall of Canada, Ltd., *Toronto*
Prentice-Hall of India Private Limited, *New Delhi*
Prentice-Hall of Japan, Inc., *Tokyo*

Preface

We have realized for some time that there is a great need for additional training of law enforcement personnel. Education in law enforcement has been expanding in colleges and universities in order to meet this need. Growth has been extremely rapid because of the tremendous impetus given to the training and education of law enforcement personnel by the President's Crime Commission.

When a police officer is hired, he encounters a mass of information which he is expected to master. He faces years of study, formal and informal: the pinning on of the shield does not instantly make him a policeman.

Criminal law is one of the most important subjects the law enforcement officer will study. It is usually among the core courses in any police science program at the college level (for instance, the programs certified by the California Commission on Peace Officers' Standards and Training). The criminal law area embraces an enormous amount of material; in fact, law students receive special instruction in this area to augment their legal education. However, the average law student still takes only six units in criminal law; an experienced police officer is often better versed in criminal law than a lawyer who has just passed the bar examination.

California criminal law is contained in many different codes but primarily in the penal code. This text brings together the codes that are most significant for the policeman. It is by no means comprehensive, but it does collect those sections which are pertinent to the law enforcement officer. In addition, it contains discussion of legal and enforcement aspects of the laws, written in nontechnical language, which will enable the new officer or the preservice student to understand the law and to apply it for enforcement. This book, which is directed specifically to the police officer's needs, is the only one we know of that is so oriented.

C.A.P.

J.C.B.

Acknowledgments

We gratefully acknowledge the prepublication reviews of two outstanding police educators, Paul B. Weston, Professor of Police Science at Sacramento State College, and Jack MacArthur, Coordinator of Police Science at Modesto City College, both of whom made invaluable contributions to this text.

We are indebted to the personnel of the Los Angeles Police Department and the Los Angeles County Sheriff's Department, who made numerous suggestions which were incorporated into the text. In addition we are grateful for the many contributions of material and the encouragement provided by members of the Southern California Police Training Officers Association and the staff of the Los Angeles District Attorney's Office (Evelle J. Younger, District Attorney). The guidance and recommendations of the California Commission on Peace Officers' Standards and Training and the Peace Officers' Training Unit of the California State Department of Education are also acknowledged.

The encouragement of police practitioners, police science students at Rio Hondo Junior College, and fellow instructors in the Police Educators Association of California stimulated and maintained our interest in preparing this book.

Lastly, we wish to express publicly our appreciation to our wives, who gave so unselfishly of their husbands' time and without whose assistance this book would never have reached the reader.

The Authors

C. A. PANTALEONI

Associate Professor and Coordinator, Police Science Department, Rio Hondo Junior College. A.B., M.S., California State College at Los Angeles; graduate work Loyola Law School and U.C.L.A. Former lecturer, University of Indiana, Citrus College, Pasadena City College and Cerritos College. Former Deputy Sheriff, Los Angeles County Sheriff's Department; former Investigator, Bureau of Investigation, Los Angeles District Attorney's Office. Consultant for American Association of Junior Colleges, National Sheriff's Association and State Department of Education, Peace Officer's Training. Past-president of Police Educators Association of California and Lambda Alpha Epsilon–Grand Chapter.

JAMES C. BIGLER

B.S., Ohio State University and United States Naval Academy; J.D., George Washington University; retired Colonel, U.S. Marine Corps. Former Chief, Bureau of Investigation, Los Angeles District Attorney's Office. Admitted to the bar in the District of Columbia; the California Bar and the U.S. Supreme Court.

Contents

I. GENERAL PROVISIONS OF CRIMINAL LAW

II. SPECIFIC CRIMINAL AREAS

A. Crimes Against Property

ix

I

GENERAL PROVISIONS
OF CRIMINAL LAW

*There are certain provisions of criminal law
that are or may be applicable to any and all crimes.
These consist of general defenses to crime, the
applicable degree of intent, the parties to the criminal act
and their degree of involvement, as well as the
procedural steps in arrest, trial, and punishment. Our
treatment of these matters will not include procedural
requirements. The general provisions of criminal law must be
considered in connection with all crimes.*

1

Introduction and General Provisions

Criminal law was the earliest form of control imposed upon man. In its earliest stages it was confused with religion. The prehistoric tribal chieftain enforced rules of conduct to protect his regime and to make wars on neighbors, but the conduct of one person toward another was controlled by the witch doctor or priest. Relationships between individuals in England, except where such relationships touched the king, were governed in this way through the Middle Ages. The King's Courts enforced title to land and the safety of the King's subjects because land and warriors were the basis of the feudal system. The Chancellor, a churchman, controlled the courts of equity, which in turn controlled relationships between persons and had the power to relieve the rigidity of the King's law when such rigidity "touched the chancellor's conscience."

As civilization emerged and tribes merged into kingdoms and empires, the criminal law became the creature of the state. It is the duty of the state to enact a consistent code of laws to control its citizens for their own protection and for the protection of the state. Consequently, the criminal law is imposed on any person, citizen or alien, who performs a proscribed act within the territorial boundaries of the state.

The law which developed in England as a result of royal edict or by

3

the recorded decisions of the judiciary became known as the common law. The common law was so named because it originated in custom and usage, and had become recognized by the courts. The common law included many facets of law and control of the community in addition to the criminal law. This whole body of law, largely unwritten, is distinguishable from the various Codes that were handed down and accepted by other peoples: for example, the Code of Hammurabi in Persia, Assyria, and the Middle East; and the Justinian Code which developed into the Napoleonic Code adopted in France and other European countries.

The common law was brought to America by the English colonists and became a large part of the law in all of the states including those settled mainly by continental Europeans. However, these people also brought with them the laws of their own countries (principally France and Spain), known as the civil law which is a codification of the Roman Law. As might be expected, the basic concepts of the civil law vary to some extent from those of the common law. All of these influences have been merged in California criminal law. California criminal law is codified primarily in the Penal Code of California. Certain other codes also contain criminal laws— the Health and Safety Code, Welfare Institutions Code, California Vehicle Code, etc. Several pertinent sections from these codes are discussed in future chapters.

No act or omission is a crime in California unless there is in force a valid statute or ordinance declaring the act therein defined to be punishable as a crime and prescribing a penalty for its violation. Similarly, no excuse or justification will afford a defense to a person charged with crime unless such defense is based on statute or ordinance. The "unwritten law" or "the law of necessity" has no standing in California.

STATUTORY REQUIREMENTS

For a criminal statute to be effective and valid it must be enacted by the legislative body and approved by the executive in accordance with constitutional requirements. Assuming that the statute in question is properly enacted, there remain several additional requirements. Briefly summarized these requirements are:

- The statute must be in English; Art. IV ss24 Calif. Const. It may not inflict punishment without a judicial trial; (A Bill of Attainder) Art. I ss16 Calif. Const.; Art. I ss9(3) U.S. Const.
- It may not operate retroactively by punishing an act committed before the enactment of the statute, by creating a crime where none existed when the act in question was committed, or by increasing the punishment or removing a defense for an act committed prior

to the enactment of the statute; (Ex Post Facto Law) Art. I ss16 Calif. Const.; Art. I ss9(3) U.S. Const.

- It may not be vague or uncertain with regard to the persons subject thereto or the acts or omissions required or thereby proscribed.

Where there are municipal ordinances in conflict with state laws, the municipal ordinance cannot authorize an act prohibited by state law nor can it prohibit an act which is specifically authorized by state law. Thus in cases of direct conflict the state law is controlling. Furthermore, where the state preempts a certain field of activity, if the legislative intent of the state appears to have been to occupy that entire field of activity, the controlling state law nullifies any municipal ordinance or regulation in that field which is not consistent with the state law. If the legislature of the state has not manifested an intention to preempt the field and there is neither duplication nor direct conflict, the municipal ordinance is valid.

Where a criminal statute is repealed without a saving clause in the repealing legislative act, the courts are without authority to proceed against any person charged with crime thereunder, subsequent to the effective date of the repeal. The California Government Code at ss9608 has a general saving clause (a restriction in a repealing act which is intended to save rights, pending proceedings, penalties, etc., from the annihilation which would result from an unrestricted repeal) for all criminal laws enacted by the state of California, *but not extending to municipal or local ordinances.* Repeal of repealing legislation does not revive the original legislation. It must be specifically reenacted to be effective. If the new legislation merely amends the former law, the courts have authority to enforce the law in effect at the time the crime was committed.

The American Law Institute has been studying the nation's criminal laws and has published a tentative draft of a Modern Penal Code. The Commissioners on Uniform State Laws have promulgated several uniform and model acts within specific fields: anti-gambling, desertion and nonsupport, narcotics legislation, reciprocal enforcement of Support Act. In 1963 the California legislature created a "Joint Legislative Committee for the Revision of the Penal Code" and appropriated substantial funds for the committee's use.

VENUE AND JURISDICTION

The problem of jurisdiction and venue is largely one of procedure. A necessary element of any criminal prosecution is that the court have jurisdiction and venue. While there is much similarity between these two terms in layman's language, venue can be defined as "geographical jurisdiction." The doctrine of venue therefore necessitates that a trial take place in the same county where the crime occurred. The law of venue determines which specific court or courts among those having jurisdiction should take cognizance of and determine a particular controversy.

Jurisdiction indicates the authority of the court. Misdemeanors are within the trial jurisdiction of municipal courts; felonies are within the trial jurisdiction of superior courts. Accordingly, no one may be tried for a felony in a municipal court as it lacks jurisdiction. As a further example of this, a person who has committed robbery in Los Angeles city must be tried in a court having appropriate jurisdiction; to wit, the superior court. Venue requires that it be a superior court in Los Angeles County. When a defendant requests a change of venue in a criminal proceeding, he is requesting a change of geographical location, but jurisdiction is still maintained by a similar court.

Here we will examine jurisdiction of the subject matter: Jurisdiction over the person is acquired by lawful arrest and appearance. Problems in jurisdiction over the person accused of a crime may arise in extradition proceedings. Jurisdiction is the authority vested in a court to take cognizance of and decide disputes and to impose sanctions, judgments, or sentences.

APPLICABLE STATUTES

California Constitution Article VI #5—*Superior Courts; Municipal Courts; Justice Courts; Jurisdiction; Days Open; Process; Judge Pro Tempore.* Sec. 5. The Superior Courts shall have original jurisdiction in all civil cases and proceedings (except as in this Article otherwise provided, and except, also cases and proceedings in which jurisdiction is or shall be given by law to Municipal or to Justices or other inferior courts); in all criminal cases amounting to felony, and cases of misdemeanor not otherwise provided for; and of all such special cases and proceedings as are not otherwise provided for; and said court shall have the power of Naturalization and to issue papers therefor.

The Superior Courts shall have appellate jurisdiction in such cases arising in Municipal and in Justices' and other inferior courts in their respective counties or cities and counties as may be prescribed by law. The Legislature may, in addition to any other appellate jurisdiction of the Superior Courts, also provide for the establishment of appellate departments of the Superior Court in any county or city and county wherein any Municipal Court is established, and for the constitution, regulation, jurisdiction, government and procedure of such appellate departments. Superior Courts and Justices' Courts in cities having a population of more than 40,000 inhabitants shall always be open, legal holidays and nonjudicial days excepted. The process of Superior Court shall extend to all parts of the state; provided, that all actions for the recovery of the possession of, quieting the title to, or for the enforcement of liens upon real estate, shall be commenced in the county in which the real estate, or any part thereof, affected by such action or actions, is situated. Said Superior Courts, and their judges shall have power to issue writs of mandamus, certiorari, prohibition, quo warranto, and habeas corpus on petition by or on behalf of any person in actual custody, in their respective counties. Injunctions and writs of prohibition may be issued and served on legal holidays and nonjudicial days. The process of any Municipal Court shall extend to all parts of the county or city and county in which the city is situated, where such court is established, and to such other parts of the state as may be provided by law, and such process may be executed or enforced in such manner as the Legislature shall provide. Upon stipulation of the parties litigant or their attorneys of record cause in the Superior Court or in a Municipal Court may be tried by a judge pro tempore who must be a member of the bar sworn to try the cause, and who shall be empowered to act in such capacity in the cause tried before him until the final determination thereof. The selection of such judge pro tempore, shall be subject to the approval and order of the court in which said cause is pending and shall also be subject to such regulations and orders as may be prescribed by the judicial council.

P.C. 1462—*Jurisdiction of Municipal Courts in misdemeanor cases.* Each municipal court shall have jurisdiction in all criminal cases amounting to misdemeanor, where the offense charged was committed within the county in which such municipal court is established except those of which the juvenile court is given jurisdiction and those of which other courts are given exclusive jurisdiction. Each municipal court shall have exclusive jurisdiction in all cases involving the violation of ordinances of cities or towns situated within the district in which such court is established.

LEGAL DISCUSSION

The superior court has jurisdiction of all felonies and of misdemeanors where there is no municipal court. If a municipal or justice court has jurisdiction of a particular misdemeanor, it ousts the superior court jurisdiction; hence *there is no concurrent jurisdiction.*

Any superior court in the state has jurisdiction to try any felony committed anywhere in the state and the same is true of municipal courts and misdemeanors. The question of venue is not determinative of whether jurisdiction has attached.

The general rule of venue is set up by statute.

APPLICABLE STATUTE

P.C. 777—*Jurisdiction of offenses committed in state.* Every person is liable to punishment by the laws of this state, for a public offense committed by him therein, except where it is by law cognizable exclusively in the courts of the United States; and, except as otherwise provided by law, the jurisdiction of every public offense is in any competent court within the jurisdictional territory of which it is committed.

LEGAL DISCUSSION

In general the state of California has jurisdiction over crimes which are in violation of the penal and other codes and are committed within the territorial boundaries of the state.

Excluded from California jurisdiction are:

- Crimes against federal statutes
- Crimes on the high seas
- Crimes on aircraft
- Crimes in enclave (on federal reservations within the state).

Included in California jurisdiction are:

Crimes committed in part within the state
a. Bringing stolen property into the state[1]
b. Aiding or abetting a crime within the state[2]
c. Commission of a California crime by means of an agent[3]
d. Acts within the state committed with intent to commit a crime (attempts) elsewhere[4]

Ordinarily venue lies in the county in which the crime was committed subject to the following qualifications and exceptions:

- Offense partially committed in County A and partially in County B may be prosecuted in either county.[5]
- Crime committed on county boundary or within 500 yards thereof may be prosecuted in either county.[6]
- Crime committed on a carrier may be prosecuted in any county through which the carrier passes or in that wherein the trip terminates.[7]
- Kidnapping, child stealing, false imprisonment or pandering may be prosecuted in (1) county where offense was committed, (2) county from which victim was taken, or (3) any county wherein an act of instigation, procuring, promoting or aiding the crime was committed.[8]
- Homicide may be prosecuted in the county (1) where fatal injury was inflicted, (2) where victim died, (3) where body was found.[9]
- If kidnapping is involved, the crime may be prosecuted in any of

the counties wherein parts of the kidnapping were committed or wherein any act necessary to the consummation of the crime was committed (as per P.C. 781; 784).

- Burglary, robbery, or theft may be prosecuted in the county in which the property was taken from the owner, or in the county into which the property was brought.[10]
- Sex crimes such as bigamy may be prosecuted in the county where (1) marriage took place; (2) cohabitation occurred; (3) defendant was apprehended.
- Sex crimes such as incest may be prosecuted in the county where (1) act of intercourse took place; (2) defendant was apprehended.
- Conspiracy may be prosecuted in any county where "any overt act tending to effect such conspiracy" was committed.[11]
- Nonsupport of minor child may be prosecuted in any county in which (1) child is cared for, (2) defendant is apprehended.
- Escape from penal institutions: If from state prison, may be prosecuted in any county in California.[12] If from county jail, may be prosecuted only in county maintaining jail from which escape was effected.[13]
- Criminal defamation: Libel by newspaper may be prosecuted in the county (a) in which paper is published, (b) where the libeled person resided at the time of publication.[14]
- Slander by radio or other device may be prosecuted in the county (1) where slander is uttered, (2) where slandered party resided at time of utterance.

Reasonable Doubt—Presumption of Innocence

Coupled with the burden of proof in criminal cases is (1) the presumption of innocence and (2) the doctrine of reasonable doubt. These principles require the prosecution to carry the burden of proof and establish the guilt of the defendant beyond a reasonable doubt.[15]

A reasonable doubt is not a captious possibility nor is it proof to a mathematical certainty. It is an honest, reasonable misgiving in the mind of a reasonable, unbiased person. Proof beyond reasonable doubt is required in the trial. There is no requirement for proof beyond reasonable doubt at a preliminary hearing. In an appeal it is presumed that the judgment is regular and valid until proved otherwise.

Notwithstanding the inflexible rule that the "burden of proof" is initially with the prosecution and remains there throughout the trial, there are various issues and phases of the trial where the "burden of proceeding" shifts to the defendant. The prosecution having established its case, the defendant must come forward with proof *and proceed*, otherwise he will be found guilty. Examples of such cases are:

1. Proof of insanity
2. Proof of entrapment
3. Proof of mitigating circumstances which justify or excuse the act constituting the crime
4. Proof of procedural defenses: illegal arrest, former jeopardy, statute of limitations, defendant who lacks capacity to commit crime, etc.
5. Good faith marriage when used as a defense for bigamy, rape, etc.

In the foregoing instances the prosecution, having carried the "burden of proof," is not required to disprove all possible defenses, but if such defense exists defendant must come forward with evidence and establish it or be convicted.

In addition to the affirmative defense which the defendant must establish if he seeks refuge behind it, there are various presumptions which, unless overcome by the defendant, will establish parts of the prosecution's case as part of its burden of proof. These presumptions arise because certain elements exist only in the mind of and to the exclusive attention of the defendant or because the presumed fact is a logical inference drawn from other facts. Most of these presumptions, whatever their reason for existence, are reduced to code provisions. Some that are of primary interest to law enforcement officers are:

P.C. 537—Presumption of *intent* to defraud an innkeeper from departure without an offer to pay.

P.C. 484—Presumption of *intent* to defraud an employee from hiring said employee without informing him of every unpaid labor claim.

B. & P. 12510—Presumption of *intent* to violate weights and measures law from possession of false weights or crooked scales.

P.C. 12023—Presumption of *intent* to commit a felony when a concealable firearm is *used* in commission of an offense against the person.

V.C. 10855—Presumption of embezzlement of a rented vehicle from wilful and intentional failure to return same within five days after expiration of the agreement.

P.C. 270—Presumption of *wilful nonsupport of a child* from proof of abandonment or desertion or failure to furnish the necessities of life.

HOW TO FIND THE LAW

California criminal law is based on the Penal Code. However, any code provision must be interpreted with regard to:

1. Its relation to other code provisions

2. The interpretation of its meaning as to:
   a. Meaning of words
   b. Expression of legislative intent
   c. Scope of its effect
3. Its constitutionality

The code provisions are, of course, set forth in the Penal Code. The interpretations for our purposes are confined to decisions of courts of appeal of California and the United States legislative hearings and decisions of courts of appeal in sister states. The opinions of acknowledged experts in the field of law may be a basis of interpretation where decisions are wanting.

In reading a decision we place greatest weight on what the court decided. What the court said in rationalizing its decision is "obiter dicta," and although it is authoritative, it does not speak with the same force and intensity as what the court did. It might be said that "dicta" is merely the opinion of the writer of the decision, but what the court decided is the collective thinking of all members, or at least a majority.

There are three principal publishers of the California Penal Code: (1) the West Company, (2) the Deering Company and (3) the Standard Codes. West publishes codes, law books (rules of law) and treatise for the entire United States which makes it easier to research into the federal law or the laws of sister states when necessary.

All publishers annotate their code works with references to pertinent cases. Some even include suggested forms.

Apart from the Code there are two writers on California criminal law who are widely read and frequently quoted: Witkin and Fricke. These works are primarily intended for use by courts and attorneys and are overly technical for police students.

The codes and the text are indexed in the usual manner (by case citation) and can be entered from these indices.

The case law is published in the Reporters and consists principally of decisions of the Supreme Court of California and of the various District Courts of Appeal. References to the form are abbreviated as follows:

Cal App or CA	for California District Court of Appeals
Cal or C	for California Supreme Court
Pac or P	for Pacific Reports
U.S.	for United States Supreme Court
2d	denotes second edition of the reporter

Cases reported by the Supreme Court are abbreviated: __Cal__or__ Cal 2d__, and to the DCA are abbreviated: __CA__and__CA 2d__. In each case there are two series to be noted. The figure which precedes the designation is the volume and the number following it is the page within that volume.

Examples of this are as follows:

21 Cal 315	Means Volume 21 of the California Reports (California Supreme Court), page 315
12 Cal App 2d 220	Means Volume 12 of the California Appellate Reports (District Court of Appeal), second edition, page 220

In addition to the foregoing, the West Company publishes the decisions of both the Supreme Court and the DCA in a single series. This series uses the indicia P (Pacific). The Pacific series consists of 300 volumes and then starts the Pacific Second. The Pacific series and the first 110 volumes of Pacific 2d contain decisions from all the Pacific States; thereafter a special series containing only California Reports was published in addition to the Pacific sectional reporter, and after volume 346 of Pacific 2d the edition containing only California decisions is called the California Reporter and starts over with Volume I. These are abbreviated: __P __, __P 2d__, and __CR__, the number preceding the letter being the volume and that following being the page within the volume.

To connect CA and C citations to P and CR citations, refer to the California Blue and White Book. The blue pages connect C and CA to P and CR whereas the white pages connect P and CR to C and CA.

There are numerous ways to research a question into the cases as follows:

Annotated Codes

The annotated codes will have following each section of the code a list or digest of the leading interpretative cases pertaining to that section with direct code citations to the Reporters.

Treatise

The treatise or law book footnotes and text references by citations to the applicable case law in the reports.

Encyclopedia

The principal encyclopedias are Corpus Juris Secundum and California Jurisprudence, second edition. You enter these through the indices the same as when entering the treatise, and here you will locate referenced material and supporting citations direct to the Reporters.

Digests

The West Company publishes what is known as a digest. All reported cases are digested under the various classifications in the Digest which correspond with the classifications used throughout the West system from texts to treatise to encyclopedia through Digests.

You will note in the head note of a case a principle of law and above it a caption—an outline of a key and a number. If you trace this caption and key number to the Digest, you will find your case insofar as the specific principle is concerned and along with it all other cases determining the same or closely analogous principles taken from other cases and citations referring to those cases.

Sheppard's Citator

Sheppard's citator consists primarily of two tables (1) under each section of a code or constitution all Reporter citations of all cases citing or interpreting that section and (2) under each case citation you will find every other case which cited, overruled, affirmed, distinguished or in any other way dealt with the case in question.

Black's Law Dictionary

A very complete list of words and phrases frequently used in legal discussions.

When using a code, encyclopedia, digest or treatise, always check to see if there are supplements in the form of pamphlets inserted in the back of the book as a pocket supplement or an additional supplemental volume. Then trace your provision through the supplement to determine if it has been modified, amended, repealed, etc.

DISCUSSION QUESTIONS

1. What is meant by statutory law?
2. Explain the transition from common law to statutory law.
3. Explain venue and jurisdiction.
4. Explain the trial jurisdiction of the superior court and the municipal court.
5. What is meant by burden of proof?
6. What is a case citation?
7. What are the names of the reporters for the California Supreme Court?

NOTES

[1]P.C. 27 (2); P.C. 789; P.C. 497.
[2]P.C. 27 (3); P.C. 778b.
[3]P.C. 778.
[4]P.C. 778a.
[5]P.C. 781.
[6]P.C. 782.
[7]P.C. 783.
[8]P.C. 784.
[9]P.C. 790.
[10]P.C. 786.
[11]P.C. 182; P.C. 184.
[12]P.C. 4701.
[13]P.C. 4702.
[14]Cal. Const. Art. 1 §59.
[15]P.C. 1096.

2

Elements of Crime

APPLICABLE STATUTES

P.C. 16—*Crimes; kinds—crimes, how defined.* Crimes are divided into:
1. Felonies; and,
2. Misdemeanors.[1]

P.C. 17—*Felony; misdemeanor; classification of offense punishable as felony or misdemeanor after sentence, on commitment to youth authority, or on probation.* A felony is a crime which is punishable with death or by imprisonment in the state prison. Every other crime is a misdemeanor. When a crime, punishable by imprisonment in the state prison, is also punishable by fine or imprisonment in a county jail, in the discretion of the court, it shall be deemed a misdemeanor for all purposes after a judgment imposing a punishment other than imprisonment in the state prison. Where a court commits a defendant to the youth authority upon conviction of a crime punishable, in the discretion of the court, by imprisonment in the state prison or fine or imprisonment in a county jail, the crime shall be deemed a misdemeanor.

(Where a court grants probation to a defendant without imposition of sentence upon conviction of a crime punishable in the discretion of the

15

court by imprisonment in the state prison or imprisonment in the county jail, the court may at the time of granting probation, or, on application of defendant or probation officer thereafter, declare the offense to be a misdemeanor.)[2]

P.C. 177—*Offense with no penalty prescribed; punishment.* When an act or omission is declared by a statute to be a public offense, and no penalty for the offense is prescribed in any statute, the act or omission is punishable as a misdemeanor.

H & S 11504—*"Felony offense"* and offense *"punishable as a felony" defined.* As used in this article "felony offense" and offense "punishable as a felony" refer to an offense for which the law prescribes imprisonment in the state prison as either an alternative or the sole penalty, regardless of the sentence the particular defendant received.

LEGAL DISCUSSION

In general a felony-misdemeanor is treated as a felony until sentence is pronounced reducing it to a misdemeanor.

This distinction between felonies and misdemeanors is important to the police officer in many ways. It affects the right of an officer to arrest and search where the crime is not committed in his presence; and the right of an officer to use deadly force to prevent a crime or the escape of a criminal. It also affects the criminal proceedings, by determining the duration of the statute of limitations; the severity of the sentence; and, in cases of homicide resulting from or in connection with the commission of another crime, the degree of the homicide. A homicide, whether intentional or unintentional, that results from the commission of certain felonies enumerated in P.C. 189[3] is first-degree murder; if it results from the commission of any other felony, it is second-degree murder; and if it results from the commission of a misdemeanor, it is manslaughter (P.C. 192 (2)).[4]

Crimes are also classified as "true crimes" and as "regulatory" or "public welfare" offenses. The first type constitutes an injury to the victim, either in his person or his property, or to civilization or the community as a whole. The second are constituted offenses by statute in the interests of the general welfare. The distinction is basically in the intent required as an element of the crime.

Intent

True crimes, as distinguished from regulatory or public welfare offenses, contain a mental element impossible of exact definition: *mens rea* or general criminal intent. Except in cases involving criminal negligence there must exist this state of mind which includes but is not limited to intent; it takes the form of "an evil purpose," "guilty knowledge," "a guilty mind," "a guilty or wrongful purpose." The U.S. Supreme Court in Morrissette v. U.S.[5] gives an elaborate historical review of *mens rea*.

Motive

Motive as distinguished from intent is the emotional urge or the state of mind which induces the particular act or acts which constitute the crime. Although it is not an element of the crime, it is frequently introduced in criminal prosecutions to establish intent, to help identify the criminal by removing doubt as to identity, to establish the sanity or insanity of the accused, or to establish justification or excusability of the act. The absence of motive may be introduced as an element of defense and taken into account in support of the presumption of innocence. However, proof of motive in a third person is excluded as too remote and speculative.[6]

Intent is proved by either direct or circumstantial evidence. There are in California law certain presumptions established by statute; although these are of small practical assistance, they are included here:

Code of Civil Procedure 1962 (1)—A malicious and guilty intent (is conclusively presumed), from the deliberate commission of an unlawful act, for the purpose of injury to another.

Code of Civil Procedure 1963 (2)—That an unlawful act was done with an unlawful intent (is a disputable presumption).

Code of Civil Procedure 1963 (3)—That a person intends the ordinary consequences of his voluntary act (is a disputable presumption).

These presumptions do not relieve the prosecution of the burden of proving necessary criminal intent as a fact by the introduction of competent evidence.

Specific Intent

Certain offenses require something more than the *mens rea* or general intent; there must be a specific intent to do some particular prohibited act. Examples of specific intent are conspiracy, assault, larceny, robbery, burglary, murder. Where a specific intent is required as an element of the offense, it presents a question of fact and must be proved by introducing evidence to show the circumstances attendant to the crime. Direct evidence proving intent is seldom available from anyone except the defendant. His testimony as to lack of intent is admissible, but its credibility and weight are to be determined by the trier of fact whether court or jury.[7]

The statutes describe other mental states by the use of the following language:

APPLICABLE STATUTES

P.C. 7 (1) The word "willfully," when applied to the intent with which an act is done or omitted, implies simply a purpose or willingness to commit the act, or make the omission referred to. It does not require any intent to violate law, or to injure another, or to acquire any advantage;

P.C. 7 (2) The words "neglect," "negligence," "negligent," and "negligently" import a want of such attention to the nature or probable consequences of the act or omission as a prudent man ordinarily bestows in acting in his own concerns;

P.C. 7 (3) The word "corruptly" imports a wrongful design to acquire or cause some pecuniary or other advantage to the person guilty of the act or omission referred to, or to some other person;

P.C. 7 (4) The words "malice" and "maliciously" import a wish to vex, annoy, or injure another person or an intent to do a wrongful act established either by proof or presumption of law;

P.C. 7 (5) The word "knowingly" imports a knowledge that the facts exist which bring the act or omission within the provisions of this code. It does not require any knowledge of the unlawfulness of such act or omission;

P.C. 7 (6) The word "bribe" signifies anything of value or advantage, present or prospective, or any promise or undertaking to give any, asked, given, or accepted, with a corrupt intent to influence, unlawfully, the person to whom it is given, in his action, vote, or opinion, in any public or official capacity.

Transferred Intent

The theory of transferred intent is applied principally in assault and homicide cases. When A intends to murder B but kills C by mistake, the intent to murder B is transferred to create the crime of murder in C's death. Similarly, where a fatality results from the intended commission of a crime, the intent to commit the crime is transferred to supply the intent to establish the homicide. (See the preceding discussion of felonies and misdemeanors.)

Absence of Intent

Those offenses which have been heretofore referred to as "regulatory offenses" or "public welfare offenses" are punishable despite the lack of a criminal intent or a specific intent. The need for their regulation is created by our complex and fast-moving civilization. A few examples are traffic offenses, pure food and drug offenses, violations of zoning and building and safety codes.

Criminal Negligence

It should be noted that under P.C. 205 and P.C. 7 (2) criminal negligence may be sufficient to constitute a crime without intent. However, where a specific intent is required, criminal negligence will not suffice. To constitute criminal negligence the act must amount to a "gross," "criminal," or "culpable" departure from the standard of due care. Omissions to act where there is a duty to act, even though not amounting to negligence, are by statute punishable as crimes in the "regulatory" or "public welfare" category; for example:

1. Failure to render tax return
2. Failure to keep adequate records
3. Failure to collect or pay taxes
4. Failure to comply with health or safety regulations
5. Failure to support spouse, child or parent

Corpus Delicti

In every prosecution for crime it is necessary to establish the corpus delicti, i.e., "the body of the crime" or the "elements of the crime" consisting of (1) the fact of injury, loss or harm; and (2) the existence of a criminal agency as its cause. Thus in homicide the showing of a dead body is not of itself establishment of a corpus delicti; it must be also shown that a criminal agency caused the death. Identity of the person responsible for the crime is not a part of corpus delicti.

No part of the corpus delicti can be proved by admissions or confessions of the defendant. Such statements cannot be admitted into evidence until the corpus delicti is established. The corpus delicti need not be shown beyond a reasonable doubt. A prima facie showing will suffice. Although confessions or admissions made outside the courtroom are excluded pending proof of the corpus delicti, a co-defendant's testimony in court will establish the corpus delicti.

The old English rule in murder cases required one of the elements of the corpus delicti to be established by direct evidence; however, the majority and the California rule permit establishment of every element of the corpus delicti by circumstantial evidence.

APPLICABLE STATUTE

P.C. 20—*To constitute crime there must be unity of act and intent.* In every crime or public offense there must exist a union, or joint operation of act and intent, or criminal negligence.

LEGAL DISCUSSION

The act and the required intent or negligence must concur in point of time and operate jointly. An intent acquired subsequent to the act constituting the crime will not sustain the proof of the crime. The act must be in violation of law.

A criminal act is usually an affirmative, voluntary physical manifestation of the defendant's will. However, the following are exceptions which satisfy the requirements:

1. Solicitation of another to commit a crime—P.C. 653f[8]
2. Agreement in conspiracy—P.C. 182[9]
3. Possession of prohibited items
   Concealed weapons—P.C. 12000
   Narcotics—H & S 11500
   Obscene Matter—P.C. 311

Although not mentioned in P.C. 20, a failure to act where required (a negative act) may be punishable. The duty to act must be established by statute or in rare cases by the relationship of the parties. Examples of statutory requirements, as noted previously, are: failure to make reports or keep records for tax purposes; failure to pay tax; failure to render aid to the victim of an accident; failure to support spouse, child or parent.

The courts have encountered great difficulty in resolving questions of mergers, concurrence, multiplicity, and inclusion of offenses. No one rule or one set of rules has been developed. These plague the lawyer in forming his indictment or information, in the form and consistency of verdicts, in enforcing the provisions against multiple punishment for a single act or omission (P.C. 654), or in determining a question of former jeopardy. Where, for example, there are several thefts each amounting to less than $200, but totaling more than that amount, is the suspect guilty of petty or grand theft? Is it a misdemeanor or a felony? What are the officer's powers of arrest, search, and use of deadly force where the crime is not committed in his presence?

Usually one act with one effect constitutes one offense. But how about the single shot that kills several persons, the single arson that kills many people, the simultaneous robbing and kidnapping of two people. California law holds that in these cases there are as many offenses as there are victims.[10]

On the other hand, examples of multiple victims, objects, or overt acts considered to be a single offense include a conspiracy with multiple object and overt acts; receipt of goods stolen from several owners;[11] defrauding an individual of property and money in a single transaction;[12] obtaining a succession of payments by a single false representation;[13] the possession of two or more firearms at one time.[14]

APPLICABLE STATUTE—MULTIPLE PUNISHMENT

> P.C. 654—*Acts made punishable by different provisions of this code.* An act or omission which is made punishable in different ways by different provisions of this code may be punished under either of such provisions, but in no case can it be punished under more than one; an acquittal or conviction and sentence under either one bars a prosecution for the same act or omission under any other. In the cases specified in sections 648, 667, and 668, the punishments therein prescribed must be substituted for those prescribed for a first offense, if the previous conviction is charged in the indictment and found by the jury.

LEGAL DISCUSSION

Generally a single act violating several statutes gives rise to as many offenses, separately indictable, and not subject to a plea of former jeopardy; but P.C. 654 prevents multiple punishment.

On the other hand separate acts violating the same statute and affecting the same victim are separately indictable, not subject to a plea of former jeopardy, and separately punishable: for example, several acts of incest.[15]

Where several similar acts involve multiple victims as in a succession of petty thefts, but each of the acts is done pursuant to a general plan, the entire transaction is regarded as a single crime amounting to a felony.[16]

If we find all of the elements of Crime A in Crime B but Crime B has some additional elements, then Crime A is a lesser included offense in Crime B. Conviction or acquittal of either "A" or "B" cannot be successfully pleaded as a former jeopardy in a subsequent trial for the other offense. Where all of the same elements are found in both crimes, they are described as necessarily included and a conviction or acquittal of one will sustain the successful interposition of a plea of former jeopardy in the second trial.

APPLICABLE STATUTE—ATTEMPTS

P.C. 664—*Penalties for attempts.* Every person who attempts to commit any crime, but fails, or is prevented or intercepted in the perpetration thereof, is punishable, where no provision is made by law for the punishment of such attempts, as follows:

1. *Offense punishable by five years or more.* If the offense so attempted is punishable by imprisonment in the state prison for five years, or more, or by imprisonment in a county jail, the person guilty of such attempt is punishable by imprisonment in the state prison, or in a county jail, as the case may be, for a term not exceeding one-half the longest term of imprisonment prescribed upon a conviction of the offense so attempted; provided, however, that if the crime attempted is one in which there is no maximum sentence set by law or in which the maximum sentence is life imprisonment or death the person guilty of such attempt shall be punishable by imprisonment in the state prison for a term of not more than 20 years.

2. *Offense punishable by less than five years.* If the offense so attempted is punishable by imprisonment in the state prison for any term less than five years, the person guilty of such attempt is punishable by imprisonment in the county jail for not more than one year.

3. *Offense punishable by fine.* If the offense so attempted is punishable by a fine, the offender convicted of such attempt is punishable by a fine not exceeding one-half the largest fine which may be imposed upon a conviction of the offense so attempted.

4. *Offense punishable by imprisonment and fine.* If the offense so attempted is punishable by imprisonment and by a fine, the offender convicted of such attempt may be punished by both imprisonment and fine, not exceeding one-half the longest term of imprisonment and one-half the largest fine which may be imposed upon a conviction of the offense so attempted.

LEGAL DISCUSSION

An attempt to commit a crime is a crime in itself, the punishment of which is related to that resulting from conviction of the completed offense. It consists of (1) the specific intent to commit a particular crime and (2) a direct, ineffectual act done toward its commission. The act must be more than mere preparation; it must, in fact, be such that the completed crime would result but for the interruption.

Where attempt is charged and the completed crime is proved, or where an attempt to commit Crime "A" results in actual completion of Crime "B," P.C. 663 and P.C. 665 control.

APPLICABLE STATUTES

P.C. 663—*Attempts to commit crimes, when punishable.* Any person may be convicted of an attempt to commit a crime, although it appears on the trial that the crime intended or attempted was perpetrated by such person in pursuance of such attempt, unless the court, in its discretion, discharges the jury and directs such person to be tried for such crime.

P.C. 665—*Restrictions upon the preceding sections.* The last two sections do not protect a person who, in attempting unsuccessfully to commit a crime, accomplishes the commission of another and different crime, whether greater or less in guilt, from suffering the punishment prescribed by law for the crime committed.

LEGAL DISCUSSION

The area of attempts is expanded by statute in specific cases to include conduct which under P.C. 664 would not constitute attempts:

- Placing flammable substances or device with requisite intent— arson (P.C. 451a)
- Entering train, interfering with controls with intent to rob—train robbery (P.C. 214)
- Statutes prohibiting the possession of deadly weapons capable of concealment or burglar's tools, etc. (P.C. 466[17] and P.C. 467)

It is frequently urged that there can be no punishable attempt where the crime is impossible of consummation, for example, where a dummy is shot in the belief that it is a wife's paramour. There appears to be no fixed concept of this law of impossibility. If there is an *apparent* ability to commit the crime in the way attempted, the attempt is indictable even though, unknown to the person making the attempt, the crime cannot be committed because the means employed are in fact unsuitable or because of extrinsic facts, such as the nonexistence of some essential object or the existence of an obstruction by the intended victim or by a third person.

APPLICABLE STATUTES

P.C. 153—*Compounding crimes.* Every person who, having knowledge of the actual commission of a crime, takes money or property of another, or any gratuity or reward, or any engagement, or promise thereof, upon any agreement or understanding to compound or conceal such crime, or to abstain from any prosecution thereof, or to withhold any evidence thereof, except in the cases provided for by law, in which crimes may be compromised by leave of court, is punishable as follows:

1. By imprisonment in the state prison not exceeding five years, or in a county jail not exceeding one year, where the crime was punishable by death or imprisonment in the state prison for life;

2. By imprisonment in the state prison not exceeding three years, or in the county jail not exceeding six months, where the crime was punishable by imprisonment in the state prison for any other term than for life;

3. By imprisonment in the county jail not exceeding six months, or by fine not exceeding five hundred dollars, where the crime was a misdemeanor.

P.C. 1377—*Certain offenses for which the party injured has a civil action may be compromised.* When the person injured by an act constituting a misdemeanor has a remedy by a civil action, the offense may be compromised as provided in the next section, except when it is committed:

1. By or upon an officer of justice, while in the execution of the duties of his office;
2. Riotously;
3. With an intent to commit a felony.

P.C. 1378—*Compromise to be by permission of the court. Order thereon to bar another prosecution.* If the person injured appears before the court in which the action is pending at any time before trial, and acknowledges that he has received satisfaction for the injury, the court may, in its discretion, on payment of the costs incurred, order all proceedings to be stayed upon the prosecution, and the defendant to be discharged therefrom; but in such case the reasons for the order must be set forth therein, and entered on the minutes. The order is a bar to another prosecution for the same offense.

LEGAL DISCUSSION

The crime of compounding crime consists of three elements:

1. Commission of crime and defendant's knowledge thereof
2. Receipt of consideration pursuant to voluntary agreement
3. Agreement not to prosecute, etc.

It is to be distinguished from misprision of felony (knowing concealment of a felony by an affirmative act) and from extortion (consideration passing under threat of prosecution).

Attention is directed to P.C. 1377, P.C. 1378, P.C. 1379, which provide the basic law to be considered in compromising of crimes limited to misdemeanors.

DISCUSSION QUESTIONS

1. Define misdemeanor and felony.
2. What is the difference between intent and motive?
3. Define corpus delicti.
4. Explain the relationship between act and intent.
5. What are the elements of the crime of attempt?
6. What is meant by former or double jeopardy?

NOTES

[1]P.C. 16, amended in the 1968 Legislature, is now: "... *Crimes and public offenses include*:
1. Felonies; ...
2. Misdemeanors; and
3. Infractions." (Changes or additions in text are indicated by underline.)

[2]P.C. 17, amended in the 1968 Legislature, is as follows: "A felony is a crime which is punishable with death or by imprisonment in the state prison. Every other crime or public offense is a misdemeanor except those offenses that are classified as infractions. When a crime, punishable by imprisonment in the state prison, is also punishable by fine or imprisonment in a county jail, in the discretion of the court, it shall be deemed a misdemeanor for all purposes after a judgment imposing a punishment other than imprisonment in the state prison. Where a court commits a defendant to the Youth Authority upon conviction of a crime punishable, in the discretion of the court, by imprisonment in the state prison or fine or imprisonment in a county jail, the crime shall be deemed a misdemeanor.

Where a court grants probation to a defendant without imposition of sentence upon conviction of a crime punishable in the discretion of the court by imprisonment in the state prison or imprisonment in the county jail, the court may at the time of granting probation, or, on application of defendant or probation officer thereafter, declare the offense to be a misdemeanor."

P.C. 1042.5 was added under the 1968 Legislature and is as follows: "1042.5 *Trial of Infraction*. Trial of an infraction shall be by the court, but when a defendant has been charged with an infraction and with a public offense for which there is a right to jury trial and a jury trial is not waived, the court may order that the offenses be tried together by jury or that they be tried separately with the infraction being tried by the court either in the same proceeding or a separate proceeding as may be appropriate."

The effect of the above legislative changes is basically administrative and procedural in nature. It deprives the individual of his right to a jury trial where his offense is an infraction rather than a misdemeanor. The police officer still handles the offender on an infraction in the same manner as he would a misdemeanor.

[3]See Homicide, Chapter 13.

[4]See Homicide, Chapter 13.

[5]342 US 246; 72 SCT 240; 96 LEd 288.

[6]People v. Perkins, 8 C 2d 502; 66 P 631; 121 ALR 1362.

[7]People v. McAuliff 154 CA 2d 332; 316 P 2d 381;
People v. Cabaltero, 31 CA 2d 52; 87 P 2d 364.

[8]See Chapter 3.

[9]See Chapter 3.

[10]People v. Majors, 65 C 138; 3 P 597;
People v. Brannon, 70 CA 225; 233 P 88;
People v. DeCausas, 150 CA 2d 274; 309 P 2d 835;
People v. Gaither, 173 CA 2d 662; 343 P 2d 799;
People v. Langonarisino, 97 CA 2d 92; 217 P 2d 124;
People v. Knowles, 35 C 2d 175; 217 P 2d 1;
Neal v. Calif., 55 C 2d 11; 9 CR 607; 357 P 2d 839.

[11]People v. Smith, 26 C 2d 854; 161 P 2d 941.

[12]People v. Woods, 37 C 2d 584; 233 P 2d 897.

[13]People v. Bailey, 55 C 2d 514; 11 CR 543; 360 P 2d 39.

[14]People v. Puppillo, 100 CA 559; 280 P 545.

[15]People v. Sanders, 103 CA 2d 200; 229 P 2d 76.

[16]People v. Bailey, 55 C 2d 514; 11 CR 543; 360 P 2d 39.

[17]See Chapter 19, Deadly Weapons Control Laws.

PRINCIPALS
ACCESSORIES
ACCOMPLICES
CONSPIRACY
SOLICITATION

3

Parties to Crime

APPLICABLE STATUTES

P.C. 30—*Classification of parties to crime.* The parties to crime are classified as:
1. Principals; and
2. Accessories.

P.C. 31—*Who are principals.* All persons concerned in the commission of a crime, whether it be felony or misdemeanor, and whether they directly commit the act constituting the offense, or aid and abet in its commission, or, not being present, have advised and encouraged its commission, and all persons counseling, advising, or encouraging children under the age of fourteen years, lunatics or idiots, to commit any crime, or who, by fraud, contrivance, or force, occasion the drunkenness of another for the purpose of causing him to commit any crime, or who, by threats, menaces, command, or coercion, compel another to commit any crime, are principals in any crime so committed.

LEGAL DISCUSSION

There are only two classifications of persons involved in the commission of crime in California:

1. Principals; and
2. Accessories.

The term "principal" has reference to all parties involved in the commission of a crime, whether it be felony or misdemeanor, while the term "accessory" refers only to felonies. There is no such thing as an accessory to a misdemeanor in California.

Under the common law these classifications were further broken down to:

1. Principals in the first degree;
2. Principals in the second degree;
3. Accessory before the fact; and
4. Accessory after the fact.

A principal in the first degree was the person who actually committed the crime, such as the one who struck the fatal blow in murder.

A principal in the second degree was the one who was actually present at the commission, who aided and abetted the perpetrator but did not actually commit the crime. Mere presence at the scene was not enough, as he might be an innocent bystander. He must aid and abet the perpetrator—for example, by acting as a lookout in a robbery or burglary—to assure success in the accomplishment of the unlawful purpose.

Principals in the first and second degree were equally guilty of the offense, and subject to identical punishments. The distinction between them, therefore, was purely one of terminology.

An "accessory before the fact" was one who counseled, commanded, procured, or otherwise encouraged the guilty party to commit the crime, but was not present at the actual commission of the offense. He was as guilty and subject to the same punishment as the principal in the first or second degree. The only distinction between a principal in the second degree and an accessory before the fact was that the former was present while the latter was not. According to the then existing procedural rules, no conviction was possible if the defendant was charged as a principal and proved to be an accessory, or was charged as an accessory and proved to be a principal. An accessory could not be tried until after the conviction of the principal unless both were tried jointly, in which case the jury could not consider the question of guilt of the accessory until after they had first found the principal to be guilty. If the principal was never apprehended, or had died, the accessory could not be brought to justice. It became apparent that the distinction among principals in the first degree, principals in the second degree, and accessories before the fact needed to be eliminated entirely and all such parties be made principals. The California legislature did just that by enacting section 971 of the Penal Code entitled: "Distinction Between Accessory Before the Fact and Principals Abrogated: All Concerned Prosecuted, etc. as Principals: Allegations," which, as amended in 1951, reads as follows:

> The distinction between an accessory before the fact and a principal, and between principals in the first and second degree is abrogated; and all persons concerned in the commission of a crime, who by the operation of other provisions of this code are principals therein, shall hereafter be prosecuted, tried and punished as principals and no other facts need be alleged in any accusatory pleading against any such person than are required in an accusatory pleading against a principal.

By the first sentence of P.C. 31—Principals—"All persons concerned in the commission of a crime, whether it be felony or misdemeanor"—we find that the designation "principal" applies to all crimes, misdemeanors as well as felonies. The next portion of that sentence, "whether they directly commit the act . . . or aid and abet in its commission," needs some explanation. The phrase "whether they directly commit the act" is self-explanatory. The word "aid" means to support, help, assist, or strengthen. It must be distinguished from its synonym "encourage," the difference being that "aid" connotes active support and assistance, while "encourage" does not; and it must be distinguished from "abet," which implies necessary criminality in the act while "aid," standing alone, does not.

The words "aid" and "abet" are nearly synonymous as generally used; but, strictly speaking, "aid" does not imply guilty knowledge or felonious intent, whereas "abet" includes knowledge of the wrongful purpose and counsel and encouragement in the commission of the crime.

Again, going back to P.C. 31—"and all persons counseling, advising, or encouraging children under the age of fourteen years, lunatics or idiots, to commit any crime. . . ." Here we have a situation where the person who commits the crime, such as a child under the age of fourteen, a lunatic or idiot, might not be guilty of any crime, as P.C. 26 refers to those people as being incapable of committing crimes; yet the person who counseled, advised, or encouraged them to perform the prohibited act would be subject to prosecution as a principal by virtue of section 31. In 1919, when San Pedro was a city separate from Los Angeles, the parents of a four-year-old child who encouraged the child to use a tricycle on the sidewalks of the city in violation of an ordinance were guilty of violation of that ordinance as principals.[1]

Again, looking at section 31—"or who, by fraud, contrivance, or force, occasion the drunkenness of another for the purpose of causing him to commit any crime . . ."—one example would be causing a person to become intoxicated by means of fraud, contrivance, or force for the purpose of making him participate in an act of sex perversion; or causing the intoxication of a married woman to induce her to commit adultery.

Section 31 continues: "or who by threats, menaces, command, or coercion, compel another to commit any crime, are principals in any crime so committed." We might group those four words—threats, menaces, command, or coercion—under one heading and call it "compulsion," for the phraseology of the section requires that the innocent partner be compelled to commit the offense through this means.

APPLICABLE STATUTE

> P.C. 32—*Who are accessories.* Every person who, after a felony has been committed, harbors, conceals or aids a principal in such felony, with the intent that said principal may avoid or escape from arrest, trial, conviction or punishment, having knowledge that said principal has committed such felony or has been charged with such felony or convicted thereof, is an accessory to such felony.

LEGAL DISCUSSION

As stated previously, there is no longer an "accessory before the fact" in California. We only have *one* type of accessory; therefore, we no longer use the terms "accessory before the fact" and "accessory after the fact" but merely the general term "accessory."

Note that section 32 begins: "Every person who, *after a felony has been committed . . .*" It applies only to felonies; there is no such thing as an accessory to a misdemeanor.

"To harbor a person" means to receive clandestinely and without lawful authority a person for the purpose of so concealing him that another having the right to lawful custody of such person shall be deprived of same.

The word "conceal," as used in this section, means more than a simple withholding of knowledge possessed by a party that a felony has been committed. It includes the element of some affirmative act on the part of the person tending to or looking toward the concealment of the commission of the felony. Mere silence after knowledge of the commission of a felony is not sufficient to constitute the party an accessory. The word "charged" as used in this section means a formal complaint, indictment, or information filed against the criminal; or possibly an arrest without warrant might be sufficient.

In order, then, to successfully prosecute a person for the crime of accessory, we have to establish in the evidence that he had actual knowledge that the principal had committed a felony, had been charged with a felony, or had been convicted thereof; that, with this knowledge, he either harbored, concealed, or aided the principal; and that he did so with a specific intent —i.e., that the harboring, concealing, or aiding of the principal would assist him in avoiding arrest, trial, conviction, or punishment.

APPLICABLE STATUTES—ACCESSORIES

P.C. 33—*Accessories; punishment.* Except in cases where a different punishment is prescribed, an accessory is punishable by a fine not exceeding five thousand dollars, or by imprisonment in the state prison not exceeding five years or in a county jail not exceeding one year, or by both such fine and imprisonment.

P.C. 791—*Of an indictment against an accessory.* In the case of an accessory, as defined in Section 32, in the commission of a public offense, the jurisdiction is in any competent court within the jurisdictional territory of which the offense of the accessory was committed, notwithstanding the principal offense was committed in another jurisdictional territory.

LEGAL DISCUSSION

Therefore, if a felony is committed in San Francisco, and the perpetrator flees to Los Angeles where someone performs an act making him an accessory to such felony, the accessory would be prosecuted in Los Angeles county, notwithstanding the fact that the principal would be prosecuted in the city and county of San Francisco.

APPLICABLE STATUTE

P.C. 1111—*Conviction on testimony of accomplice.* A conviction can not be had upon the testimony of an accomplice unless it be corroborated by such other evidence as shall tend to connect the defendant with the commission of the offense; and the corroboration is not sufficient if it merely shows the commission of the offense or the circumstances thereof.

An accomplice is hereby defined as one who is liable to prosecution for the identical offense charged against the defendant on trial in the cause in which the testimony of the accomplice is given.

LEGAL DISCUSSION

A person who knowingly, voluntarily, and with common intent with the principal offender unites in the commission of a crime is an accomplice. The purpose of this section is to define an accomplice and the rule of evidence governing accomplicity.

An "accomplice" is one "associated with and culpably implicated with others in the commission of a crime, all being principals." One who could be prosecuted as a principal would be an accomplice. The term is used to define a situation from which certain collateral consequences flow, such as the need of corroboration of testimony or the competency of an accomplice as a witness. It is commonly applied to those testifying against their fellow-criminals; if in the course of a trial any of the latter are called as witnesses, although they are principals, they are referred to as accomplices. We might say, therefore, that any principal or any conspirator, when called upon to testify in the trial of his co-conspirators, becomes identified as an accomplice.

APPLICABLE STATUTE

P.C. 182—*Criminal conspiracy: Acts constituting; punishment; venue.* If two or more persons conspire:

1. To commit any crime.
2. Falsely and maliciously to indict another for any crime, or to procure another to be charged or arrested for any crime.
3. Falsely to move or maintain any suit, action or proceeding.
4. To cheat and defraud any person of any property, by any means which are in themselves criminal, or to obtain money or property by false pretenses or by false promises with fraudulent intent not to perform such promises.
5. To commit any act injurious to the public health, to public morals, or to pervert or obstruct justice, or the due administration of the laws.
6. To commit any crime against the person of the President or Vice-President of the United States, the governor of any state or territory, any United States justice or judge, or the secretary of any of the executive departments of the United States.

They are punishable as follows:

When they conspire to commit any crime against the person of any official specified in subdivision 6, they are guilty of a felony and are punishable by imprisonment in the state prison for not less than 10 years.

When they conspire to commit any other felony, they shall be punishable in the same manner and to the same extent as is provided for the punishment of the said felony. If the felony is one for which different punishments are prescribed for different degrees, the jury or court which finds the defendant guilty thereof shall determine the degree of the felony defendant conspired to commit. If the degree is not so determined, the punishment for conspiracy to commit such felony shall be that prescribed for the lesser degree, except in the case of conspiracy to commit murder, in which case the punishment shall be that prescribed for murder in the first degree.

If the felony is conspiracy to commit two or more felonies which have different punishments and the commission of such felonies constitutes but one offense of conspiracy, the penalty shall be that prescribed for the felony which has the greater maximum term.

When they conspire to do an act described in subdivision 4 of this section, they shall be punishable by imprisonment in the state prison for not more than 10 years or by imprisonment in the county jail for not more than 1 year, or by a fine not exceeding five thousand dollars ($5,000), or both.

When they conspire to do any of the other acts described in this section they shall be punishable by imprisonment in the county jail for not more than one year, or in the state prison for not more than three years, or by a fine not exceeding five thousand dollars ($5,000), or both.

All cases of conspiracy may be prosecuted and tried in the superior court of any county in which any overt act tending to effect such conspiracy shall be done.

LEGAL DISCUSSION

As regards conspirators as parties to crimes, we can define a conspiracy as a criminal partnership wherein two or more persons agree to participate in some illegal activity.

The elements of this crime would therefore include:

1. The *agreement* to do a prohibited act.

2. *Two or more persons*—a violation cannot result in conviction where only one defendant is involved; however, all co-conspirators do not have to be prosecuted. They may be accomplices and testify. Hence a conspiracy may have involved many persons but the prosecution of only two defendants. This frequently occurs in bookmaking cases where all bettors are "technical" or "legal" accomplices.

3. *Overt Act*—This may be an act of preparation as well as one of furtherance or completion. It need only be done by one co-conspirator; his act is binding on all parties to the conspiracy. The act need not be sufficient to amount to an attempt, but it must show "the meeting of the minds" and must have progressed further than just the agreement.

All conspiracies are felonious. Hence a felony charge may be filed for conspiracy to commit a misdemeanor, for example, petty theft. The charge of conspiracy is in addition to the substantive charge; hence a charge of conspiracy to commit robbery as well as a charge of robbery itself are possible. The crime itself or the attempted crime may constitute one of the overt acts of the conspiracy.

Contrary to concepts of common law and previous case decisions a conspiracy involving only husband and wife is prosecutable.[2] The courts now hold that the arithmetic of "one and one make two" applies, so that the charge is logical.

It is interesting to note the various penalties applied to this crime. Also, section 182 applies to agreements to commit acts that are not necessarily crimes. In general subsections 2, 3, 4, and 5 deal with obstructing the administration of justice or with injurious acts involving public health or morals.

One overt act in any prosecutable conspiracy must have been committed within the state. Venue for trial is in any county within which an overt act takes place.

ENFORCEMENT ASPECTS

Section 182 is one of primary applicability to police officers. Whenever there are two or more defendants involved in an offense, consideration should be given to a possible conspiracy complaint.

Discretion should be exercised to avoid unintended use of this section by indiscriminate attempts to "upgrade misdemeanors into felonies." The prosecuting attorney will normally make the decision. The section has been used very effectively in prosecutions of individuals who have defrauded the public through false representations which constitute petit theft. Throughout the nation there are unscrupulous persons who prey on local homeowners and households relying on the lack of complaint on the part of the victim. There have been roofs repaired which have been guaranteed forever, and by the first rainfall the suspects are in another town making more claims to new victims. While the Music Man is a well-known play, it is not uncommon that musical instruments have been sold with representations of lessons, talent and band participation that have bilked local communities. Here the victim thought that he had purchased an entire program of lessons assuring his child's fame and fortune, and then realized that he has only paid an exorbitant price for an inferior horn. Under certain flagrant instances these types of cases constitute petit theft and may be prosecuted under the conspiracy section.

A charge of conspiracy requires the prosecutor to prepare an individual complaint. There are no general forms for this as the overt acts will vary in each case. Therefore, there exists a degree of unfamiliarity with these pleadings. The police officer may assist the prosecutor by having available information on possible overt acts.

At least one or more overt acts must be alleged in a conspiracy indictment or information. However, other acts not alleged may be introduced to further establish the conspiracy. Therefore, the admissibility of other acts may be a material factor for a successful prosecution.

Often one of the co-conspirators is the more active in a crime. The "master-mind" is, however, bound by the acts of any other co-conspirator. There is no apportioning of guilt in this charge; all parties are equally guilty.

Police officers should remember that accomplices (co-conspirators) may establish the corpus delicti of the crime, but additional corroborative evidence is required for conviction.

APPLICABLE STATUTE

P.C. 653f.—*Soliciting commission of a crime.* Every person who solicits another to offer or accept or join in the offer or acceptance of a bribe, or to commit or join in the commission of murder, robbery, burglary, grand theft, receiving stolen property, extortion, rape by force and violence, perjury, subornation of perjury, forgery, or kidnapping, is punishable by imprisonment in the county jail not longer than one year or in the state prison not longer than five years, or by fine of not more than five thousand dollars. Such offense must be proved by the testimony of two witnesses, or of one witness and corroborating circumstances.

LEGAL DISCUSSION

Common law made it a misdemeanor to solicit a person to commit a felony. Today's statutes recognize the crime but, as in the California statute, restrict it to certain named crimes. Sections of the California Codes deal with specific forms of solicitation, in addition to those enumerated in P.C. 653f., as follows:

- Solicitation for a prostitute—P.C. 266h
- Solicitation of a minor's participation in narcotics offenses— H & S 11502
- Solicitation of a woman to submit to treatment inducing miscarriage—P.C. 276
- Solicitation of sabotage—Military or Veterans Code 1673

Solicitation itself is a distinct offense. The solicitor is guilty of the offense even though the person solicited immediately rejects the request or proposal. But if the crime is committed, the solicitor is guilty both of soliciting and of committing the crime.

Solicitation as distinguished from conspiracy does not require an agreement to act nor an overt act. If the solicitor believes the crime or act can be committed, it is immaterial that such act or crime is either impossible of commission at the time or becomes impossible before commission.

In California the law on solicitation is a misdemeanor-felony, and it must be proved by the testimony of two witnesses, or of one witness and corroborating circumstances.

ENFORCEMENT ASPECTS

It should be noted that police investigation should emphasize that the person being solicited in all likelihood will become a pseudo-accomplice. The fact that the person agrees to go along with the solicitor under the direction of law enforcement officials does not amount to entrapment.

In order to issue a complaint, the prosecuting attorney must be shown evidence that a crime was actually solicited. Not only must it be one of the specific crimes covered in the Code section, but the corpus delicti of the crime must be indicated. Law enforcement officers must expend every effort to secure the necessary corroborating evidence. Frequently this is one of the difficult areas.

SUMMARY AND GENERAL CONSIDERATIONS

Identification of the principals to a crime is extremely important, for it involves the identity of persons to be arrested. A law enforcement officer should always clearly identify the persons who are likely suspects.

The principals may be co-conspirators or accomplices, at the discretion of the prosecuting attorney. Whenever an officer deals with an accomplice, keep in mind that the testimony must be sufficient to establish the corpus delicti (required only to a prima facie degree). Proof of guilt, however, will have to be established by corroborating evidence. "Legal" accomplices may sometimes be the chief witnesses. This happens frequently, as we have noted, in bookmaking cases where the individual bettors (probably the victims) are legal accomplices. Rarely is there any thought of prosecuting them, and they frequently give testimony in the trial which charges the bookmaker. The matter of corroborating evidence becomes extremely important when the officer realizes that the testimony of 100 bettors is not sufficient to convict a bookmaker but merely establishes the corpus of the crime (P.C. 337a).

DISCUSSION QUESTIONS

1. Define principals.
2. Define accessories.
3. Define accomplice.
4. What are the elements of the crime of conspiracy?
5. Discuss the difference in the overt act for conspiracy as compared to attempt.
6. Give an example of a crime of solicitation.

NOTES

[1]Mueller v. Standard Oil, 180 C 260; 180 P 605.
[2]People v. Pierce, 163 CA 2d 460; 329 P 2d 508.

4

Defenses to Crime

APPLICABLE STATUTE

P.C. 26—*Who are capable of commiting crimes.* All persons are capable of committing crimes except those belonging to the following classes:

One—Children under the age of fourteen, in the absence of clear proof that at the time of committing the act charged against them, they knew its wrongfulness;

Two—Idiots;

Three—Lunatics and insane persons;

Four—Persons who committed the act or made the omission charged under an ignorance or mistake of fact, which disproves any criminal intent;

Five—Persons who committed the act charged without being conscious thereof;

Six—Persons who committed the act or made the omission charged through misfortune or by accident, when it appears that there was no evil design, intention, or culpable negligence;

Seven—Married women (except for felonies) acting under the threats, command, or coercion of their husbands;

Eight—Persons (unless the crime be punishable with death) who committed the act or made the omission charged under threats or menaces sufficient to show that they had reasonable cause to and did believe their lives would be endangered if they refused.

LEGAL DISCUSSION

One—Infants

In view of the juvenile courts' jurisdiction the criminal courts seldom encounter a defense of infancy. Offenders under fourteen (14) years of age are, with few exceptions, remanded to the juvenile courts and the juvenile authorities.

Two and Three—Idiots, Lunatics and Insane Persons

Some psychiatrists contend that all persons who commit crimes are mentally deficient. The public, the legislature, and the judiciary do not necessarily agree. To establish a defense of idiocy under P.C. 26(2), it must be established that the defendant lacks the mental capacity to appreciate the character of his act, or to know that his act would violate the rights of another, or to know that the act is in itself wrong. He must be incapable of comprehending the consequences of his act.[1] Mere feeble-mindedness not amounting to idiocy or insanity will not suffice.

In California the issue of sanity is raised by separate plea and is tried in a separate trial.[2] The defendant is presumed sane and the burden of proving insanity rests on him. The rule in effect in California is the McNaughten Rule, which states: "To establish a defense on the ground of insanity it must be clearly proved that at the time of committing the acts comprising the crime the defendant was laboring under such defect of reason from disease of the mind as not to know the nature and quality of the act he was doing or as not to know that what he was doing was wrong." This is frequently described as the inability to distinguish right from wrong. California does not recognize the following forms of insanity which are frequently referred to in literature and in the press:

- Moral or emotional insanity—A disturbed emotional state wherein the mind is not deranged but the moral sense is perverted.
- Irresistible impulse (also known as moral insanity)—
- The theory that a defendant is not responsible for his act if he is irresistibly impelled to commit it despite his knowledge and understanding that his act is wrong.

The Durham Rule

(Also known as the New Hampshire Rule) excuses the defendant when his crime is the product of mental disease or defect.

The Proposed Model Penal Code Rule

A person is not responsible for criminal conduct if at the time of such conduct, as a result of mental disease or defect, he lacks substantial capacity either to appreciate the criminality of his conduct or to conform his conduct to the requirements of the law. The term "mental disease or defect" does not include an abnormality manifested solely by repeated criminal or otherwise antisocial conduct.

Miscellaneous Mental Disorders

The defense of insanity has been refused in some cases to persons suffering from melancholia, epilepsy, unbalanced mind, psychopathic personality, defective reasoning, morphine addiction, irrationality, nomadic traits and homosexuality, monomania, excessive use of alcohol, nervous disorders, criminalistic inclinations, weak will power, sadistic tendencies, sexual perversion, hallucinations, etc.

In recent times several psychiatrists throughout the world have been evaluating the relationship between insanity and chromosomes in the body. The importance and legal significance of chromosomes has been recognized in the Olympic games where several female contestants have been officially declared to be ineligible to compete as females. In Australia the supreme court has upheld an insanity plea based on the chromosome formation. Authorities agree that possibly one in three hundred have chromosome conditions that could constitute insanity. Many legal authorities view with concern and alarm the expanding theories on insanity which may eventually affect criminal law.

Delirium Tremens

Brought on by excessive use of alcohol has been treated as a temporary condition induced by a voluntary act and within the rule excluding voluntary intoxication as a defense.

The Theory of Diminished Responsibility

Has been accepted by the English courts as a modification to the McNaughten Rule. It permits mental disease or defect to diminish the gravity of the crime. For example, derangement which is not a defense under the McNaughten Rule may cause a sentence to be reduced from first- to second-degree murder or from murder to manslaughter.

Four—Person Acting Under a Mistake of Fact

It is necessary that the alleged mistaken facts be carefully scrutinized to insure that the mistake is not one of law (discussed below) instead of fact.

Where a corporation relies on the advice of its attorney that a permit for the sale of stock is unnecessary, the mistake is one of law and not excusable; but where a corporation relies on the information of its attorney that a permit has been issued when in fact none has been issued, it is a mistake of fact and excusable.

In the public welfare offenses which do not require a *mens rea*, a mistake of fact is not a defense; but where the statute requires willfulness or knowledge, a mistake of fact will generally be accepted as a defense negating such willfulness or knowledge. Certain offenses against public morals have been traditionally enforced without acceptance of the mistake of fact defense. Examples are statutory rape and contributing to the delinquency of a minor where mistake regarding the victim's age is no defense. Formerly bigamy was in this category, but this was repudiated in 1956.[3]

Five—Unconscious Persons

This section would appear to be restricted to cases of somnambulism or unconsciousness from cranial injury. It also applies to persons while under epileptic seizure. Where a person knows that he is subject to periods of blackout or epileptic seizure, yet knowing this, continues to operate a car, a crime arising from his unconsciousness has been held to be excused.[4] A victim of involuntary intoxication falls into this class of unconscious person. Involuntary intoxication would exist where an individual had consumed an alcoholic beverage in the belief that it contained no alcohol, or where drugs were administered to an individual without his knowledge.

Where an individual conceives of a crime, plans it in general, and then produces a state of intoxication or unconsciousness through alcohol or drugs, with a view to reducing the degree of his responsibility, he will be denied the benefits of his own self-induced unconsciousness.

Six—Misfortune or Accident

Misfortune as used here has been judicially pronounced analogous to "mis-adventure."[5] A rare example of a defense based on misfortune or accident would be the case of a passenger in a taxicab who is not licensed to operate a motor vehicle but who brings the cab to a stop after the cab driver has jumped from the moving vehicle.[6]

Seven—Married Women

Inasmuch as the defense of coercion is available to anyone, this section has been given effect by holding that a wife need not show threats which influenced her action but only such influence from her husband as causes her to obey his directions.[7] (This applies only to misdemeanors.)

Eight—Duress

Many jurisdictions by statute or by judicial decision hold fear of great bodily harm sufficient to excuse a criminal act.[8] It has been argued that the distinction between fear of danger to life and fear of great bodily harm "has become rather unrealistic in the light of recent psychological research," but in California the solid consensus of judicial opinion restricts the defense of duress to those instances where fear of danger to life is established.[9] Furthermore, the duress or coercion must involve a present peril. Mere threat of future injury will not suffice. There must be "immediacy and imminency" of the threatened action.

Lack of Intent, Malice or Corruption

In those crimes requiring a specific intent a lack thereof is a defense to crime. Some of the factors affecting the existence of intent have been covered in the preceding discussion (mistake of fact, mistake of law, idiocy, insanity, misfortune or inadvertance, duress).

Proof that an individual knew the law and intended to violate it is not required. Specific intent is the intent to do the proscribed act, not the intent to violate the law. The case where a person is ignorant of his legal rights or duties must be distinguished. For example, where one takes property in the mistaken belief that he is the legal owner, it isn't his ignorance of the law which defeats larceny; it is the fact that, because he believed he owned the property, there was no specific intent to steal.

Reliance on advice of counsel is not an excuse to crime; but where the regulatory control body is an administrative agency, reliance on the interpretation of an officer thereof has been held to be an excuse.

Compulsion

P.C. 26, subsection eight (quoted above) covers the question of threat or duress—as defense against a criminal act—fear of danger to life or great bodily harm, and threat of future injury.

When the criminal act is committed as a result of an order issued by a person in authority, such compulsion will not excuse the commission of crime. The fact that the person issuing the order is one in authority who can enforce his order by various forms of sanctions such as military discipline and/or discharge from civil employment, corporal punishment of a child, etc., does not excuse the crime.

Consent, Condonation, Compromise

In those crimes where lack of consent is an element (rape, theft, robbery) the existence of consent is a defense. However, consent obtained by fraud is not consent; and a person could be incapable of giving his consent. The mere absence of resistance is not of itself proof of consent, because resistance is not required under circumstances where the party realizes resistance would be futile. Consent obtained by threat, force, or duress is not consent.

In other crimes wherein lack of consent is not an element of the crime, the existence of consent is immaterial to the existence of crime except that consent is not a defense to assault and battery. However, a valid contest (legal boxing match, football game, or wrestling match) is an exception to this rule. Where there is an illegal contest (boxing match, etc.), the fight itself is a breach of the peace, and consent of the parties will not excuse the resultant batteries.

Condonation and compromise are distinguished from consent in that they exist after the act whereas consent exists prior to and during the criminal act. Ordinarily the injured party cannot compromise or condone the criminal act because the criminal act offends the state as well as the victim. However, there are some statutory exceptions.

P.C. 269 condones the crime of seduction on intermarriage of the parties.

Where the victim of a misdemeanor through his civil action or otherwise acknowledges receipt of satisfaction, the court may excuse the defendant.[10] There is also the practical situation where the victim declines to make criminal complaint and where a showing of restitution will influence the court to grant probation, etc.

Entrapment

The defendant is entrapped where he never contemplated the crime, the crime having originated in the minds of police officers and defendant having acted at the instigation of the police. If, on the other hand, the defendant conceived the crime and the police stood idly by and did not interfere although they were fully apprised of the contemplated crime, there is no entrapment.

The defense of entrapment has no foundation in statute. It is applied where the entrapment was established by (a) police officers of the prosecuting jurisdiction, (b) police officers of a foreign jurisdiction, and (c) various official persons or organizations working with law enforcement officials; however, the defense has never been allowed where the entrapment was made by a private citizen devoid of connection with any police agencies.

Definition of "Person"

In Re Corporation—Capacity to Commit Crime (Business Association), P.C. 7 includes a corporation in the word "person." It is well established that a corporation is subject to criminal liability for public welfare offenses and other offenses which do not require a specific intent, such as police regulations. There is some uncertainty as to whether a corporation can commit a crime involving a specific intent. The modern view holds the corporation liable.

Since a partnership is considered not to be a legal entity and P.C. 7 doesn't include a partnership, a partnership is not held responsible for a crime involving specific intent, but the partners may be held responsible as individuals. Obviously under these circumstances a partner can't be convicted of a crime which he did not personally commit and of which he had no culpable knowledge, simply because he was a member of the partnership. However, when it is a crime like the sale of impure food, mislabeled products, etc., all partners are equally liable criminally.[11]

APPLICABLE STATUTE—DRUNKENNESS

P.C. 22—*Drunkenness no excuse for crime. When it may be considered.* No act committed by a person while in a state of voluntary intoxication is less criminal by reason of his having been in such condition. But whenever the actual existence of any particular purpose, motive, or intent is a necessary element to constitute any particular species or degree of crime, the jury may take into consideration the fact that the accused was intoxicated at the time, in determining the purpose, motive, or intent with which he committed the act.

LEGAL DISCUSSION

Voluntary intoxication results when a person knowingly and intentionally consumes a drug or intoxicant even though he had no intention of becoming intoxicated and even though the amounts and circumstances of the consumption would not normally have resulted in intoxication. If the drug or intoxicant is unknowingly injected or forced on a defendant, the intoxication is involuntary and the defendant would probably be considered an unconscious person under P.C. 26—if the degree of intoxication was sufficient to impair the mental faculties. Writers on criminal law have repeatedly commented that they could find no examples of involuntary intoxication.

In those crimes requiring a specific intent or a specific state of mind, intoxication can be shown to prove the defendant could not entertain such intent or state of mind, thereby reducing the degree of the crime under P.C. 22.

APPLICABLE STATUTES—FORMER JEOPARDY

Constitution of the United States—Amendment 5. No person shall be held to answer for a capital, or otherwise infamous crime, unless on a presentment or indictment of a grand jury, except in cases arising in the land or naval forces, or in the militia, when in actual service in time of war or public danger; nor shall any person be subject for the same offense to be twice put in jeopardy of life or limb; nor shall be compelled in any criminal case to be a witness against himself, nor be deprived of life, liberty, or property, without due process of law; nor shall private property be taken for public use, without just compensation.

Constitution of California—Article I, Sec. 13: Criminal cases; speedy and public trial; process for witnesses; appearance and defense; counsel; double jeopardy; self-incrimination; due process; failure to explain or deny; depositions. In criminal prosecutions, in any court whatever, the party accused shall have the right to a speedy and public trial; to have the process of the court to compel the attendance of witnesses in his behalf, and to appear and defend, in person and with counsel. No person shall be twice put in jeopardy for the same offense; nor be compelled, in any criminal case, to be a witness against himself; nor be deprived of life, liberty, or property without due process of law; but in any criminal case, whether the defendant testifies or not, his failure to explain or to deny by his testimony any evidence or facts in the case against him may be commented upon by the court and by counsel, and may be considered by the court or the jury. The legislature shall have power to provide for the taking, in the presence of the party accused and his counsel, of depositions of witnesses in criminal cases, other than cases of homicide when there is reason to believe that the witness, from inability or other cause, will not attend at the trial.

P.C. 654—Acts made punishable by different provisions of this code. [Quoted in Chapter 2.]

P.C. 656—Foreign conviction or acquittal. Whenever on the trial of an accused person it appears that upon a criminal prosecution under the laws of another state, government, or country, founded upon the act or omission in respect to which he is on trial, he has been acquitted or convicted, it is a sufficient defense.

P.C. 687—*Second prosecution for the same offense prohibited.* No person can be subjected to a second prosecution for a public offense for which he has once been prosecuted and convicted or acquitted.

P.C. 793—*Conviction or acquittal in another state a bar, where the jurisdiction is concurrent.* When an act charged as a public offense is within the jurisdiction of another state or country, as well as of this state, a conviction or acquittal thereof in the former is a bar to the prosecution or indictment therefor in this state.

P.C. 794—*Conviction or acquittal in another county a bar, where the jurisdiction is concurrent.* When an offense is within the jurisdiction of two or more courts, a conviction or acquittal thereof in one court is a bar to a prosecution therefor in another.

P.C. 1023—*Conviction, acquittal, or jeopardy; bar to another indictment, etc., for a higher offense, effect of.* When the defendant is convicted or acquitted, or has been once placed in jeopardy upon an accusatory pleading, the conviction, acquittal, or jeopardy is a bar to another prosecution for the offense charged in such accusatory pleading, or for an attempt to commit the same, or for an offense necessarily included therein, of which he might have been convicted under that accusatory pleading.

P.C. 1101—*Effect of such discharge.* The order mentioned in the last two sections is an acquittal of the defendant discharged, and is a bar to another prosecution for the same offense.

P.C. 1188—*Defendant, when to be held or discharged.* If, from the evidence on the trial, there is reason to believe the defendant guilty, and a new indictment or information can be framed upon which he may be convicted, the court may order him to be recommitted to the officer of the proper county, or admitted to bail anew, to answer the new indictment or information. If the evidence shows him guilty of another offense, he must be committed or held thereon, and in neither case shall the verdict be a bar to another prosecution. But if no evidence appears sufficient to charge him with any offense, he must, if in custody, be discharged: or if admitted to bail, his bail is exonerated; or if money has been deposited instead of bail, it must be refunded to the defendant or to the person or persons found by the court to have deposited said money on behalf of said defendant: and the arrest of judgment shall operate as an acquittal of the charge upon which the indictment or information was founded.

P.C. 1387—*Dismissal of actions. Order bar to other prosecution.* An order for the dismissal of the action, made as provided in this chapter, is a bar to any other prosecution for the same offense if it is a misdemeanor, but not if it is a felony.

LEGAL DISCUSSION

To constitute former jeopardy a defendant must be (1) placed on trial (2) for the same offense (3) on a valid indictment or information or other accusatory pleading (4) before a competent tribunal (5) including (a) a competent jury duly impanelled, sworn and charged with the case or (b) if jury is waived the court must have been "entered upon." There is no jeopardy until defendant has been placed on trial under circumstances where if completed a valid sentence could be imposed.

Where a trial has commenced but is interrupted before completion through no action of the defendant, in general it constitutes a former jeopardy.

In general where an accused is convicted of a lesser included offense and appeals his conviction, resulting in retrial, he cannot be convicted of a greater offense than that of which he was convicted in his first trial. Conviction of the same degree of crime on second trial cannot result in a greater punishment than was imposed on the first trial.

The complexity of our criminal laws has developed a defense which on its surface extends the defense of former jeopardy past its constitutional limitations by adopting into criminal law or rather criminal procedure a doctrine of the civil courts, namely, collateral estoppel. The principle as applied to criminal action has no foundation in federal or state constitutions and none in statute.

Where several crimes against several jurisdictions or several defendants arise from the same set of operative facts and it is apparent that the defense of former jeopardy is not available, the courts have declined to redetermine a specific question of fact which was previously resolved by another court in a separate proceeding.

In U.S. v. Oppenheim[12] the U.S. Supreme Court held that a determination of the applicability of a statute made in the first trial was binding on the court in a second trial involving different issues. And again in U.S. v. Sealfon[13] where the defendant in his first trial for fraud against the United States was found not guilty of conspiracy and in a subsequent trial was found guilty of conspiracy involving the same agreement, the Supreme Court reversed the conviction on the basis of the earlier determination.

On the other hand in Hoag v. New Jersey[14] the defendant pleaded his acquittal in a first trial for robbing A in his second trial for robbing B; although both robberies were committed by the same acts of the defendant the court affirmed the conviction. The California courts appear to have followed the Hoag case.[15]

Because of the nebulous state of the laws in regard to collateral estoppel in criminal cases and the complexity of the problem, it is recommended that the peace officer be aware of the principles involved but make no detailed inquiry into the applicability of the doctrine until he is confronted with a specific problem.

APPLICABLE STATUTES

P.C. 197 (2), (3) and (4)—*Justifiable Homicide.* [Quoted in Chapter 13.]

P.C. 198—*Bare fear not to justify killing.* [Quoted in Chapter 13.]

P.C. 835 a.—*Reasonable force to effect arrest, prevent escape is permissible.* [Quoted in Chapter 5.]

P.C. 843—*What force may be used.* [Quoted in Chapter 5.]

LEGAL DISCUSSION

There is in California *No Need to Retreat.* Defendant may stand his ground and resist.[16]

Nor does defendant have to adopt specific defensive action to avoid confrontation such as avoiding certain streets and highways that he would otherwise normally use.[17]

The privilege of self-defense is not available to the aggressor—or trespassor. But after retreat, withdrawal, and detachment conducted in *such manner as to reasonably inform the opponent* of the retreat or withdrawal, he then acquires the privilege to defend himself from continued or persistent attack by said opponent.

A similar situation is involved when "A," a nonfelonious aggressor (simple assault, trespass), is confronted with an unreasonable amount of force from "B," the victim of this first aggression, amounting to a felonious assault. "A" has the full right of self-defense and may employ reasonable force in his own defense.

In all of these cases the right of use of extraordinary force in self-defense ends with the aggression except where the defendant must pursue his attacker to insure his safety from future danger.[18] The pursuit must not be for revenge or to inflict punishment but must be in good faith solely for the purpose of defense against further aggression and must be based on reasonable apprehension of such further aggression.

Ordinarily the right of self-defense does not extend to the right to defend a third person. California by statute extends it to "wife, husband, parent, child, master, mistress or servant."[19]

Justification for crime committed in defense of property is primarily limited to a defense of one's own habitation.[20] This does not mean one can kill a nonfelonious trespasser who threatens no violence or felony. On the other hand, if the intruder resists ejection and assaults the lawful occupant, the occupant may use such force as is necessary to eject but *may not use deadly force* unless he honestly believes that he is in danger of great bodily harm.

The law of justification contains special provisions applicable to peace officers acting as such.

APPLICABLE STATUTE

P.C. 196—*Justifiable homicide by public officers.* [Quoted in Chapter 13.]

LEGAL DISCUSSION

A killing is justified if reasonably necessary to effect an arrest of a person who has committed a felony in the peace officer's presence or of a person who has been charged with felony, or where the officer has reasonable cause to believe that a felony has been committed.[21]

Compare P.C. 196 (3) with P.C. 197 (4) and note the distinction. The private citizen must establish that it *was necessary* for him to kill and the deceased must have been actually guilty of a felony.

Neither a peace officer nor a private person is justified in killing a misdemeanant. The peace officer may employ deadly force to effect the arrest, prevent escape or overcome resistance (see P.C. 835a) if the warrant has been issued or the misdemeanor was committed in the peace officer's presence.

There is no statutory basis and no direct case law supporting a defense of necessity; nevertheless, most writers in this field appear to accept the principle. Illustrations of necessity which are frequently used appear to stem from human relations and transactions which from their very nature are most unlikely to result in arrest or prosecution; e.g., stealing to prevent starvation of self or family, sacrificing the life of another to save one's own life. It must be remembered that necessity as a defense would only apply as such in cases where self-defense, governmental authority, and other recognized and accepted defenses were inapplicable.

APPLICABLE STATUTES—STATUTE OF LIMITATIONS

P.C. 801—*Limitation of one year in misdemeanors.* An indictment for any misdemeanor must be found or an information or complaint filed within one year after its commission.

P.C. 1426a—*Complaint for misdemeanor.* A complaint for any misdemeanor triable in a justice court must be filed within one year after its commission.

P.C. 800—*Limitation: felonies; acceptance of bribe.* An indictment for any other felony than murder, the embezzlement of public money, the acceptance of a bribe by a public official or a public employee, or the falsification of public records, must be found, and information filed, or case certified to the superior court, within three years after its commission. An indictment for the acceptance of a bribe by a public official or a public employee, a felony, must be found, and the information filed, or case certified to the superior court, within six years after its commission.

P.C. 17—*Classification of public offenses.* [Quoted in Chapter 2.]

APPLICABLE STATUTES

P.C. 799—*No time limitation for commencement of prosecution in certain crimes.* There is no limitation of time within which a prosecution for murder, the embezzlement of public moneys, and the falsification of public records must be commenced. Prosecution for murder may be commenced at any time after the death of the person killed, and for the embezzlement of public money or the falsification of public records, at any time after the discovery of the crime.

P.C. 802—*Computation of time; exclusion of defendant's absence from state.* If, when or after the offense is committed, the defendant is out of the state, an indictment may be found, a complaint or an information filed or a case certified to the superior court, in any case originally triable in the superior court, or a complaint may be filed, in any case originally triable in any other court, within the term limited by law; and no time during which the defendant is not within this state, is a part of any limitation of the time for commencing a criminal action.

LEGAL DISCUSSION

Although included as a legal defense created by law, the Statute of Limitations as applied to prosecutions is jurisdictional. The prosecution must prove timely prosecution within the applicable period.

The courts have resolved the question of applicability of the Statute of Limitations consistent with P.C. 17 by holding that P.C. 800, the statute applicable to felonies, applies.[22] However if one is charged with a felony after one year has expired and is convicted of a misdemeanor, the one-year limitation applies.[23]

The time is computed by excluding the day the crime was committed and including the day the indictment was found or the accusatory pleading was filed. In computing the statutory period, periods in which the defendant was absent from the jurisdiction are excluded.

Since the period runs from the commission of the crime and in conspiracy we have an agreement and an overt act or several overt acts, the period runs from the commission of the *last* overt act. However, a conspiracy to conceal the first conspiracy is not such overt act.[24]

Immunity

There are special statutes granting immunity for specific purposes:

APPLICABLE STATUTES

California Constitution, Article IV, Sec. 35—*Lobbying; legislator influenced by reward, etc.* Any person who seeks to influence the vote of a member of the legislature by bribery, promise of reward, intimidation or any other dishonest means, shall be guilty of lobbying, which is hereby declared a felony; and it shall be the duty of the legislature to provide, by law, for the punishment of this crime. Any member of the legislature who shall be influenced in his vote or action upon any matter pending before the legislature by any reward, or promise of future reward, shall be deemed guilty of a felony, and upon conviction thereof, in addition to such punishment as may be provided by law, shall be disfranchised and forever disqualified from holding any office or public trust. Any person may be compelled to testify in any lawful investigation or judicial proceeding against any person who may be charged with having committed the offense of bribery or corrupt solicitation, or with having been influenced in his vote or action, as a member of the legislature, by reward or promise of future reward, and shall not be permitted to withhold his testimony upon the ground that it may criminate himself or subject him to public infamy; but such testimony shall not afterwards be used against him in any judicial proceeding, except for perjury in giving such testimony.

Corporation Code #25354—*Self-incrimination; immunity from prosecution; perjury.* No person shall be excused from testifying or from producing any book, document, or other thing under his control upon any such examination, audit, investigation, or hearing upon the ground that his testimony, or the book, document, or other thing required of him, may tend to incriminate him, or may have a tendency to subject him to punishment for a felony, or to a penalty or forfeiture; but no person shall be prosecuted, punished, or subjected to any penalty or forfeiture for or on account of any act, transaction, matter, or thing concerning which he is so compelled to testify under oath. No person so testifying is exempt from prosecution or punishment for perjury committed by him in his testimony.

Government Code #9410—*Immunity from prosecution, penalty or forfeiture; evidence; privilege; perjury.* A person sworn and examined before the senate or assembly, or any committee, cannot be held to answer criminally or be subject to any penalty or forfeiture for any fact or act touching which he is required to testify. Any statement made or paper produced by such witness is not competent evidence in any criminal proceeding against the witness. The witness cannot refuse to testify to any fact or to produce any paper touching which he is examined for the reason that his testimony or the production of the paper may tend to disgrace him or render him infamous. Nothing in this section exempts any witness from prosecution and punishment for perjury committed by him on examination.

P.C. 1324—*Evidence demanded before grand jury.* In any felony proceeding or in any investigation or proceeding before a grand jury for any felony offense if a person refuses to answer a question or produce evidence of any other kind on the ground that he may be incriminated thereby, and if the district attorney of the county in writing requests the superior court in and for that county to order that person to answer the question or produce the evidence, a judge of the superior court shall set a time for hearing and order the person to appear before the court and show cause, if any, why the question should not be answered or the evidence produced, and the court shall order the question answered or the evidence produced unless it finds that to do so would be clearly contrary to the public interest, or could subject the witness to a criminal prosecution in another jurisdiction, and that person shall comply with the order. After complying, and if, but for this section, he would have been privileged to withhold the answer given or the evidence produced by him, that person shall not be prosecuted or subjected to penalty or forfeiture for or on account of any fact or act concerning which, in accordance with the order, he was required to answer or produce evidence. But he may nevertheless be prosecuted or subjected to penalty or forfeiture for any perjury, false swearing or contempt committed in answering, or failing to answer, or in producing, or failing to produce, evidence in accordance with the order.

LEGAL DISCUSSION

The general effect of the immunity statute is to assure a witness freedom from prosecution for any crime disclosed by his testimony. If the immunity suffices to protect the witness from prosecution, he can be compelled to testify by contempt proceedings. Laxity in law enforcement or nonuniform enforcement of the law is not a defense of crime.[25]

This defense must be considered in connection with the "equal protection of the laws" provisions of the Constitution, particularly where racial discrimination or discrimination against political groups is involved. An example is a strict and injurious enforcement of gambling laws in Negro areas coupled with little or no enforcement in other areas.[26]

Untenable Defenses

California does not recognize the unwritten law (right to avenge a wrong to a female member of one's family),[27] or a mercy killing of a person suffering from incurable pain. There is even less possibility that the California courts would accept religious convictions or onerous social customs as a defense for crime. Repentance may be a ground for mitigation of punishment but is not a defense to crime. Abandonment and withdrawal from a crime, unless it occurs before the crime is completed (the overt act in a conspiracy), is not a defense to a completed crime.

Unless otherwise excused, the past criminal conduct of the deceased is no justification for killing him. By "otherwise excused," we mean self-defense, lawful exercise of the power of arrest, etc. In the same vein, ordinarily the contributory negligence of the decedent does not furnish a defense. The exception to this rule lies in vehicle manslaughter cases where the decedent's conduct appears to be the sole proximate cause of his death.

DISCUSSION QUESTIONS

1. Identify the classes of persons who are incapable of committing a crime.
2. Explain the current rule on insanity (McNaughten Rule).
3. Explain entrapment and give an example.
4. Explain the statute of limitations as it affects misdemeanors.
5. What crimes have no statute of limitations?
6. Explain immunity and give an example.

NOTES

[1]People v. Oxnam, 170 C 211; 149 P 165;
  People v. Keyes, 178 C 794; 175 P 6.
[2]P.C. 1016 (5); 1017 (5).
[3]People v. Vogel, 46 C 2d 798; 299 P 2d 850.
[4]People v. Freeman, 61 CA 2d 110; 142 P 2d 435.
[5]People v. Gorgol, 122 CA 2d 281; 265 P 2d 69.
[6]People v. Acosta, 45 C 2d 538; 250 P 2d 1.

[7]People v. Stately, 91 CA 2d Supp 943; 206 P 2d 76.

[8]People v. Otis, 174 CA 2d 119; 344 P 2d 342.

[9]People v. Hart, 98 CA 2d 514; 220 P 2d 595;
People v. Lindstrom, 128 CA 111; 16 P 2d 1003.

[10]In re Casperson, 69 CA 2d 441; 159 P 2d 88;
People v. Schoning, 74 CA 109; 239 P 413.

[11]P.C. 1377; 1378.

[12]U.S. v. Oppenheim, 242 US 83; 37 SCT 68; 61 LEd 161.

[13]U.S. v. Sealfon, 332 US 575; 68 SCT 237; 92 LEd 180.

[14]Hoag v. New Jersey, 356 US 464; 78 SCT 829; 2 LEd 2d 913.

[15]People v. Beltran, 94 CA 2d 197; 210 P 2d 238.

[16](a) Defense of Life
    P.C. 197 (3)
    People v. Finali, 31 CA 479; 160 P 850;
    People v. Armstrong, 106 CA 2d 490; 235 P 2d 242.
  (b) Defense of Property (Habitation)
    P.C. 198

[16](b) People v. Reese, 65 CA 2d 329; 150 P 2d 571
  (c) Defense of Property (other than habitation)
    Nakashimo v. Takase, 8 CA 2d 35; 46 P 2d 1020

[17]People v. Gonzalez, 71 C 569; 12 P 783.

[18]People v. Hackett, 56 CA 2d 20; 137 P 2d 51.

[19]P.C. 197; 198.

[20]P.C. 197 (2).

[21]People v. Kilvington, 105 C 86; 37 P 799.

[22]Doble v. Sup. Ct., 197 C 556; 241 P 852.
Davis v. Sup. Ct., 175 CA 2d 8; 345 P 2d 513.

[23]People v. Meyers, 39 CA 244; 178 P 965;
People v. Angelo, 24 CA 2d 626; 75 P 2d 614.

[24]Gruenwald v. U.S., 353 US 391; 77 SCT 963; 1 LEd 2d 931.

[25]People v. Montgomery, 47 CA 2d 1; 117 P 2d 437;
In re Finn, 54 C 2d 807; 8 CR 741; 356 P 2d 685;
In re Oreek, 74 CA 2d 215; 168 P 2d 186.

[26]People v. Harris, 182 CA 2d Supp 837; 5 CR 852.

[27]People v. Youn, 70 CA 2d 28; 160 P 2d 132.

5

Laws of Arrest

APPLICABLE STATUTES—ARREST

P.C. 834—*Arrest Defined. By Whom Made.* An arrest is taking a person into custody, in a case and in the manner authorized by law. An arrest may be made by a peace officer or by a private person.

P.C. 835—*How an Arrest Is Made and What Restraint Allowed.* An arrest is made by an actual restraint of the person, or by submission to the custody of an officer. The person arrested may be subjected to such restraint as is reasonable for his arrest and detention.

P.C. 841—*Arrest, How Made.* The person making the arrest must inform the person to be arrested of the intention to arrest him, of the cause of the arrest, and the authority to make it, except when the person making the arrest has reasonable cause to believe that the person to be arrested is actually engaged in the commission of or an attempt to commit an offense, or the person to be arrested is pursued immediately after its commission, or after an escape. The person making the arrest must, on request of the person he is arresting, inform the latter of the offense for which he is being arrested.

LEGAL DISCUSSION

The elements required to constitute an arrest are therefore:

1. Notification of the *intent* or purpose to arrest. This may be done by a simple verbal statement or physical action may suffice if it is reasonable. Efforts should be made to satisfy this requirement even though failure to do so does not constitute false imprisonment.

2. Informing the subject of the reason or *cause* for the arrest. This may be in general terms and should include a descriptive title of the crime and the Penal Code section number if the subject requests this information.

3. *Authority* for the arrest must be shown. A uniformed officer would indicate the necessary authority. Display of identification, credentials, badge, etc., would satisfy the requirement.

4. *Effective or actual restraint* is the last element which indicates the subject has been "taken into custody." Usually there is voluntary submission by the subject. Historically this act has been performed by the placing of the officer's hand on the shoulder of the subject. This is not required, but control over the subject must reasonably be shown. It should be pointed out that every person being arrested by a peace officer has a duty to refrain from using force or any weapon to resist such arrest.[1]

An "arrest" depends entirely upon the context in which it is used. To determine whether an "arrest" has been made, the entire circumstances surrounding the incident should be examined to determine if there has been an "actual restraint" or "submission to custody." The same holds true for temporary detention: to establish the propriety of a stopping and questioning, the facts must be testified to fully so that a reviewing court is in a position to approve the conduct of the police. The officer may have to call upon his expertise, his training, or his past experience as a trained observer to establish to the court his justification for both temporary detention and arrest. Temporary detention for questioning cannot be divorced from the law of arrest. For, in a sense, temporary detention for questioning can amount to an "actual restraint of the person." The line between arrest and detention is thin indeed. In California there is no statutory or constitutional authority to stop and question; the right to do so having been established only by judicial interpretation. To warrant stopping and questioning, the courts have, in effect, stated that there can be some interference with a person's freedom of movement, short of actual restraint or submission to custody, which need not be a statutory arrest.

Not every interference with absolute freedom of action is an arrest. Numerous instances could be cited in which the police may have insufficient knowledge to establish probable cause to arrest but enough to constitute a breach of duty if they did not investigate. The daily life of an officer is full of situations in which questioning short of an arrest is called for. California recognizes that the police must have the power to detain and question a person without necessarily making an arrest when the circumstances are such as would indicate to a reasonable man in a like position that such a course is necessary to the proper discharge of his duties.

The concept of detention is becoming more widespread, and the courts are recognizing the importance and necessity for this action. To give a hypothetical example: An officer responding to a family-dispute call sees, as he arrives on the scene, the defendant leaning inside a car and swinging his fists; at the same time he observes a woman's legs extending out of the car and hears a woman's screams. The officer restrains the defendant and places him in the squad car but does not formally place him under arrest. Our hypothetical defendant was ultimately convicted as a result of an assault later committed on the officer during the course of the investigation. On appeal, he contends his original arrest was unlawful. The court would no doubt hold that the defendant was not under arrest at the time he was first restrained from assaulting the woman and placed in the police car; he was merely being detained until the officer could complete his investigation. The pre-arrest detention would be proper. The court would recognize that the officer had probable cause to arrest in any event. Pre-arrest detention is consistent with proper police work, permitting a reasonable investigation without the necessity of formally placing someone under arrest. As the hypothetical officer came upon a scene that was not altogether free from doubt, he could have even asked the defendant for a general explanation of his conduct without the need for a statement of constitutional rights.

Family-dispute cases frequently resolve themselves at the scene. Officers can often restrain the parties, conduct an investigation, hopefully allow tempers to cool—all without the necessity of immediate arrest.

ENFORCEMENT ASPECTS

Law enforcement officers should note specifically the exceptions under P.C. 841. Police procedures for safeguarding the officer are necessary. If the officer has reasonable cause to believe the suspect is actually engaged in committing or attempting a crime or if the suspect is being immediately pursued after the commission, there is no requirement to comply with notification of intent, cause, and authority. Thus officers viewing an armed robbery in progress should not procrastinate in long legal explanations but instead should cry out: "Police! Do not move. Drop your weapons!" Extreme caution must be exercised when stopping dangerous criminals in the midst of their acts.

As regards pursuit of a suspect, it should be noted that it must be reasonably prompt. The same officer need not be in constant pursuit. In fact the suspect need not be in continuous view. Thus a suspect may be chased by several officers who may even be from different agencies. If the suspect vehicle is lost from sight and then relocated, the suspect is still being pursued. The test therefore requires that police be in reasonably fresh pursuit of the suspect from the crime scene.

We turn now to definitions of magistrates and peace officers, which need to be included in a discussion of arrest.

APPLICABLE STATUTES

P.C. 807—*Magistrate Defined.* A magistrate is an officer having power to issue a warrant for the arrest of a person charged with a public offense.

P.C. 808—*Who are Magistrates?* The following persons are magistrates:
1. The Justices of the Supreme Court;
2. The Justices of the District Courts of Appeal;
3. The Judges of the Superior Court;
4. The Judges of the Municipal Court;
5. The Judges of the Justice Courts.

P.C. 830—Any person who comes within the provisions of this chapter and who otherwise meets all standards imposed by law on a peace officer is a peace officer, and notwithstanding any other provision of law, no person other than those designated in this chapter is a peace officer. The restriction of peace officer functions of any public officer or employee shall not affect his status for purposes of retirement.

P.C. 830.1—Any sheriff, undersheriff, or deputy sheriff, regularly employed and paid as such, of a county, any policeman of a city, any policeman of a district authorized by statute to maintain a police department, any marshal or deputy marshal of a municipal court, or any constable or deputy constable, regularly employed and paid as such, of a judicial district, is a peace officer. The authority of any such peace officer extends to any place in the state:

(a) As to any public offense committed or which there is probably cause to believe has been committed within the political subdivision which employs him; or

(b) Where he has the prior consent of the chief of police, or person authorized by him to give such consent, if the place is within a city or of the sheriff, or person authorized by him to give such consent, if the place is within a county; or

(c)　As to any public offense committed or which there is probably cause to believe has been committed in his presence, and with respect to which there is immediate danger to person or property, or of the escape of the perpetrator of such offense.

P.C. 830.2—(a)　Any member of the California highway patrol is a peace officer whose authority extends to any place in the state; provided, that the primary duty of any such peace officer shall be the enforcement of the provisions of the Vehicle Code or of any other law relating to the use or operation of vehicles upon the highways, as that duty is set forth in the Vehicle Code. Provided further, that he shall not act as a peace officer in enforcing any other law except (i) when in pursuit of any offender or suspected offender or (ii) to make arrests for crimes committed in his presence or upon any highway.

(b)　Any member of the California State Police Division is a peace officer; provided, that the primary duty of any such peace officer shall be the protection of state properties and occupants thereof, and he shall not act as a peace officer in enforcing any law except (1) when in pursuit of any offender or suspected offender or (2) to make arrests for crimes committed in his presence or upon state properties.

P.C. 830.3—(a)　The Deputy Director and the Assistant Director of the Department of Justice, the Chief, Assistant Chief, and special agents of the Bureau of Criminal Identification and Investigation, the Chief, Assistant Chief, and narcotics agents of the Bureau of Narcotic Enforcement, and such investigators who are so designated by the Attorney General, are peace officers.

The authority of any such peace officer extends to any place in the state as to a public offense committed or which there is probable cause to believe has been committed within the state.

(b)　Any inspector or investigator regularly employed and paid as such in the office of a district attorney is a peace officer.

The authority of any such peace officer extends to any place in the state:

(1)　As to any public offense committed, or which there is probably cause to believe has been committed, within the county which employs him; or

(2)　Where he has the prior consent of the chief of police, or person authorized by him to give such consent, if the place is within a city or of the sheriff, or person authorized by him to give such consent, if the place is within a county; or

(3)　As to any public offense committed or which there is probably cause to believe has been committed in his presence, and with respect to which there is immediate danger to person or property, or of the escape of the perpetrator of such offense.

(c)　The Director of the Department of Alcoholic Beverage Control and persons employed by such department for the enforcement of the provisions of Division 9 (commencing with Section 23000) of the Business and Professions Code are peace officers; provided, that the primary duty of any such peace officer shall be the enforcement of the laws relating to alcoholic beverages, as that duty is set forth in Section 25755 of the Business and Professions Code. Any such peace officer is further authorized to enforce any penal provision of law while, in the course of his employment, he is in, on, or about any premises licensed pursuant to the Alcoholic Beverage Control Act.

(d) The Chief and investigators of the Division of Investigation of the Department of Professional and Vocational Standards are peace officers; provided, that the primary duty of any such peace officer shall be the enforcement of the law as that duty is set forth in Section 160 of the Business and Professions Code.

(e) Members of the Wildlife Protection Branch of the Department of Fish and Game deputized pursuant to Section 856 of the Fish and Game Code, deputies appointed pursuant to Section 851 of such code, and county fish and game wardens appointed pursuant to Section 875 of such code are peace officers; provided, that the primary duty of deputized members of the Wildlife Protection Branch, and the exclusive duty, except as provided in Section 1509.7 of the Military and Veterans Code, of any other peace officer listed in this subdivision, shall be the enforcement of the provisions of the Fish and Game Code, as such duties are set forth in Sections 856, 851 and 878, respectively, of such code.

(f) The State Forester and such employees or classes of employees of the Division of Forestry of the Department of Conservation and voluntary fire wardens as are designated by him pursuant to Section 4156 of the Public Resources Code are peace officers; provided, that the primary duty of any such peace officer shall be the enforcement of the law as that duty is set forth in Section 4156 of such code.

(g) Officers and employees of the Department of Motor Vehicles designated in Section 1655 of the Vehicle Code are peace officers; provided, that the primary duty of any such peace officer shall be the enforcement of the law as that duty is set forth in Section 1655 of such code.

(h) The secretary, chief investigator, and racetrack investigators of the California Horse Racing Board are peace officers; provided, that the primary duty of any such peace officer shall be the enforcement of the provisions of Chapter 4 (commencing with Section 19400) of Division 8 of the Business and Professions Code and Chapter 10 (commencing with Section 330) of Title 9 of Part 1 of the Penal Code. Any such peace officer is further authorized to enforce any penal provision of law while, in the course of his employment, he is in, on, or about any horseracing enclosure licensed pursuant to the Horse Racing Law.

(i) Police officers of a regional park district, appointed or employed pursuant to Section 5561 of the Public Resources Code, and officers and employees of the Department of Parks and Recreation designated by the director pursuant to Section 5008 of such code are peace officers; provided, that the primary duty of any such peace officer shall be the enforcement of the law as such duties are set forth in Sections 5561 and 5008, respectively, of such code.

(j) Members of the University of California police department appointed pursuant to Section 23501 of the Education Code are peace officers; provided, that the primary duty of any such peace officer shall be the enforcement of the law as that duty is set forth in Section 23501 of the Education Code.

(k) Policemen of the San Francisco Port Authority are peace officers; provided, that the primary duty of any such peace officer shall be the enforcement of the laws relating to the San Francisco Harbor, as that duty is set forth in Part 1 (commencing with Section 1690) of Division 6 of the Harbors and Navigation Code.

(l) The State Fire Marshal and assistant or deputy state fire marshals appointed pursuant to Section 13103 of the Health and Safety Code are peace officers; provided that the primary duty of any such peace officer shall be the enforcement of the law as that duty is set forth in Section 13104 of such code.

(m) Members of an arson investigating unit, regularly employed and paid as such, of a fire protection agency of the state, of a county, city, or district, are peace officers; provided, that the primary duty of any such peace officer shall be the detection and apprehension of persons who have violated or who are suspected of having violated any fire law.

(n) The Chief and such inspectors of the Bureau of Food and Drug Inspections as are designated by him pursuant to subdivision (a) of Section 216 of the Health and Safety Code are peace officers; provided that the exclusive duty of any such peace officer shall be the enforcement of the law as that duty is set forth in Section 216 of such code.

(o) The authority of any peace officer listed in subdivisions (c) through (n), inclusive, extends to any place in the state; provided, that except as otherwise provided in this section, Section 830.6, or Section 1509.7 of the Military and Veterans Code, any such peace officer shall be deemed a peace officer only for purposes of his primary duty, and shall not act as a peace officer in enforcing any other law except:

(1) When in pursuit of any offender or suspected offender; or

(2) To make arrests for crimes committed, or which there is probable cause to believe have been committed, in his presence while he is in the course of his employment; or

(3) When, while in uniform, such officer is requested, as a peace officer, to render such assistance as is appropriate under the circumstances to the person making such request, or to act upon his complaint, in the event that no peace officer otherwise authorized to act in such circumstances is apparently and immediately available and capable of rendering such assistance or taking such action.

P.C. 830.4—Security officers of the California State Police Division, the Sergeant at Arms of each house of the Legislature, guards and messengers of the Treasurer's office, the Director of the Department of Harbors and Watercraft and employees of such department designated by him pursuant to Section 71.2 of the Harbors and Navigation Code, members of a state college police department appointed pursuant to Section 24651 of the Education Code, the hospital administrator of a state hospital under the jurisdiction of the Department of Mental Hygiene and police officers designated by him pursuant to Section 4312 of the Welfare and Institutions Code, any railroad or steamboat company policeman commissioned by the Governor pursuant to Section 8226 of the Public Utilities Code, persons designated by a cemetery authority pursuant to Section 8325 of the Health and Safety Code, special officers of the Department of Airports of the City of Los Angeles commissioned by the city police commission, the chief of toll services, captains, lieutenants, and sergeants employed by the Department of Public Works on vehicular crossings pursuant to Chapter 13 (commencing with Section 23250) of Division 11 of the Vehicle Code, and persons employed as members of a security patrol of a school district pursuant to Section 15832 of the Education Code are peace officers while engaged in the performance of the duties of their respective employments.

The authority of any such peace officer extends to any place in the state as to a public offense committed or which there is probable cause to believe has been committed with respect to persons or property the protection of which is the immediate duty of such officer.

P.C. 830.5—(a) Any parole officer of the State Department of Corrections, placement or parole officer of the Youth Authority, probation officer, or deputy probation officer is a peace officer. Except as otherwise provided in this subdivision, the authority of any such peace officer shall extend only as to conditions of parole or of probation by any person in this state on parole or probation, or to the escape of any inmate or ward from a state institution, or to the transportation of such persons. The authority of any parole officer of the State Department of Corrections shall further extend to violations of any penal provisions of law which are discovered in the course of and arise in connection with his employment.

(b) Any warden, superintendent, supervisor, or guard employed by the Department of Corrections, and any officer or employee of each institution for delinquents of the Department of Youth Authority, is a peace officer. The authority of any such peace officer shall extend only as is necessary for the purpose of carrying out the duties of his employment. When he is carrying out his duties, any such supervisor, guard, officer or employee who is engaged in transportation of prisoners or apprehension of prisoners or wards who have escaped is a peace officer whether acting within or without this state.

(c) When, pursuant to Nevada law, an officer or employee of. the Nevada State Prison has in his custody in California a prisoner of the State of Nevada whom he is transporting from the Nevada State Prison or any honor or forest camp in Nevada to another point in Nevada for the purposes of firefighting or conservation work, such officer or employee of the Nevada State Prison shall have the power to maintain custody of the prisoner in California and to retake the prisoner if he should escape in California to the same extent as if such officer or employee were a peace officer appointed under California law and the prisoner had been committed to his custody in proceedings under California law.

P.C. 830.6—(a)   Whenever any qualified person is deputized or appointed by the proper authority as a reserve or auxiliary sheriff or city policeman, or as a deputy sheriff, and is assigned specific police functions by such authority, such person is a peace officer; provided, that the authority of such person as a peace officer shall extend only for the duration of such specific assignment.
(b)   Whenever any person is summoned to the aid of any uniformed peace officer, such person shall be vested with such powers of a peace officer as are expressly delegated him by the summoning officer or as are otherwise reasonably necessary to properly assist such officer.

LEGAL DISCUSSION AND ENFORCEMENT ASPECTS

The new codification and definition of peace officers affects numerous other codes. The most important changes however have been cited above. Under P.C. 830.1, the authority of a peace officer is extended to any place in the State with specific provisions. Sub-section (a) considers the employing municipality and, referring back to common law, as well as recent case decisions, the employee is a peace officer within his own "bailiwick." Sub-section (b) acknowledges the right of a chief law enforcement officer to authorize other peace officers to act in his jurisdiction. Sub-section (c) is a partial answer to a policeman's dilemma which existed prior to the change in the law. When an officer is outside his jurisdiction he may be for all legal purposes a "badge carrying" private person. Now, however, he is given peace officer status whenever he has probable cause, or, when in fact, a public offense is committed in his presence and where there is an immediate danger to person or property, or the possible escape of the suspect.

The effect of section P.C. 830.2 (a) deals solely with the California Highway Patrol and grants them statewide jurisdiction. Highway Patrolmen are restricted to enforcement of provisions in the Vehicle Code or other laws upon highways, and specifically directed *not* to act as a peace officer enforcing other laws, i.e. resident burglary, embezzlement, etc. They are, of course, exempt when in fresh pursuit, or for crimes committed in their presence or upon any highway.

The legislature was quite clear in granting peace officer status to all officers who observed crimes committed in their presence. An example of this is an off-duty police officer who is cashing his paycheck in another geographical sub-division when the place is robbed. He is now morally and legally obligated and authorized to act as a full-fledged peace officer throughout the State of California.

The reader's attention is called to section P.C. 830.3 (o) which limits all those persons listed in sub-division (c) through (n). Those classes of people are deemed peace officers only for the purpose of their respective primary duties, and shall not act as peace officers except,

1. when in fresh pursuit
2. when making arrests for crimes committed in their presence while in the course of their respective employment.
3. when in uniform if requested to act as a peace officer and render assistance as long as no other authorized peace officer is in the area or capable of rendering immediate assistance.

Auxiliary and reserve policemen or sheriffs are limited peace officers. Such limitations are restricted to the specific police functions assigned by the appointing authority.

Persons who are summoned to assist a peace officer are now also vested by the same powers and authority as would be necessary to assist the summoning officer. This section now allows peace officers to transfer their authority to a private person during emergency situations or whenever they deem the circumstances necessitate.

While the authority of a peace officer has been broadened there are still many occasions when a policeman on duty may be acting as a private person. It is most important that police officers determine prior to taking action that they are in fact peace officers at that moment. An example of this would be when two detectives are investigating a misdemeanor offense in their jurisdiction and follow leads to the suspect in another jurisdiction. If the officers have not obtained prior consent from the local police chief, and if circumstances require that they make an arrest for a crime that does not take place in their presence, they must realize that they are making the arrest pursuant to the laws of arrest of a private person (P.C. 837). Whenever an officer is in a position that his status is questionable he must make a determination and act in the best interest of justice and his employer.

The legislature did not decree firemen or animal regulation officers to be peace officers. This was undoubtedly an oversight, and will be rectified in the very near future, but the processing of violations charged with unlawful burnings or leash-law violations has been hampered. These officers can no longer act under their authority as peace officers and issue citations to the offender. They now must contact a police officer and file a complaint with him. The policeman can then issue the citation or if necessary take the suspect into custody after the fireman or animal regulation officer has made a private person's arrest. Surely the legislature will move promptly to facilitate justice prevailing in these types of matters.

APPLICABLE STATUTES—USE OF FORCE

P.C. 835a—*Reasonable Force to Effect Arrest, Prevent Escape Is Permissible.* Any peace officer who has reasonable cause to believe that the person to be arrested has committed a public offense may use reasonable force to effect the arrest, to prevent escape or to overcome resistance. A peace officer who makes or attempts to make an arrest need not retreat or desist from his efforts by reason of the resistance or threatened resistance of the person being arrested; nor shall such officer be deemed an aggressor or lose his right to self-defense by the use of reasonable force to effect the arrest or to prevent escape or to overcome resistance.

P.C. 843—*What Force May Be Used.* When the arrest is being made by an officer under the authority of a warrant, after information of the intention to make the arrest, if the person to be arrested either flees or forcibly resists, the officer may use all necessary means to effect the arrest.

P.C. 844—*Arrests, Entries for.* To make an arrest, a private person, if the offense be a felony, and in all cases a peace officer, may break open the door or window of the house in which the person to be arrested is, or in which they have reasonable grounds for believing him to be, after having demanded admittance and explained the purpose for which admittance is desired.

P.C. 845—*Same.* Any person who has lawfully entered a house for the purpose of making an arrest, may break open the door or window thereof if detained therein, when necessary for the purpose of liberating himself, and an officer may do the same, when necessary for the purpose of liberating a person who, acting in his aid, lawfully entered for the purpose of making an arrest, and is detained therein.

P.C. 846—*Weapons May Be Taken from Persons Arrested.* Any person making an arrest may take from the person arrested all offensive weapons which he may have about his person, and must deliver them to the Magistrate before whom he is taken.

LEGAL DISCUSSION

As regards the use of "reasonable force" by an arresting officer it must be emphasized that there is a definite limitation on the use of deadly weapons by police officers with a concomitant responsibility to justify its use as being reasonable in each specific case. Justifiable homicide (P.C. 196) is discussed in Chapter 13.

The use of force to enter a premises is authorized provided the purpose of the officer's presence is announced and he has demanded admittance. The courts, however, have been most lenient in this regard if it is shown that the required action would have jeopardized the officer's safety. A speedy entry into a premises is also permitted if it is reasonably indicated that evidence might be disposed of by delay or announcement of the officers, as in cases of narcotic arrests.

ENFORCEMENT ASPECTS

The amount of force which an officer may use while making an arrest is a matter of special importance. The legal authority revolves around the *reasonable necessity* for force. For a *FELONY*, when apparently necessary to a reasonable man, the officer has a right to use deadly force![2] *For a misdemeanor deadly force is never authorized!*

Every Police Agency has a policy or departmental order regarding the use of firearms. The discharge of a weapon (Warning Shot) is not unlawful when the officer reasonably believes that a felony has been committed. However, most agencies do not recommend this action and in fact prohibit it. Discretion is the policeman's guide in the use of firearms. The authors strongly recommend the following rule of thumb: IF YOU HAVE TIME TO THINK BEFORE SHOOTING—DON'T SHOOT!

Field Interrogation Guidelines

The "stop and frisk" right of a police officer has consistently been upheld by the courts.[3] The authority for a "pat-down" or "cursory search" for weapons is a necessary protective right for law enforcement officers to maintain. As long as officers conduct this search in good faith, evidence is admissible, i.e., a firearm discovered in the course of an arrest could be admissible in a prosecution under the Deadly Weapons Control Act. However, this would not be true in the case of narcotics found in the suspect's pockets. The search must be restricted to possible offensive weapons; anything further would be a violation of Constitutional guarantees. In general the following guidelines are applicable:

1. Police may detain and question a person when the circumstances are such as would indicate to a reasonable man in like position that such a course of conduct is necessary to the proper discharge of his duties.

2. Temporary detention for questioning permits reasonable investigation, without necessarily making an arrest.

3. Although police have the power to detain and question, there must be probable cause to detain.

4. Probable cause to detain requires that there be some unusual or suspicious circumstances, or other demonstrable reasons, warranting the investigation. Such factors as time, location, number of people, demeanor and conduct of a suspect, a recently reported crime, and the gravity of the crime reported are relevant.

5. In the absence of probable cause to detain, any evidence seized incidental to the unlawful detention is inadmissible.

6. In determining whether the restraint imposed on an individual is an arrest or a detention, the intent of the officer is relevant. A stopping followed by an immediate search, other than a pat-down search, indicates an intention to arrest. A stopping after which the officers question the suspect in good faith with respect to the reason for the detention indicates the detention was for investigation, not arrest.

7. In the event of a recently reported crime in the neighborhood, police may, with probable cause to detain, stop a suspect and return him to the scene of the crime for investigation.

8. Where the circumstances warrant it, officers may request a suspect to alight from the car for questioning.

ARREST BY WARRANT

The general definition of a warrant is a writ or precept from a competent authority in pursuance of law, directing the doing of an act, and addressed to an officer or person competent to do the act, and affording him protection from damage if he does it. The legal definition of a warrant of arrest is an order in writing, in the name of the people, signed by a magistrate, commanding the arrest of the defendant.

The general forms of a warrant are set forth in P.C. 814 for a felony and P.C. 1427 for a misdemeanor. These warrants are issued based on a complaint. Bench warrants are a different type and are issued by the court or clerk upon the order of the court.[4]

To be valid on its face a warrant must specify the name of the defendant (John Doe is a name used in case the true name of a defendant is not known); the date of issuance; the city, county or township where issued; and the signature of the issuing magistrate (a facsimile signature is acceptable).[5] Section 153 of the Code of Civil Procedure provides that the court seal must be on a warrant. The bail must also be on the warrant.[6] It should be noted that "NO BAIL" satisfies this requirement in that bail has been set—to wit: "NO BAIL."

Felony warrants may be served at any time. Misdemeanor warrants must have an approved endorsement for nighttime service. Usually the warrant form will have the printed notice "This warrant may be served in the nighttime." Without this endorsement the misdemeanor warrant can only be served during daylight hours (P.C. 840).

Warrants of arrest are directed to peace officers in the state, and only they may execute the warrants. An arrest warrant may not be served by a private person. An officer need not have an arrest warrant in his possession, but, if requested by the defendant, it must be shown to him as soon as practicable.[7] As long as a warrant is regular on its face, the peace officer is required to execute it regardless of any defect in the proceedings.[8] The officer is exempt from liability in execution of a warrant as long as he acts without malice and reasonably believes the arrestee is the proper party.[9] A warrant is valid indefinitely; there is no statute of limitations. However, a warrant can be recalled by the court.

A telegraphic warrant or a teletype abstract of warrant is as valid as the original in the hands of the receiving officer. This warrant also should be shown to the arrestee as soon as practicable upon request.

LAWS OF ARREST (WITHOUT WARRANT)

Most arrests are made without warrants and usually under stress situations. Every officer must know the limits and authority he possesses. This may well be the most important area of knowledge that a good officer must understand and be able to apply.

There are many cases that can be lost forever at the moment of arrest or initial police contact. The importance of this is reflected in possibilities of false arrest suits; search and seizure rules excluding evidence; self-incrimination warnings which make confessions and admissions inadmissible;[10] and the right to resist a potentially unlawful arrest.

APPLICABLE STATUTES

P.C. 836—*Arrests by peace officers.* A peace officer may make an arrest in obedience to a warrant, or may, without a warrant, arrest a person:

1. Whenever he has reasonable cause to believe that the person to be arrested has committed a public offense in his presence.

2. When a person arrested has committed a felony, although not in his presence.

3. Whenever he has reasonable cause to believe that the person to be arrested has committed a felony, whether or not a felony has in fact been committed.

P.C. 836.3—*Arrest by peace officer.* A peace officer may make an arrest in obedience to a warrant delivered to him, or may, without a warrant, arrest a person who, while charged with or convicted of a misdemeanor, has escaped from any county or city jail, prison, industrial farm or industrial road camp or from the custody of the officer or person in charge of him while engaged on any county road or other county work or going to or returning from such county road or other county work or from the custody of any officer or person in whose lawful custody he is when such escape is not by force or violence.

P.C. 837—*Arrests by private persons.* A private person may arrest another:

1. For a public offense committed or attempted in his presence.

2. When the person arrested has committed a felony, although not in his presence.

3. When a felony has been in fact committed, and he has reasonable cause for believing the person arrested to have committed it.

LEGAL DISCUSSION

Although undefined by statute, an understanding of "reasonable cause" is an essential of proper police officer training. The term "probable cause" is frequently used interchangeably. Briefly we are discussing a state of facts which would lead an ordinary and prudent person to conscientiously believe or possess a strong suspicion of a particular fact based upon the specific circumstances.

The authority for arrest by a peace officer has certain similarities to that of a private person, but the distinction is extremely important. Whenever a peace officer is acting as a private person, his authority is correspondingly limited. It behooves the officer to be certain that he maintains his peace officer status, as previously discussed in this chapter. When the officer makes an arrest acting as a private person, he must follow the same procedures as required of the private persons. Subsequent acts, such as issuing a citation only or other acts as a peace officer, invalidate the original arrest. The term "citizen's arrest" may sometimes be misleading. The arrest is performed by a private person who may or may not be a citizen of the United States. The same arrest authority is possessed by aliens.

Under subsection 1 of Sec. 836 and Sec. 837 the key phrase is "in his presence." This means that the arresting person must be able to establish all the elements of the crime from his own personal knowledge; hence he must have acquired this from his natural senses. The difference of authority revolves around the peace officer having the "reasonable belief" that the crime is being committed in his presence. Therefore, if a woman is screaming for help and is struck by a man, an arrest by a peace officer is certainly justified based upon the reasonableness of the circumstances. If a private person makes the arrest and it turns out the man and woman were merely "practicing for a theatrical play," there is a false arrest. The private person has no leeway regarding reasonable cause; there must actually be an offense committed in his presence. This then is the major difference between the two authorities. Both of these sections refer to public offenses (misdemeanor and felony). As a practical matter most arrests made under this section would be for misdemeanors.

As to subsection 2 of each of the laws of arrest it should be noted that they are virtually identical. They are very rarely used, and the authors do not recommend arrests or bookings under these sections. Practically speaking the subsections are stating that felons may be arrested at any time in any area by anybody. Furthermore the subsections may authorize an arrest "retroactively." For example, if an arrest were to be made of the very next person to enter through a doorway, this could turn out to be a legal arrest if the person had committed a felony. This fact would be unknown at the time of arrest.

As to subsection 3 of each of the laws, note that this refers to *felonies* only. The main distinction between the peace officer and the private person is that the felony crime must actually have been committed in order for the private person to arrest lawfully. The felony having been committed, the private person need have only reasonable cause for believing the person arrested to have committed it. In effect, then, we consider the actual commission of the crime (to wit a felony) and the reasonable belief that the suspect was the perpetrator. If a person is seen crawling into the window of a residence late at night and is arrested by a peace officer, this may constitute a lawful arrest. Certainly it is reasonable to believe a burglary (felony) may have been attempted as it is most unusual for a person to crawl into residence windows at a late and unusual hour. However, if the facts reveal that the suspect was the son of the owner and had just been discharged from the armed services, we have a different arrest situation for the private person. There is as a matter of fact no crime (felony) committed despite the suspiciousness of the circumstances. Hence an arrest by a private person would be unlawful no matter how much good faith and intent he may have exercised.

ENFORCEMENT ASPECTS

Peace officers must understand and apply the laws of arrest as a minister must know and apply the gospel. Time does not allow for a complete discussion, and actual experience is needed to thoroughly learn these laws of arrest. However, a few guidelines should be noted.

1. Whenever possible an arrest should be made by warrant.
2. When a police officer makes an arrest without a warrant, if he is acting as a police officer within the scope of his authority as such, he is performing a private person's arrest and his conduct is governed by the law pertaining thereto.
3. Subsection 1 of both arrest laws deals with misdemeanors. As a peace officer are you acting with reasonable cause? As a private person can you alone establish the corpus delicti of the crime?
4. Under P.C. 836 (3) as a peace officer are you sure you have probable cause to believe that the person arrested has committed a *felony*? As a private person can you be sure the *felony* has been committed? When booking a suspect so arrested, all bookings should be under Sec. 836 (3) and the specific felony. The booking should read 836 (3) of 211 (Robbery).
5. As a peace officer be sure to advise citizens when they have authority to make arrests inasmuch as this may be the only way to proceed in practical police problems; i.e., where there is a nonfelonious assault resulting in minor injury and such assault was not witnessed by the peace officer, the suspect may be arrested by the victim.
6. The officer must always exercise discretion when accepting custody of a person arrested by a "private person." For example, a child could arrest an adult who had molested him, whereas an obviously intoxicated person might not be capable of making an effective arrest by a private person.
7. The fact that a person has been arrested does not mean he in turn cannot arrest another person or in fact arrest the officer. These are certainly rare instances but nonetheless they should be considered as they could be possible even if civil claims for damages might follow.
8. Remember that any person making an arrest may summon assistance from all males over 18 years of age.[11]

SPECIAL ARREST CIRCUMSTANCES AND CONSIDERATIONS

Arrests without warrants may also be made under the following conditions:

1. Upon authorization or order of a magistrate.
2. Under the Uniform Fresh Pursuit Act.
3. An escape from prison or county jail.
4. A California bail bondsman whose client has not complied with court orders.
5. Probation violation.
6. Parole violation.
7. Persons released on their own recognizance by a court who do not appear when ordered to do so.

Exemptions from Arrest

Rarely used, but necessary to the discussion of this topic, are the exemptions which stem from the U.S. Constitution, Article 1, Section 6, and the California Constitution, Article IV, Section 11. Diplomatic immunity is conferred by and through the U.S. State Department. These are true and valid representatives of the sovereign authority of a foreign country including ambassadors and other diplomatic officials. The immunity is for civil and criminal process and extends also to the families and the official households. The only authorization for police contact would be in preventing acts of violence by these persons. Arrests are voidable by these persons, and they must establish their immunity in a judicial proceeding.

Members of the state, county or municipal legislature bodies are exempt from civil process and criminal process in matters which arose before their entrance into the state.[12] They must also be granted a reasonable time to leave the state after the trial or court appearance.

CONCLUSION AND GENERAL SUMMARY

Peace officers cannot assume their actions are under a peace officer status simply because they carry a "badge." The Penal Code and judicial interpretations have set additional criteria to be considered. "Private persons" arrests by peace officers will become more prevalent in view of the limitation imposed by "scope of authority." The need for complete awareness and knowledge of the laws of arrest becomes most essential.

DISCUSSION QUESTIONS

1. Define arrest in general and legal terms.
2. What are the hours of service for misdemeanor and felony warrants?
3. What legally is necessary to constitute an arrest?
4. What is required on a warrant of arrest?
5. Who are magistrates?
6. Who are peace officers?
7. Explain the laws of arrest of a peace officer without a warrant.
8. What force may be used in making an arrest?
9. Explain the laws of arrest of a private person.
10. Explain the effect of jurisdiction and venue on a peace officer's authority.

NOTES

[1]P.C. 834a.
[2]People v. Brite, 9 C 2666; 72 P 2d 122.
  People v. Adams, 85 C 231; 24 P 629.
[3]Gisske v. Sanders, 9 CA 13; 98 P 43.
[4]P.C. 979–986; 1195–1196.
[5]P.C. 815; 1427.
[6]P.C. 815a.
[7]P.C. 842.
[8]CCP 262.1.
[9]CC 43.5
  People v. Marquez, 237 ACA 741.
[10]Miranda v. Arizona, 384 US 436.
[11]P.C. 150.
[12]P.C. 1334.4–1334.5.

II

SPECIFIC
CRIMINAL AREAS

*Criminal laws can be divided into three
major categories: crimes against the individual person or
persons; crimes against property; and
crimes against the public or society itself. The lines of
demarcation are not always clear. For
example, robbery is intended to be a crime against property,
but it directly affects the person's right to be
free of fear. Lynching is a crime against the public, but
it most certainly is a crime against the
victim. We have arbitrarily classified crimes in these
three categories in order to present the
laws in a logical sequence.*

IIA

CRIMES
AGAINST PROPERTY

*Crimes against property include crimes
against property rights as well as against tangible property.
For example, the title to property can
be offended by forgery. There is, as we have noted,
some overlap between crimes against
the person and crimes against property, as in the case
of robbery and extortion. We have selected
the prime moving factor, namely, the property sought, as
the guiding principle in classing these crimes
as crimes against property.*

6

Theft and Related Offenses

APPLICABLE STATUTES—THEFT

P.C. 484—*Theft defined*. (a) Every person who shall feloniously steal, take, carry, lead, or drive away the personal property of another, or who shall fraudulently appropriate property which has been entrusted to him, or who shall knowingly and designedly, by any false or fraudulent representation or pretense, defraud any other person of money, labor, or real or personal property, or who causes or procures others to report falsely of his wealth or mercantile character and by thus imposing upon any person, obtains credit and thereby fraudulently gets or obtains possession of money or property or obtains the labor or service of another, is guilty of theft. In determining the value of the property obtained, for the purposes of this section, the reasonable and fair market value shall be the test, and in determining the value of services received the contract price shall be the test. If there be no contract price, the reasonable and going wage for the service rendered shall govern. For the purposes of this section, any false or fraudulent representation or pretense made shall be treated as continuing, so as to cover any money, property or service received as a result thereof, and the complaint, information or indictment may charge that the crime was committed on any date during the particular period in question. The hiring of any additional employee or employees without advising each of them of every labor claim due and unpaid and every judgment that the employer has been unable to meet shall be prima facie evidence of intent to defraud.

(b) Except as provided in Section 10855 of the Vehicle Code, intent to commit theft by fraud is presumed if one who has leased or rented the personal property of another pursuant to a written contract fails to return the personal property to its owner within 20 days after the owner has made written demand by certified or registered mail following the expiration of the lease or rental agreement for return of the property so leased or rented, or If one presents to the owner identification which bears a false or fictitious name or address for the purpose of obtaining the lease or rental agreement.

(c) The presumptions created by subdivision (b) are presumptions affecting the burden of producing evidence.

(d) Within 30 days after the lease or rental agreement has expired, the owner shall make written demand for return of the property so leased or rented. Notice addressed and mailed to the lessee or renter at the address given at the time of the making of the lease or rental agreement and to any other known address shall constitute proper demand. Where the owner fails to make such written demand the presumption created by subdivision (b) shall not apply.

P.C. 490a—*"Theft" substituted for larceny, embezzlement or stealing.* Wherever any law or statute of this state refers to or mentions larceny, embezzlement, or stealing, said law or statute shall hereafter be read and interpreted as if the word "theft" were substituted therefor.

P.C. 486—*Degrees of theft.* Theft is divided into two degrees, the first of which is termed grand theft; the second, petty theft.

P.C. 489—*Punishment of grand theft.* Grand theft is punishable by imprisonment in the county jail for not more than one year or in the state prison for not more than 10 years.

P.C. 490—*Punishment of petty theft.* Petty theft is punishable by fine not exceeding five hundred dollars, or by imprisonment in the county jail not exceeding six months, or both.

P.C. 514—*Embezzlement, penalty for.* Every person guilty of embezzlement is punishable in the manner prescribed for theft of property of the value or kind embezzled; and where the property embezzled is an evidence of debt or right of action, the sum due upon it or secured to be paid by it must be taken as its value; if the embezzlement or defalcation is of the public funds of the United States, or of this state, or of any county or municipality within this state, the offense is a felony, and is punishable by imprisonment in the state prison not less than one nor more than 10 years; and the person so convicted is ineligible thereafter to any office of honor, trust, or profit in this state.

LEGAL DISCUSSION

The reader should note that the general theft statute (P.C. 484) does not differentiate grand theft from petty theft. This section does, however, merge all former crimes of larceny, embezzlement, and bunco crimes into "straight theft."

The charge of theft may be general and need not specify the method of the theft.[1] In fact, the judge or jury may have full discretion in arriving at their decision without determining the form of theft. Often theft by trick or device and theft by false pretenses overlap so that a verdict may be justified on either theory. The basic elements of the crime of theft require:

1. There must be control over the subject of the theft. A person cannot be charged with the theft of an item over which he cannot exercise control. There must also be a movement of the property so that the thief has actually exercised dominion over the goods. This control, movement, and dominion are referred to as the asportation element of theft. The statute specifies the taking and carrying away of the goods.[2]

2. Intent to *permanently* deprive the owner of the property is an important element of the crime of theft. Proof is generally shown by circumstantial evidence. In this type of case unity of act and intent is emphasized. Even with the most malicious intent, a person cannot be charged with the theft of his own property as in the situation where a person believes he is stealing someone else's hat and coat and it is later discovered to be his own.

ENFORCEMENT ASPECTS

It is most important for the reader to realize that grand theft is a felony and that other types of theft are misdemeanors. The arrest implications have been stressed previously in Chapter 5. It is very difficult for a field officer to make an on-the-spot decision as to the severity of the crime (theft). Accordingly, the authors urge study and evaluation of the facts and circumstances *prior* to exercising felony authority. The old hue and cry of "Stop thief, stop!" spurs the apprehending officer to action, but there is still the question whether the crime is a felony or a misdemeanor.

Many officers have regretted their swift action based solely on the victim's loud laments and frantic accusations.

APPLICABLE STATUTES

P.C. 487—*Grand theft defined.* Grand theft is theft committed in any of the following cases:
1. When the money, labor or real or personal property taken is of a value exceeding two hundred dollars ($200); provided, that when domestic fowls, avocados, olives, citrus or deciduous fruits, nuts and artichokes are taken of a value exceeding fifty dollars ($50); provided, further, that where the money, labor, real or personal property is taken by a servant, agent or employee from his principal or employer and aggregates two hundred dollars ($200) or more in any 12 consecutive month period, then the same shall constitute grand theft.
2. When the property is taken from the person of another.
3. When the property taken is an automobile, firearm, horse, mare, gelding, any bovine animal, any caprine animal, mule, jack, jenny, sheep, lamb, hog, sow, boar, gilt, barrow or pig.

P.C. 487a—*Stealing the carcass of an animal.* (a) Every person who shall feloniously steal, take, transport or carry the carcass of any bovine, caprine, equine, ovine, or suine animal or of any mule, jack or jenny, which is the personal property of another, or who shall fraudulently appropriate such property which has been entrusted to him, is guilty of grand theft. (b) Every person who shall feloniously steal, take, transport, or carry any portion of the carcass of any bovine, caprine, equine, ovine or suine animal or of any mule, jack or jenny, which has been killed without the consent of the owner thereof, is guilty of grand theft.

P.C. 487b—*Grand theft of real property.* Every person who converts real estate of the value of fifty dollars ($50) or more into personal property by severance from the realty of another, and with felonious intent to do so, steals, takes, and carries away such property is guilty of grand theft and is punishable by imprisonment in the state prison for not less than one year nor more than 14 years.

P.C. 487c—*Petit theft of real property.* Every person who converts real estate of the value of less than fifty dollars ($50) into personal property by severance from the realty of another, and with felonious intent to do so steals, takes, and carries away such property is guilty of petit theft and is punishable by imprisonment in the county jail for not more than one year, or by a fine not exceeding one thousand dollars ($1,000), or by both such fine and imprisonment.

P.C. 487d—*Grand theft of gold dust, amalgam, or quicksilver.* Every person who feloniously steals, takes, and carries away, or attempts to take, steal, and carry from any mining claim, tunnel, sluice, undercurrent, riffle box, or sulfurate machine another's gold dust, amalgam, or quicksilver is guilty of grand theft and is punishable by imprisonment in the state prison for not less than one year nor more than 14 years.

P.C. 488—*Petty theft defined.* Theft in other cases is petty theft.

LEGAL DISCUSSION

Grand theft under P.C. 487 is defined in three ways. The first is in relation to the value of the item taken; the second is in relation to the area where the theft occurs—to wit, the person; the third covers certain specific items which are statutorily declared to constitute a felonious theft.

As determination of value is necessary, note that it must be estimated exclusively in lawful money of the United States.[3] Value of property is determined by the fair market value. This is usually established by the testimony of the purchaser, a qualified appraiser, or a tradesman of the goods. It is not necessary for the prosecution to show that the defendant was aware of the value of goods taken.[4]

A single taking of two one hundred dollar ($100) bills would constitute petty theft. However, an employee who steals a total of two hundred dollars ($200) within twelve consecutive months by several takings would be charged with grand theft. The reader should note the penny discrepancy in this type of theft as the statute reads "over $200" in one case and "$200 or more" in the other.

The agricultural history of our nation has accorded value to certain fruits and animals so that the theft of the enumerated items of a value exceeding fifty dollars ($50) is decreed grand theft. Farm animals have been included as subjects of grand theft, a provision that can be traced back to the horse rustler and cattle thief of old. In metropolitan areas these crimes are rare.

Every theft from the person of a victim which involves the use of force or fear is a robbery. (See Chapter 10 on robbery.) Therefore, each theft from the person or immediate presence of the victim must be carefully scrutinized to ascertain whether force and/or fear was involved.

Included in the list of felonious takings are firearms. These occur most frequently in urban areas. The firearm listing is of recent origin and stems primarily from conditions of civil unrest and attempts to reduce unlawful acts involving firearms.

Theft from the person disregards value completely. These thefts are usually evident and include pickpockets and purse snatchers.

Where the property is an automobile, the element of "permanently" depriving the owner is essential in proving grand theft. An unlawful taking of an automobile is not alone sufficient to sustain a grand theft charge. "Joyriding" or "borrowing" of an auto is more properly prosecuted under Section 10851 of the Vehicle Code, which states:

> Any person who drives or takes a vehicle not his own, without the consent of the owner thereof and with intent to either permanently or temporarily deprive the owner thereof of his title to or possession of such vehicle, whether with or without intent to steal the same, or any person who is a party or accessory to or an accomplice in any such driving or unauthorized taking or stealing is guilty of a felony, and upon conviction thereof shall be punished by imprisonment in the state prison for not less than one year nor more than five years or in the county jail for not more than one year or by a fine of not more than five thousand dollars ($5,000) or by both such fine and imprisonment. The consent of the owner of a vehicle to its taking or driving shall not in any case be presumed or implied because of such owner's consent on a previous occasion to the taking or driving of such vehicle by the same or a different person.

To constitute this offense there must be a moving to satisfy the asportation element. This section describes a felony which may be "broken down" to a misdemeanor conviction by sentence of the court. The fact that a defendant rode as a passenger in the stolen vehicle would not, alone, be sufficient for conviction.[5]

ENFORCEMENT ASPECTS

An important consideration in thefts by employees involves the statute of limitations. The section states "any" consecutive 12-month period; hence the investigation can go back to a 36-month period (felony statute of limitations being three years). If thefts of $200 or more can be shown within any 12-month period, a felony charge can be sustained. If not, then a series of misdemeanor thefts have been committed, some of which may not be prosecutable as the statute may have tolled (misdemeanor statute of limitations being one year).

The discussion to this point has involved a straight taking, stealing, or larceny of goods. It should be noted that this would be impossible if the goods were real property. How does one "take" an acre of ground? However, under areas of embezzlement or theft by false pretenses, real property may very well be the subject of theft.[6] Inherently unlawful property such as a betting marker or lottery ticket is not a subject of theft. Certain other thefts are defined in the following sections:

APPLICABLE STATUTES

P.C. 491—*Dogs are personal property*. Dogs are personal property, and their value is to be ascertained in the same manner as the value of other property.

P.C. 492—*Larceny of written instruments*. If the thing stolen consists of any evidence of debt, or other written instrument, the amount of money due thereupon, or secured to be paid thereby, and remaining unsatisfied, or which in any contingency might be collected thereon, or the value of the property the title to which is shown thereby, or the sum which might be recovered in the absence thereof, is the value of the thing stolen.

P.C. 493—*Value of passage tickets*. If the thing stolen is any ticket or other paper or writing entitling or purporting to entitle the holder or proprietor thereof to a passage upon any railroad or vessel or other public conveyance, the price at which tickets entitling a person to a like passage are usually sold by the proprietors of such conveyance is the value of such ticket, paper, or writing.

P.C. 494—*Written instruments completed but not delivered*. All the provisions of this chapter apply where the property taken is an instrument for the payment of money, evidence of debt, public security, or passage ticket, completed and ready to be issued or delivered, although the same has never been issued or delivered by the makers thereof to any person as a purchaser or owner.

P.C. 495—*Severing and removing part of the realty declared larceny*. The provisions of this chapter apply where the thing taken is any fixture or part of the realty, and is severed at the time of the taking, in the same manner as if the thing had been severed by another person at some previous time.

P.C. 499—*Stealing water*. Every person who, with intent to injure or defraud, connects or causes to be connected, any pipe, tube, or other instrument, with any main, service pipe, or other pipe or conduit or flume for conducting water, for the purpose of taking water from such main, service pipe, conduit or flume, without the knowledge of the owner thereof, and with intent to evade payment therefor, and every person who, with intent to injure or defraud, injures or alters any watermeter, watermeter seal, service valve, or other service connection, is guilty of a misdemeanor.

P.C. 499a—*Theft of electricity*. Every person who shall willfully, and knowingly with intent to injure or defraud, make or cause to be made any connection in any manner whatsoever with any electric wire or electric appliance of any character whatsoever operated by any person, persons or corporation authorized to generate, transmit and sell electric current, or who shall so willfully and knowingly with intent to injure or defraud, use or cause to be used any such connection in such manner as to supply any electric current for heat or light or power to any electric lamp, or apparatus or device, by or at which electric current for heat or light or power is consumed or otherwise used or wasted, without passing through a meter for the measuring and registering of the quantity passing through such electric wire or apparatus, or who shall knowingly and with like intent injure, alter or procure to be injured or altered any electric meter, or obstruct its working, or procure the same to be tampered with or injured, or use or cause to be used any electric meter, or appliance so tampered with or injured, shall be deemed guilty of a misdemeanor.

P.C. 499b—*Taking vehicle for temporary use.* Any person who shall, without the permission of the owner thereof, take any automobile, bicycle, motorcycle, or other vehicle, or motorboat or vessel, for the purpose of temporarily using or operating the same, shall be deemed guilty of a misdemeanor, and upon conviction thereof, shall be punished by a fine not exceeding two hundred dollars ($200), or by imprisonment not exceeding three months, or by both such fine and imprisonment.

P.C. 499d—*Taking of aircraft.* Any person who operates or takes an aircraft not his own, without the consent of the owner thereof, and with intent to either permanently or temporarily deprive the owner thereof of his title to or possession of such vehicle, whether with or without intent to steal the same, or any person who is a party or accessory to or an accomplice in any operation or unauthorized taking or stealing is guilty of a felony, and upon conviction thereof shall be punished by imprisonment in the state prison for not less than one year nor more than five years or in the county jail for not more than one year or by a fine of not more than five thousand dollars ($5,000) or by both such fine and imprisonment.

APPLICABLE STATUTES—EMBEZZLEMENT

P.C. 503—*"Embezzlement" defined.* Embezzlement is the fraudulent appropriation of property by a person to whom it has been intrusted.

P.C. 504—*Fraudulent appropriation of property by officers of state or any association.* Every officer of this state, or of any county, city, city and county, or other municipal corporation or subdivision thereof, and every deputy, clerk, or servant of any such officer, and every officer, director, trustee, clerk, servant, or agent of any association, society, or corporation (public or private), who fraudulently appropriates to any use or purpose not in the due and lawful execution of his trust, any property which he has in his possession or under his control by virtue of his trust, or secretes it with a fraudulent intent to appropriate it to such use or purpose, is guilty of embezzlement.

P.C. 504a—*Fraudulent removal of leased property, embezzlement.* Every person who shall fraudulently remove, conceal or dispose of any goods, chattels or effects, leased or let to him by any instrument in writing, or any personal property or effects of another in his possession, under a contract of purchase not yet fulfilled, and any person in possession of such goods, chattels, or effects knowing them to be subject to such lease or contract of purchase who shall so remove, conceal or dispose of the same with intent to injure or defraud the lessor or owner thereof, is guilty of embezzlement.

P.C. 504b—*Debtor's fraudulent appropriation of proceeds from sale of property covered by security agreement.* Where under the terms of a security agreement, as defined in Section 9105 of the Commercial Code, the debtor has the right to sell the property covered thereby and is to account to the secured party for, and pay to the secured party the indebtedness secured by the security agreement from, the proceeds of the sale of any of the said property, and where such debtor, having sold the property covered by the security agreement and having received the proceeds of such sale, willfully and wrongfully, and with the intent to defraud, fails to pay to the secured party the amounts due under the security agreement, or the proceeds of such sale, whichever is the lesser amount, and appropriates such money to his own use, said debtor shall be guilty of embezzlement and shall be punishable as provided in Section 514.

P.C. 506—*Misappropriations by persons controlling or intrusted with property.* Every trustee, banker, merchant, broker, attorney, agent, assignee in trust, executor, administrator, or collector, or person otherwise intrusted with or having in his control property for the use of any other person, who fraudulently appropriates it to any use or purpose not in the due and lawful execution of his trust, or secretes it with a fraudulent intent to appropriate it to such use or purpose, and any contractor who appropriates money paid to him for any use or purpose, other than for that which he received it, is guilty of embezzlement, and the payment of laborers and materialmen for work performed or material furnished in the performance of any contract is hereby declared to be the use and purpose to which the contract price of such contract, or any part thereof, received by the contractor shall be applied.

P.C. 506a—*Collector of accounts or debts defined.* Any person who, acting as collector, or acting in any capacity in or about a business conducted for the collection of accounts or debts owing by another person, and who violates the provisions of section five hundred six of the Penal Code, shall be deemed to be an agent or person as defined in said section five hundred six of the Penal Code, and subject for a violation of the provisions of said section five hundred six of the Penal Code, to be prosecuter, tried, and punished in accordance therewith and with law: and the word collector herein set forth shall include and be held to mean every such person who collects, or who has in his possession or under his control property or money for the use of any other person, whether in his own name and mixed with his own property or money, or otherwise, or whether he has any interest, direct or indirect, in or to such property or money, or any portion thereof, and who fraudulently appropriates to his own use, or the use of any person other than the true owner, or person entitled thereto, or secretes such property or money, or any portion thereof, or interest therein not his own, with a fraudulent intent to appropriate it to any use or purpose not in the due and lawful execution of his trust.

P.C. 507—*When bailee, tenant, or lodger guilty of embezzlement.* Every person intrusted with any property as bailee, tenant, or lodger, or with any power of attorney for the sale or transfer thereof, who fraudulently converts the same or the proceeds thereof to his own use, or secretes it or them with a fraudulent intent to convert to his own use, is guilty of embezzlement.

P.C. 508—*When clerk, agent, or servant guilty of embezzlement.* Every clerk, agent, or servant of any person who fraudulently appropriates to his own use, or secretes with a fraudulent intent to appropriate to his own use, any property of another which has come into his control or care by virtue of his employment as such clerk, agent, or servant, is guilty of embezzlement.

P.C. 511—*Claim of title a ground of defense.* Upon any indictment for embezzlement, it is a sufficient defense that the property was appropriated openly and avowedly, and under a claim of title preferred in good faith, even though such claim is untenable. But this provision does not excuse the unlawful retention of the property of another to offset or pay demands held against him.

P.C. 512—*Intent to restore property.* The fact that the accused intended to restore the property embezzled is no ground of defense or mitigation of punishment, if it has not been restored before an information has been laid before a magistrate, or an indictment found by a grand jury, charging the commission of the offense.

P.C. 513—*Actual restoration authorizes mitigation of punishment.* Whenever, prior to an information laid before a magistrate, or an indictment found by a grand jury, charging the commission of embezzlement, the person accused voluntarily and actually restores or tenders restoration of the property alleged to have been embezzled, or any part thereof, such fact is not a ground of defense, but it authorizes the court to mitigate punishment, in its discretion.

LEGAL DISCUSSION

The basic elements of embezzlement require the following:

1. Fiduciary relationship—a trust relationship must exist between the defendant and the victim.

2. The property must come into the defendant's possession while title or ownership remains with the victim. Thus we differentiate ownership or title from possession.

3. The property is received in the course of the defendant's employment. Refer to the various other specific relationships as noted previously in P.C. 506, 506a, 507, 508. The Insurance Code of California also enumerates insurance agents as being a proper subject for embezzlement.[7]

4. The defendant must appropriate the property to his own use or some other use not intended with the intent to deprive the owner. This is really the wrongful element necessary for the crime. A distinct taking is not required.[8] In fact, the defendant need not benefit by the diversion of the funds.[9] Property subject to embezzlement may be money, goods, chattels, real property, or evidence of debt.[10]

In addition to the general embezzlement laws, public officers are specifically and additionally covered under P.C. 424, which states:

Public officers, embezzlement and falsification of accounts by. Each officer of this state, or of any county, city, town, or district of this state, and every other person charged with the receipt, safekeeping, transfer, or disbursement of public moneys, who either:
1. Without authority of law, appropriates the same, or any portion thereof, to his own use, or to the use of another; or,
2. Loans the same or any portion thereof: makes any profit out of, or uses the same for any purpose not authorized by law; or,
3. Knowingly keeps any false account, or makes any false entry or erasure in any account of or relating to the same; or,
4. Willfully refuses or omits to pay over, on demand, any public moneys in his hands, upon the presentation of a draft, order, or warrant drawn upon such moneys by competent authority; or,
5. Willfully omits to transfer the same, when such transfer is required by law; or,
6. Willfully omits or refuses to pay over to any officer or person authorized by law to receive the same any money received by him under any duty imposed by law so to pay over the same;
Is punishable by imprisonment in the state prison for not less than one nor more than ten years, and is disqualified from holding any office in this state.
As used in this section, "public moneys" includes the proceeds derived

from the sale of bonds or other evidence of indebtedness authorized by the legislative body of any city, county, district, or public agency.

This section is amplified by section 504, included earlier in this chapter.

ENFORCEMENT ASPECTS

The police officer must keep in mind the elements of embezzlement, as a theft may have been committed instead of an embezzlement. He must always be alert for a partnership relationship. This does not constitute embezzlement; in fact, it is not possible to prosecute one partner for taking property from the partnership. This becomes completely civil and often presents a difficult public relations problem in dealing with the irate victim. A claim of title to the property may constitute a defense to this crime; hence, investigation should preclude this possibility.

There is no legal requirement that demand be made upon the defendant by the victim. However, from an investigative point it is always advisable to show that demand was made. The time and method of demand is immaterial. It avoids the embarrassment of having the defendant state after arrest: "Here is the money—they never asked for it!"

The officer and victim should also realize that restitution does not bar prosecution. There is no requirement to *permanently* deprive the owner of his property in embezzlement. If the circumstances are flagrant, a charge may be sustained when the money was "borrowed" or just "temporarily diverted" or thereafter returned.

Police departments are in receipt of numerous claims by agencies that have sold appliances, etc. on conditional sales contracts and the purchaser has concealed or disposed of the property. This offense would fall within P.C. 504a and is an embezzlement. In most cases the repossessors try to bring pressure to bear on the purchaser and are more interested in getting the property or the money than in prosecution. Wherever possible the repossessors should be left to their civil recovery, and if officers do investigate such a case they should emphasize the fact that they are not repossessors.

APPLICABLE STATUTES—RECEIVING STOLEN PROPERTY

All previously discussed statutes are applicable. There are a few related sections which cover theft committed in this manner. Legal and investigative considerations are the most important phase, but the following sections should be noted.

P.C. 496—*Buying, receiving, or concealing stolen property.*
1. Every person who buys or receives any property which has been stolen or which has been obtained in any manner constituting

theft or extortion, knowing the same to be so stolen or obtained, or who conceals, withholds or aids in concealing or withholding any such property from the owner, knowing the same to be so stolen or obtained, is punishable by imprisonment in a state prison for not more than 10 years, or in a county jail for not more than one year.

2. Every person whose principal business is dealing in or collecting used or secondhand merchandise or personal property, and every agent, employee or representative of such person, who buys or receives any property which has been stolen or obtained in any manner constituting theft or extortion, under such circumstances as should cause such person, agent, employee or representative to make reasonable inquiry to ascertain that the person from whom such property was bought or received had the legal right to sell or deliver it, without making such reasonable inquiry, shall be presumed to have bought or received such property knowing it to have been so stolen or obtained. This presumption may, however, be rebutted by proof.

3. When in a prosecution under this section it shall appear from the evidence that the defendant's principal business was as set forth in the preceding paragraph, that the defendant bought, received, or otherwise obtained, or concealed, withheld or aided in concealing or withholding from the owner, any property which had been stolen or obtained in any manner constituting theft or extortion, and that the defendant bought, received, obtained, concealed or withheld such property under such circumstances as should have caused him to make reasonable inquiry to ascertain that the person from whom he bought, received, or obtained such property had the legal right to sell or deliver it to him, then the burden shall be upon the defendant to show that before so buying, receiving, or otherwise obtaining such property, he made such reasonable inquiry to ascertain that the person so selling or delivering the same to him had the legal right to so sell or deliver it.

P.C. 332—*Winning at play by fraudulent means.* Every person who by the game of "three-card monte," so-called, or any other game, device, sleight of hand, pretensions to fortune telling, trick, or other means whatever, by use of cards or other implements or instruments, or while betting on sides or hands of any such play or game, fraudulently obtains from another person money or property of any description, shall be punished as in case of larceny of property of like value.

P.C. 530—*Receiving money or property in a false character.* Every person who falsely personates another, in either his private or official capacity, and in such assumed character receives any money or property, knowing that it is intended to be delivered to the individual so personated, with intent to convert the same to his own use, or to that of another person, or to deprive the true owner thereof, is punishable in the same manner and to the same extent as for larceny of the money or property so received.

P.C. 532—*Obtaining money, property, or labor by false pretenses.* Every person who knowingly and designedly, by any false or fraudulent representation or pretense, defrauds any other person of money, labor, or property, whether real or personal, or who causes or procures others to report falsely of his wealth or mercantile character, and by thus imposing upon any person obtains credit, and thereby fraudulently gets possession of money or property, or obtains the labor or service of another, is punishable in the same manner and to the same extent as for larceny of the money or property so obtained.

P.C. 537—*Defrauding proprietors of hotels, inns, etc.* Any person who obtains any food or accommodations at an hotel, inn, restaurant, boarding house, lodging house, apartment house, bungalow court, motel, or auto camp, without paying therefor, with intent to defraud the proprietor or manager thereof, or who obtains credit at an hotel, inn, restaurant, boarding house, lodging house, apartment house, bungalow court, motel, or auto camp by the use of any false pretense, or who, after obtaining credit, food, accommodations, at an hotel, inn, restaurant, boarding house, lodging house, apartment house, bungalow court, motel, or auto camp, absconds, or surreptitiously, or by force, menace, or threats, removes any part of his baggage therefrom without paying for his food or accommodations is guilty of a misdemeanor.

Evidence that such person left the premises of such an hotel, inn, restaurant, boarding-house, lodging-house, apartment house, bungalow court, motel or auto camp, without paying or offering to pay for such food or accommodation shall be prima facie evidence that such person obtained such food or accommodations with intent to defraud the proprietor or manager.

P.C. 72—*Presenting false claims.* Every person who, with intent to defraud, presents for allowance or for payment to any state board or officer, or to any county, town, city, district, ward or village board or officer, authorized to allow or pay the same if genuine, any false or fraudulent claim, bill, account, voucher, or writing, is guilty of a felony.

LEGAL DISCUSSION AND ENFORCEMENT ASPECTS

The most important difference between "trick and device" and false pretenses is that no corroboration is required in theft by trick and device. Most bunco schemes involve the greed or avariciousness of the victim. Often the victim was trying to "make a fast buck" and would have been most happy if the scheme had worked. While the authors are not sympathetic to these victims, it should be recognized that the "confidence rackets" take full advantage of human weaknesses. From the "fortune teller" to the "marriage bunc" these persons prey on society. The investigator must tread a narrow road separating civil and criminal fraud. It is highly recommended that close liaison be maintained with the county prosecutor so as to assure proper case preparation. In large metropolitan areas the district attorney maintains special fraud units to assist in complex cases.

Trick and device is a form of swindle where the property is taken by trick, device, fraud, or artifice. Often an appeal to the sympathy or emotions of the victim by fake and fraudulent representations becomes the vehicle to part the goods from the owner. The important element of this type of theft is that the defendant intends to steal the property, but the victim never intends that title should pass. In fact the victim grants *possession* of the goods to the defendant based on the false representations or inducements given by the defendant. The intent to deprive the owner is present when the possession changes. In embezzlement the suspect usually receives the goods without intent to steal; thereafter he converts or diverts the monies to his own purposes.

It is important to closely examine the act, intent, title, and possession of the property from both the victim's and the defendant's standpoint. Procuring a signature on a promissory note under false promises;[11] money switch or "pigeon drop" schemes;[12] use of false and dishonest gaming devices—these are but a few examples of theft by trick and device.

There is no inconsistency between P.C. 532 (at the beginning of this section) and the general theft statutes, but rather a clarification and amplification of the governing laws. The elements of this type of theft are:

1. *Intent to defraud*—shown by the "profit motive," which is usually evident. However, it should be kept in mind that the defendant need not benefit from the transaction; he need only have the fraudulent intent.
2. There must be an actual fraud perpetrated. If the theft is not actually committed, it becomes impossible to prosecute as an attempted theft by attempted false representations.
3. False pretenses must be used. In order to sustain this charge there must be a false statement or representation given by the defendant.
4. Reliance on the false pretense—the victim must rely on the representation. In fact, he must have parted with his money because of his reliance on the representations.

The investigator must seek evidence which will satisfy the elements. To prove the intent to defraud, it is important to bring out guilty knowledge by the defendant of the falsity of the representations. If the defendant believed his representations to be true, his intent could not be to defraud.[13] The false pretenses may be made by legal or illegal acts of the defendant, and monies received because of the victim's reliance on the false representations are proper subjects for theft prosecution. There must of course always be a causal relationship between the false representation and the reason why the victim gives the money to the defendant. In false pretense theft, title or ownership of the goods passes to the defendant by virtue of the representation or inducement. This is one of the main factors differentiating it from theft by trick and device.

The reliance on a false statement which is totally immaterial to the transaction is not sufficient to establish this offense. The representation must be more than an opinion or a promise to do a future act. It must relate to a past or present fact. There can be no prosecution if promises are made in the future. There would be no way of showing the defendant's intent to defraud at the time he receives the money. Hence, no matter how ridiculous or false the statements are, they must always relate to a present or past fact.

In contrast to theft by trick and device, false pretense *must* be corroborated.

> **P.C. 1110**—*False pretenses, evidence of.* Upon a trial for having, with an intent to cheat or defraud another designedly, by any false pretense, obtained the signature of any person to a written instrument, or having obtained from any person any labor, money, or property, whether real or personal, or valuable thing, the defendant cannot be convicted if the false pretense was expressed in language unaccompanied by a false token or writing, unless the pretense, or some note or memorandum thereof is in writing, subscribed by or in the handwriting of the defendant, or unless the pretense is proven by the testimony of two witnesses, or that of one witness and corroborating circumstances; but this section does not apply to a prosecution for falsely representing or personating another, and, in such assumed character, marrying, or receiving any money or property.

The theory requiring corroboration is to show that the false representation was in fact made. Unfortunately some of the victims in these cases "misunderstand" and seek criminal rather than civil recourse.

APPLICABLE STATUTES—PRIOR CONVICTION

> **P.C. 666**—*Punishment after prior conviction of petit theft.* Every person who, having been convicted of petit larceny or petit theft and having served a term therefor in any penal institution or having been imprisoned therein as a condition of probation for such offense, commits any crime after such conviction is punishable therefor as follows:
>
> 1. If the offense of which such person is subsequently convicted is such that, upon a first conviction, an offender could be punished by imprisonment in the state prison for any term exceeding five

years, such person may be punished by imprisonment in the state prison for the maximum period for which he might have been sentenced if such offense had been his first offense, but in no case less than five years.

2. If the subsequent offense is such that upon a first conviction, the offender would be punishable by imprisonment in the state prison for five years, or any less term, then the person convicted of such subsequent offense is punishable by imprisonment in the state prison not exceeding ten years.

3. If the subsequent conviction is for petit theft, then the person convicted of such subsequent offense is punishable by imprisonment in the county jail not exceeding one year, or in the state prison not exceeding five years.

P.C. 667—*Punishment of petty theft after conviction of felony.* Every person who, having been convicted of any felony either in this state or elsewhere, and having served a term therefor in any penal institution or having been imprisoned therein as a condition of probation for such offense, commits petty theft after such conviction, is punishable therefor by imprisonment in the county jail not exceeding one year or in the state prison not exceeding five years.

LEGAL DISCUSSION AND ENFORCEMENT ASPECTS

It should be noted that these sections make misdemeanor acts felonious if the defendant has a prior conviction *and has been imprisoned in a penal institution.* A county jail, state, or federal prison qualifies as a "penal institution."[14] The defendant need not have served all of his previous sentence; it is necessary only that he should have served time.

From an investigative standpoint this is a difficult arrest problem. Usually criminal record checks do not include the disposition of the person's arrests. Accordingly, the arresting officer should consider the arrest as a misdemeanor until he can ascertain the record *and* disposition of the prior record. Bail and investigation should take account of the possibility that it may become a felony arrest.

CONCLUSION AND GENERAL SUMMARY

The consolidation of all types of theft into one crime simplifies the prosecution and formal pleadings. However, there still remain individual characteristics of each offense which must be proven. The corpus delicti of each method of theft is similar yet distinct. Restudy of each of the crimes and their elements, with emphasis on the differences and similarities, is strongly recommended.

SUMMARY OF THEFT (P.C. 484)

THEFT INCLUDES	LARCENY (STEALING)	OBTAINING PROPERTY BY FALSE PRETENSES	OBTAINING PROPERTY BY TRICK OR DEVICE	EMBEZZLEMENT (TRUST RELATIONSHIP)
ACT	Must be a taking and carrying away, known as intent to steal. This original taking is a trespass.	Property is obtained by the false representation of some past or present existing fact, not matters of opinion or future promises with no present intent to perform.	Property obtained through false promises of any kind, usually in bunco form to be used for specific purpose.	Putting the property to defendant's own use or to the use of another contrary to the terms of the trust. No intent to steal required.
INTENT	Is to deprive rightful owner of his property permanently but not in jest, under claim of right or temporarily.	Intent to defraud, that is, to get the property by means of these false representations.	Intent to defraud, that is, to get the property by means of these false promises or schemes.	Must be fraudulent, that is, with intent to use the property contrary to the terms of the trust.

TITLE	Remains in owner.	Passes to defendant (because of the inducement).	Remains in owner.	Remains in owner.
PROPERTY	Only personal. (See P.C. 495)	Real or personal.	Real or personal.	Real or personal.
POSSESSION	Unlawfully obtained by defendant.	Passes to defendant (because of the inducement).	Owner parts with custody for a limited purpose only.	Lawfully obtained by the defendant as agent, servant, bailee, or trustee.
CUSTODY	Unlawfully obtained by defendant.	Passes to defendant (because of the inducement).	Owner parts with custody for a limited purpose only.	Lawfully obtained by the defendant.
CORROBORATION	Not needed.	Needed (See P.C. 1110).	Not Needed.	Not Needed.

DISCUSSION QUESTIONS

1. Define, in general terms, theft.
2. What are the three main divisions of grand theft? Explain each.
3. Under what conditions can employee petty theft become felonious? Explain.
4. What is meant by a fiduciary relationship?
5. What is meant by asportation?
6. What differentiates auto theft under the Penal Code from auto theft under the Vehicle Code?

NOTES

[1] P.C. 952.
[2] People v. Meyer, 75 C 383; 17 P 431.
[3] P.C. 678.
[4] People v. Earle, 222 CA 2d 476; 35 CR 265.
[5] People v. Rabb, 202 C 409; 261 P 303.
  People v. Roland, 134 CA 675; 26 P 2d 517.
[6] People v. Rabb, 202 C 409; 261 P 303;
  People v. Roland, 144 CA 675; 26 P 2d 517.
[7] Cal. Insurance Code §1730.
[8] P.C. 509.
[9] People v. Pierce, 110 CA 2d 598; 243 P 2d 585.
[10] P.C. 510;
  People v. Haub, 98 CA 2d 514; 220 P 2d 595.
[11] People v. Cichetti, 107 CA 631; 290 P 600.
[12] People v. Watson, 35 CA 2d 587; 96 P 2d 374.
[13] People v. Griffith, 122 C 212; 54 P 725.
[14] People v. James, 155 CA 2d 604; 318 P 2d 175.

7

Arson and Related Offenses

The reader should be aware in advance that nearly all the applicable statutes refer to felonious burnings. The term "arson" has a very restricted use and is confined to section P.C. 447a, although the word is loosely applied to most unlawful burnings. The significant difference is in the subject of the burnings.

APPLICABLE STATUTES—ARSON

P.C. 447a—*Arson: Burning dwelling house, trailer, etc.* Any person who willfully and maliciously sets fire to or burns or causes to be burned or who aids, counsels or procures the burning of any trailer coach, as defined in section 635 (Sec. 25106) of the Vehicle Code, or any dwelling house, or any kitchen, shop, barn, stable, or other outhouse that is parcel thereof, or belonging to or adjoining thereto, whether the property of himself or of another, shall be guilty of arson, and upon conviction thereof, be sentenced to the penitentiary for not less than two or more than 20 years.

P.C. 448a—*Burning of private buildings other than dwellings.* Any person who willfully and maliciously sets fire to or burns or causes to be burned or who aids, counsels or procures the burning of any barn, stable, garage or other building, whether the property of himself or of another, not a parcel of a dwelling house; or any shop, storehouse, warehouse, factory, mill or other building, whether the property of himself or of another; or any church, meeting house, courthouse, work house, school, jail or other public building or any public bridge; shall, upon conviction thereof, be sentenced to the penitentiary for not less than 2 nor more than 20 years.

P.C. 449a—*Burning personal property.* Any person who willfully and maliciously sets fire to or burns or causes to be burned or who aids, counsels or procures the burning of any barrack, cock, crib, rick or stack of hay, corn, wheat, oats, barley or other grain or vegetable product of any kind; or any field of standing hay or grain of any kind; or any pile of coal, wood or other fuel; or any pile of planks, boards, posts, rails or other lumber; or any streetcar, railway car, ship, boat, or other watercraft, automobile or other motor vehicle; or any other personal property not herein specifically named except a trailer coach, as defined in section 635 of the Vehicle Code: (such property being of the value of twenty-five dollars ($25) and the property of another person) shall upon conviction thereof, be sentenced to the penitentiary for not less than one nor more than three years. Note: The amendment of section 449a by section 2 of this act shall not bar the prosecution or punishment of any person who violates the said section 449a by the burning of any trailer coach prior to the effective date of this act.

P.C. 600—*Malicious burning of bridge, structure, etc., not subject to arson.* Every person who willfully and maliciously burns any bridge exceeding in value fifty dollars ($50), or any structure, snowshed, vessel, or boat, not the subject of arson, or any tent, or any stack of hay or grain or straw of any kind, or any pile of baled hay or straw, or any pile of potatoes, or beans, or vegetables, or produce, or fruit of any kind, whether sacked, boxed, crated, or not, or any fence, or any railroad car, lumber, cordwood, railroad ties, telegraph or telephone poles, or shakes, or any tule-land or peat-ground of the value of twenty-five dollars ($25) or over, not the property of such person is punishable by imprisonment in the state prison for not less than one year, nor more than 10 years.

P.C. 600.5—*Malicious burning of crops, grass, timber, etc.* Every person who willfully and maliciously burns any growing or standing grain, grass or tree, or any grass, forest, woods, timber, brush-covered land, or slashing, cutover land, not the property of such person is punishable by imprisonment in the state prison for not less than one year, nor more than 10 years.

LEGAL DISCUSSION

Burning a building does not by the act alone constitute arson. The critical element is the term "maliciously." P.C. 7 defines this term as "importing a wish to vex, annoy, or injure another person, or an intent to do a wrongful act, established either by proof or presumption of law." Arson requires specific intent; the burning must therefore be intentional or of incendiary origin. This is usually established by circumstantial evidence.

In order to sustain a conviction the property need not be destroyed. As long as some part of the intended property is burned, it is sufficient for prosecution. Any burning adjacent to a building which thereafter burns the building is basis for a valid charge of arson so long as the act is intentional. The existence of a prompt method of extinguishing a fire does not preclude the charge.

As regards the burnings under P.C. 600 and P.C. 600.5, it should be noted that these were enacted after P.C. 449a. Therefore, all burnings which can come under the P.C. 600 and P.C. 600.5 sections should be prosecuted under these. While P.C. 449a was not rescinded, it has been to some extent superseded by specified property burning and penalties. These sections apply not to arson but to felonious burnings.

APPLICABLE STATUTE—ATTEMPTED ARSON

P.C. 451a—*Attempts to burn defined.* Any person who willfully and maliciously attempts to set fire to or attempts to burn or to aid, counsel or procure the burning of any of the buildings or property mentioned in the foregoing sections, or who commits any act preliminary thereto, or in furtherance thereof, shall upon conviction thereof, be sentenced to the penitentiary for not less than one nor more than two years or fined not to exceed one thousand dollars.

The placing or distributing of any flammable, explosive or combustible material or substance, or any device in or about any building or property mentioned in the foregoing sections in an arrangement or preparation with intent to eventually willfully and maliciously set fire to or burn same, or to procure the setting fire to or burning of the same shall, for the purposes of this act constitute an attempt to burn such building or property.

LEGAL DISCUSSION

It is interesting to note that the "Law of Attempts" was already in force prior to the enactment of this section. Therefore this section creates a new offense. It includes the attempt but also includes preliminary acts that are in furtherance of the burning. This in effect makes prosecutable an overt act of preparation toward an unlawful burning with specific intent. As the reader has previously noted, attempts require an overt act toward *further-*

ance of the crime as well as specific intent to commit the crime. Hence this section is more inclusive and specific.

ENFORCEMENT ASPECTS

Frequently investigation in these types of cases is undertaken by the arson detail of a fire department. Regardless who the investigator is, it is most important that the initial response to the potential crime scene (the burning building) be by persons experienced in arson investigation. Fire personnel should be cautioned to note the origin and spread of fire. Color photos are often revealing. Another critical phase of crime scene care is during fire department cleanup. All too frequently evidence is lost or destroyed in the cleanup period after a fire. There are many different types of incendiary devices. Mechanical, electrical, and chemical applications usually leave traces which may be the basic evidence in establishing the corpus of arson.

In cases where the corpus delicti cannot be proven under the "burning statutes" the investigator may be able to establish a crime under fraud perpetrated on the insurer. Motive, while never required, often is important in these types of investigations.

APPLICABLE STATUTES—DEFRAUDING INSURANCE COMPANIES

P.C. 450a—*Burning with intent to defraud insurer.* Any person who willfully and with intent to injure or defraud the insurer sets fire to or burns or causes to be burned or who aids, counsels or procures the burning of any goods, wares, merchandise or other chattels or personal property of any kind, whether the property of himself or of another, which shall at the time be insured by any person or corporation against loss or damage by fire, shall upon conviction thereof, be sentenced to the penitentiary for not less than one nor more than five years.

P.C. 548—*Burning or destroying, etc. insured property.* Every person who willfully burns or in any other manner injures, destroys, secretes, abandons, or disposes of any property which at the time is insured against loss or damage by fire, theft, or embezzlement, or any casualty with intent to defraud or prejudice the insurer, whether the same be the property or in the possession of such person, is punishable by imprisonment in the state prison for not less than one year and not more than ten years.

INSURANCE CODE, Sec. 556—It is unlawful to:
A. Present or cause to be presented any false or fraudulent claim for the payment of a loss under a contract of insurance.

B.   Prepare, make, or subscribe any writing with intent to present or use the same, or to allow it to be presented or used in support of any such claim. Every person who violates any provision of this section is punishable by imprisonment in the state prison not exceeding three years, or by fine not exceeding one thousand dollars, or both.

LEGAL DISCUSSION AND ENFORCEMENT ASPECTS

The specific intent required under these sections refers to defrauding of the insurance company. Hence, it is essential to prove that the defendant knew that the property was in fact insured. In order to complete the violation an arson or felonious burning may have occurred. In this case two separate crimes may have been committed and could be charged.

Under section 450a the person who aids must do so knowingly. Hence, the defendant must be shown to have directly and willfully set the fire or had knowledge that he was aiding in the burning.

The insurance investigator working closely with law enforcement may be able to be of great assistance. The files and records of the insurance companies may be available. The National Fire Underwriters maintain insurance records on a national level that are often most helpful.

Whenever suspicious fires are set, the prime suspect may avoid apprehension until the statute of limitations has run. Under the Insurance Code each time a claim, proof of loss, or other document enters the file, it starts the offense. Many persons are prosecuted for these violations three or four years after the fires. These offenses are against the insurance company and are not related directly to the fire. Information may develop years later, indicating by circumstantial evidence the felonious burning. Usually when questions arise on a fire claim, the matter is not settled until there is additional investigation. The final settlement may in fact be the overt act chargeable to prove a defrauding.

APPLICABLE STATUTE—FIRE BOMBS

P.C. 653.1—*Possession of fire bomb, misdemeanor. Definition.* Every person who possesses a fire bomb is guilty of a misdemeanor.

For the purpose of this section a "fire bomb" is a breakable container containing a flammable liquid with a flash point of 150 degrees fahrenheit or less, having a wick or similar device capable of being ignited, but no device commercially manufactured primarily for the purpose of illumination shall be deemed to be a fire bomb for the purpose of this section.

This section shall not prohibit the authorized use or possession of such fire bomb by a member of the armed forces of the United States or by police officers, peace officers, or law enforcement officers authorized by the properly constituted authorities for the enforcement of law or ordinances; nor shall this section prohibit the use or possession of such fire bomb when used solely for scientific research or educational purposes.

ENFORCEMENT ASPECTS

This section was very much needed. During a search of an auto containing teenagers who were suspected of participating in gang fights, officers saw in the trunk compartment several six-pack "coke" bottles filled with gasoline with cloth stoppers. Because of these "homemade Molotov cocktails" the juveniles were detained under the Welfare and Institutions Code for being in danger of injury and then were released. The subsequent enactment of this law aided law enforcement officers during disorder and riot situations. The law also aids in the establishing of probable cause for search and seizure requirements.

GENERAL CONCLUSION AND SUMMARY

While felonious burnings are occasionally committed, the crime of arson is rare. The distinguishing characteristics of the crime relate primarily to the specific subject of the burning. Physical evidence is most important in the investigation of fires with incendiary origin.

Defrauding of insurance companies may often be a means of bringing a suspect to justice. Still felonious but sometimes easier to prove, such violations in effect prolong the statute of limitations.

The "fire bomb" section grants law enforcement agencies a misdemeanor section helpful in crime prevention.

DISCUSSION QUESTIONS

1. What type of structures are enumerated under the arson section (P.C. 447a)?
2. What are the monetary value requirements under P.C. 600 for property?
3. Explain "attempted arson." How does it differ from the general law of attempt?
4. When does the statute of limitations start on crimes defrauding insurance companies?
5. What is a fire bomb? Give several examples.

8

Burglary

APPLICABLE STATUTE—BURGLARY

P.C. 459—*Definition.* Every person who enters any house, room, apartment, tenement, shop, warehouse, store, mill, barn, stable, outhouse or other building, tent, vessel, railroad car, trailer coach as defined by the Vehicle Code, vehicle as defined by said code when the doors of such vehicle are locked, aircraft as defined by the Harbors and Navigation Code, mine or any underground portion thereof, with intent to commit grand or petit larceny[1] or any felony is guilty of burglary.

LEGAL DISCUSSION

Elements of the Crime

(1) the entry; (2) of a building or one of the areas named in the statute; (3) with specific intent to commit petit or grand theft or any felony.

The criminal act, therefore, is the entry itself. In California no "breaking or entering" is necessary. Any form of entry suffices. This covers entry by use of a "fishing pole" or other apparatus wherein the suspect does not

105

set foot into the building.[2] Reaching through a door or window consummates the act sufficiently for prosecution. The entry may be lawful and even by invitation; it need not amount to a trespass. During business hours store doors are open to the public, and the entry at this time is sufficient as long as the specific intent is present. (Shoplifters using booster equipment[3] oftentimes may be prosecuted for burglary.[4])

The building or area must qualify by definition as being included in the statute. Generally, a building or house is a structure which has walls on all sides and is covered by a roof.[5] The building need not have been one intended as a habitation for human beings nor is the size of the building a definitive criterion. A telephone booth having a roof, walls on three sides, and a glass door on the fourth side is a "building" within the statute.[6] However, a shed, carport, or bin is not included. There is no specification of construction for a wall, but it must be solid (glass, wood, metal, etc.); hence any fencing on a side disqualifies the structure under this section. Note, however, that if there is a fourth wall that is a door (even if open) the structure qualifies.[7] A chicken house, cave, dugout, or a showcase within the property line and sheltered by the roof and sidewalls of a building are all subjects of burglary.

Other areas subject to burglary are defined or described as follows:

- Aircraft—any contrivance used or designed for flying except a parachute or other contrivance used primarily for safety.
- Trailer coach—a vehicle without motive power designed for human habitation and for carrying persons and property.
- Vessel—includes ships of all kinds, steamboats, canalboats, barges, and every structure adapted to be navigated from place to place for the transportation of merchandise or persons.
- Tent—"a portable shelter consisting of a covering of canvas, or formerly skins, stretched over poles and attached to stakes."
- Mine—"an excavation made in the earth, from which to extract metallic ores, coal, precious stones or other minerals." The shaft and surface equipment or supplies are part of the mine; hence theft may constitute burglary.[8]
- Vehicle—A "vehicle" is a device by which any person or property may be propelled, moved, or drawn upon a highway, excepting a device moved by human power or used exclusively upon stationary rails or tracks.[9]

    Vehicle must have all doors locked (the trunk or deck lid is considered a door).[10]

Specific intent to commit theft or any felony is required as the third element. This must exist at the time of entry. The intent need not be consummated, and the subject could even change his intent after entry. The crime being committed is an evidence of the intent as far as the charge of burglary is concerned.

ENFORCEMENT ASPECTS

For a practical police approach the officer should picture the real "victim" of a burglary as being the building.

The method of entry as well as exit is important in reflecting the intent of the perpetrator at the time of entry. Burglary is usually secretive and the entry is quickly accomplished; hence most perpetrators are caught after the crime has been committed. Even when the suspects are caught inside the premises, there may be a need to prove their intent at time of entry. Circumstantial evidence is usually all that is available. This necessity to prove the intent at the time of entry lends importance to the methods of entry or exit. Identifying possible "tools" used by the suspects may also tend to show their intent. A forcible and unlawful entry reasonably and justifiably implies the necessary element of specific intent to commit theft or a felony.

APPLICABLE STATUTE—DEGREE OF BURGLARY

P.C. 460—*Degrees; construction of section.* 1. Every burglary of an inhabited dwelling, house, trailer coach as defined by the Vehicle Code,[11] or building committed in the nighttime, and every burglary, whether in the daytime or nighttime, committed by a person armed with a deadly weapon, or who while in the commission of such burglary arms himself with a deadly weapon, or who while in the commission of such burglary assaults any person, is burglary of the first degree. 2. All other kinds of burglary are of the second degree. 3. This section shall not be construed to supersede or affect Section 464 of the Penal Code.

LEGAL DISCUSSION

First-degree burglary includes one of the following:

1. During the *nighttime* (period between sunset and sunrise) upon entering a trailer coach or inhabited dwelling. The term "inhabited" applies also to "building."[12]
2. During the daytime or nighttime if at any time the subject arms himself with a deadly weapon (blackjack, slingshot, billy, sandbag, metal knuckles, dirk, dagger, pistol, revolver, or other fire-

arm, any knife with blade longer than five inches, any razor with unguarded blade, and any pipe or bar used or intended to be used as a club).[13]
3.   Without regard to time of day if the suspect assaults any person.[14]

Second-degree burglary is any burglary which is not first degree.

ENFORCEMENT ASPECTS

The element of "nighttime" when required may be easy to establish by expert testimony, i.e., weather bureau. However, it becomes more difficult to establish the exact time the crime was committed. Therefore, any physical evidence indicating time of entry should be properly noted.

The "inhabited" element may be a little more difficult to establish. The law does not require the inhabitants to actually be inside. The persons may be out or on vacation, or the building could be used as a summer cottage.[15] If the building entered is a "Mamma-Pappa" type store where living quarters are in the rear or above on a balcony-type structure, this constitutes habitation. The main criterion to establish is the general purpose and use of the building as a dwelling.

Whenever the perpetrator is armed, or in the commission of the crime he arms himself with a deadly weapon, the element of the weapon must be decided by the jury. The person must actually *arm* himself; hence taking ten revolvers in a sealed crate from a sporting goods store would not be sufficient.[16] The intent of using the weapon offensively or defensively as well as the availability of the weapon should be considered. The theft of a deadly weapon would not automatically qualify the burglary as first degree. Instrumentalities with which a burglar arms himself which are capable of inflicting great bodily harm also may be considered under the first-degree statute.

APPLICABLE STATUTES

P.C. 461—*Punishment.* Burglary is punishable as follows:
1.   Burglary in the first degree: by imprisonment in the state prison for not less than five years.
2.   Burglary in the second degree: by imprisonment in the county jail not exceeding one year in the state prison for not less than one year or more than fifteen years.

P.C. 464—*Burglary with explosives defined; punishment.* Any person who, with intent to commit crime, enters, either by day or by night, any building, whether inhabited or not, and opens or attempts to open any vault, safe, or other secure place by use of acetylene torch or electric arc or nitroglycerine, dynamite, gunpowder, or any other explosive, is guilty of burglary with explosives.

Any person duly convicted of burglary with explosives shall be deemed to be guilty of a felony and shall be punished by imprisonment in the state prison for a term of not less than ten years nor more than forty years.

LEGAL DISCUSSION

The specific *intent* to commit crime is more general under this section. Also it should be noted that this section includes fireboxes and other non-vault security boxes. This section increases the penalty for burglary.

ENFORCEMENT ASPECTS

This section has to do with "safe burglary" as it covers the "burn" and "blow" jobs. It is important for officers to determine the method of entry into a safe so as to establish a violation under this section. A safe which is carried off by burglars would not constitute a violation under this section.

APPLICABLE STATUTE—BURGLAR TOOLS

P.C. 466—*Burglars' tools; possession.* Every person having upon him or in his possession a picklock, crow, keybit, or other instrument or tool with intent feloniously to break or enter into any building, or who shall knowingly make or alter, or shall attempt to make or alter, any key or other instrument above named so that the same will fit or open the lock of a building, without being requested so to do by some person having the right to open the same, or who shall make, alter, or repair any instrument or thing, knowing or having reason to believe that it is intended to be used in committing a misdemeanor or felony, is guilty of misdemeanor. Any of the structures mentioned in section four hundred and fifty-nine of this Code shall be deemed to be a building within the meaning of this section.

LEGAL DISCUSSION

The elements of this misdemeanor are:

1. The *possession* of the instrument and felonious intent to commit burglary, or
2. the making, altering or repairing of a key or instrument to open a lock on a building for an unauthorized person, or

3. having reason to believe the key made or being altered is intended to be used in committing a crime and going ahead and making the key or instrument.

ENFORCEMENT ASPECTS

This section is applicable to locksmiths and persons who make duplicate keys. Modern machinery has made it possible for unskilled clerks to duplicate keys, hence this section aids law enforcement in crime prevention more than apprehension.

The major police use of this section will be after valid and lawful searches of suspects are conducted and picklocks, etc., are discovered. The nature of the instrument may be considered toward establishing the necessary intent.

GENERAL POLICE ASPECTS AND CONCLUDING COMMENTS

The crime of burglary is most often committed without eyewitnesses. Accordingly, several investigation procedures will be mentioned as they reflect and relate to the elements of the crime.

Identity of perpetrator is not required for establishing the corpus delicti but is necessary for conviction; hence protection of the crime scene is most important. Areas of entry, exit, and surrounding objects stolen are to be examined for proof of identity and specific intent.

Establishing the entry is most often done by the testimony of witnesses who locked the premises and who discovered the crime. This establishes the general time limits during which the crime was committed. The time may become significant in establishing the degree. The fact that no permission to enter was given reflects on intent, as does the method of entry.

Intoxication of the defendant is admissible only to show his inability to form the specific intent necessary to commit the crime.

Attempted burglary oftentimes is the arresting charge. A burglary arrest is frequently made upon reasonable cause.[17]

DISCUSSION QUESTIONS

1. What are the elements of burglary?
2. Give examples of several areas or structures that could be subjects of burglary.
3. What constitutes first-degree burglary?

4. What is the punishment for burglary with explosives?

5. Discuss intent as it affects burglary.

6. Discuss the arrest possibilities for a suspect who is in a commercial area at a late hour and possesses a crowbar. Is it a felony or a misdemeanor arrest?

NOTES

[1] "Theft" and "larceny" can be substituted for each other (P.C. 490a).

[2] People v. Barry, 94 C 481; 29 P 1026.

[3] Booster equipment consists of various devices for concealing goods and merchandise on the person, e.g., trick packages, garments with concealable pockets and suspension equipment, etc.

[4] People v. Carrol, 60 CA 2d 66; 140 P 2d 172;
People v. Vitos, 62 CA 2d 157; 144 P 2d 393.

[5] People v. Stickman, 34 C 242.

[6] People v. Clemison, 105 CA 2d 679; 233 P 2d 924.

[7] People v. Picaroni, 131 CA 2d 612; 281 P 2d 45.

[8] People v. Silver, 16 C 2d 714; 108 P 2d 4.

[9] People v. Toomes, 148 CA 2d 465; 306 P 2d 953.

[10] Vehicle Code §670.

[11] P.C. 463.

[12] People v. Black, 73 CA 13; 238 P 374.

[13] P.C. 3024(f).

[14] Chapter 12 (Assaults).

[15] People v. Stewart, 113 CA 2d 687; 248 P 2d 768.

[16] People v. Black, 73 CA 13; 238 P 374.

[17] P.C. 836.3.

FORGERY INCLUDING NEGOTIABLE INSTRUMENT
FRAUDS
STATUTORY FORGERY
COUNTERFEITING
FORGERY AND ALTERATION OF PUBLIC RECORDS
ENFORCEMENT ASPECTS

9

Forgery

APPLICABLE STATUTES

P.C. 470—*Forgery of wills, conveyances, etc.* Every person who with intent to defraud, signs the name of another person, or of a fictitious person, knowing that he has no authority so to do, or falsely makes, alters, forges, or counterfeits, any charter, letters-patent, deed, lease, indenture, writing obligatory, will, testament, codicil, bond, covenant, bank bill or note, postnote, check, draft, bill of exchange, contract, promissory note, due bill for the payment of money or property, receipt for money or property, passage ticket, power of attorney, or any certificate of any share, right, or interest in the stock of any corporation or association, or any controller's warrant for the payment of money at the treasury, county order or warrant, or request for the payment of money, or the delivery of goods or chattels of any kind, or for the delivery of any instrument of writing, or acquittance, release, or discharge of any debt, account, suit, action, demand, or other thing, real or personal, or any transfer or assurance of money, certificate of shares of stock, goods, chattels, or other property whatever, or any letter of attorney, or other power to receive money, or to receive or transfer certificates of shares of stock or annuities, or to let, lease, dispose of, alien, or convey any goods, chattels, lands, or tenements, or other estate, real or personal, or

112

any acceptance or indorsement of any bill of exchange, promissory note, draft, order, or any assignment of any bond, writing obligatory, promissory note, or other contract for money or other property; or counterfeits or forges the seal or handwriting of another; or utters, publishes, passes, or attempts to pass, as true and genuine, any of the above named false, altered, forged, or counterfeited matters, as above specified and described, knowing the same to be false, altered, forged or counterfeited, with intent to prejudice, damage or defraud any person; or who with intent to defraud, alters, corrupts, or falsifies any record of any will, codicil, conveyance, or other instrument, the record of which is by law evidence, or any record of any judgment of a court or the return of any officer to any process of any court, is guilty of forgery.

P.C. 476—*Making, passing or uttering fictitious bills, etc.* Every person who makes, passes, utters, or publishes, with intention to defraud any other person, or who, with the like intention, attempts to pass, utter, or publish, or who has in his possession, with like intent to utter, pass, or publish, any fictitious bill, note, or check, purporting to be the bill, note, or check, or other instrument in writing for the payment of money or property of some bank, corporation, copartnership, or individual, when, in fact, there is no such bank, corporation, copartnership, or individual in existence, knowing the bill, note, check, or instrument in writing to be fictitious, is punishable by imprisonment in the county jail for not more than one year, or in the state prison for not more than fourteen years.

P.C. 476a—*Issuing bank checks, etc., with intent to defraud; presumption from protest; "credit" defined.* (a) Any person who for himself or as the agent or representative of another or as an officer of a corporation, willfully, with intent to defraud, makes or draws or utters or delivers any check, or draft or order upon any bank or depositary, or person, or firm, or corporation, for the payment of money, knowing at the time of such making, drawing, uttering or delivering that the maker or drawer or the corporation has not sufficient funds in, or credit with said bank or depositary, or person, or firm, or corporation, for the payment of such check, draft or order and all other checks, drafts, or orders upon such funds then outstanding, in full upon its presentation, although no express representation is made with reference thereto, is punishable by imprisonment in the county jail for not more than one year, or in the state prison for not more than fourteen years.

(b) However, if the total amount of all such checks, drafts or orders that the defendant is charged with and convicted of making, drawing or uttering does not exceed one hundred dollars ($100), the offense is punishable only by imprisonment in the county jail for not more than one year, except that this subdivision shall not be applicable if the defendant has previously been convicted of a violation of sections 470, 475, or 476 of this code, or of this section of this code, or of the crime of petty theft in a case in which defendant's offense was a violation also of sections 470, 475, or 476 of this code of this section, or if the defendant has previously been convicted of any offense under the laws of any other state or of the United States which, if committed in this state, would have been punishable as a violation of sections 470, 475, or 476 of this code or of this section of this code or if he has been so convicted of the crime of petty theft in a case in which, if defendant's offense had been committed in this state, it would have been a violation also of section 470, 475, or 476 of this code, or of this section.

(c)   Where such check, draft, or order is protested, on the grounds of insufficiency of funds or credit, the notice of protest thereof shall be admissible as proof of presentation, nonpayment and protest and shall be presumptive evidence of knowledge of insufficiency of funds or credit with such bank or depositary, or person, or firm, or corporation.

(d)   The word "credit" as used herein shall be construed to mean an arrangement or understanding with the bank or depositary or person or firm or corporation for the payment of such check, draft or order.

(e)   If any of the preceding paragraphs, or parts thereof, shall be found unconstitutional or invalid, the remainder of this section shall not thereby be invalidated, but shall remain in full force and effect.

LEGAL DISCUSSION

Forgery consists of the making or altering of a writing of legal efficacy providing the falsification alters the effect or result of the document. It usually consists of the making of a false signature, discussed below. It can also consist of the signing of one's own name with the knowledge and intent that it may be mistaken for the name of another. The question is further complicated by the matter of authority because the signature of another made with authority or permission is not forgery.

In all cases, except those involving public records hereinafter noted, there must be an intent to defraud; that is, to create a right, privilege, obligation or disability where none existed before.

Aside from the negotiable instruments (notes, bills, checks, etc.) covered by P.C. 476 and P.C. 470, any other instrument or writing may be forged by making a false writing or a false signature which causes the instrument to be something which it is not. Signing as agent where agency does not exist or signing another's name as agent, or as per *John Doe*, may be "false pretenses" but is *not* forgery. Furthermore, the issuance of a worthless check (N.S.F.) is not forgery because the check is what it genuinely purports to be. The fact that it is worthless does not disestablish its genuineness.

Note the limitation regarding the distinction between misdemeanor and felony as affected by previous conviction in section 476b.

Where there is fraudulent delivery of a check which purports to be valid in exchange for property or services, the offense is obtaining same by false pretenses and the party may be convicted of theft. In the absence of property or services, the *bad check law* above is applicable even though the person passing the check gains nothing thereby.

The crime is committed when:

a. the check is "made or drawn," or

b. the check is "uttered or delivered."

There is no requirement that the check be presented and dishonored or payment refused, nor is there any requirement that the victim suffer loss.[1]

The word "credit" refers to any understanding with the depositary on whom the check or draft is drawn. Note the following circumstances which do not satisfy the "credit" requirements:

1. Funds in another branch of same bank[2]
2. Funds in a savings account in same bank but no authority in bank to draw on same[3]
3. Commercial paper deposited for collection and no arrangement with the bank to draw on same[4]

The lack of credit must be coupled with a knowledge of the lack of same. This knowledge must be established by direct evidence or drawn from inferences. Direct evidence would include bank notice to the individual, the closing of the account, etc. Inferences could be drawn from repeated notices of overdraft without corresponding deposits.

Note in P.C. 476a an implied requirement that funds and credit available must cover all outstanding checks. This acts directly on those parties who make use of *"the float."* A float is the taking advantage of the time interval between the issuance of a check or draft and its presentation for payment by using the funds on deposit against which it was drawn for other purposes. In truth and fact it is an overdraft based on known or calculated transmission intervals.

One should not overlook the fact that notice of protest is presumptive evidence of insufficiency of funds or credit *and knowledge thereof.*

The forgery of an endorsement is separate from the forgery of the check. It is not a part of the instrument but the same rules apply to its execution as in the forgery of the instrument, namely the authority to sign existure of agency, identity of names, etc.

ENFORCEMENT ASPECTS

"Straight forgery" under P.C. 470 is not a violation frequently investigated by the patrolman. Keep in mind that criminals in this area are often committing grand theft as well. The intent to defraud must be proven to establish the corpus of the offense. Therefore, profit or gain is usually the motive and circumstantially at least tends to prove the intent.

It is important in these offenses to locate the alleged person whose signature was forged. He will testify not only that the signature is not his but also that he gave no one permission to sign his name. This testimony is important, and the lack of this type of testimony is what makes fictitious names hard to prove. How does the prosecution prove that a person who doesn't exist didn't give permission to the defendant to sign his name? This can only be done circumstantially and to a prima facie degree sufficient to shift the burden of proof to the defendant.

As regards the problem of "paperhangers" (criminals specializing in passing worthless checks), we should realize that this is usually investigated by a special detail in the detective division. The professional forgers are in the most lucrative area of crime today. The act of making or passing is often specialized by criminal groups. Frequently, forgery rings will burglarize business establishments with the hope of securing blank checks, check writing equipment, sample signatures, etc. Therefore, every officer investigating a burglary where nothing appears to be taken in a business area should inspect closely the firm's checkbook. Remember that if every third or fourth check is taken from a large commercial type checkbook it cannot be detected unless closely examined. Often the check loss is not discovered for many days, giving time for the suspects to pass the checks.

Nonsufficient fund (N.S.F.) check investigation requires diligence on the part of the officer to prove the intent to defraud. Post-dated checks are not N.S.F. (forgery) violations. The person who accepts a post-dated check is actually loaning the suspect the money. There is only a civil credit liability at this point which precludes criminal prosecution. A check for which payment was stopped also cannot be a violation.

As mentioned previously, a check may constitute the "false token" for a grand theft violation under trick or device.

The first thing an investigator must do for N.S.F. checks is to verify the bank account. Accordingly, the officers should maintain good rapport with the local bank officials. Upon viewing the account it is necessary to show that there was not a mere bookkeeping error on the part of the defendant. Some law enforcement agencies have local departmental policies which do not allow an investigation until two or more N.S.F. checks are reported; others place a minimum limit on the amount of money involved. The account statement will usually be used to prove the intent. Thus, if a defendant's balance for several months averaged under $100, his check for $1,500 could not have been a mere bookkeeping error. Also if his bank balance were $10 and ten $25 checks were written and passed, there would be sufficient evidence to show the intent to defraud.

APPLICABLE STATUTES

P.C. 115—*Offering false or forged instruments to be filed of record.* Every person who knowingly procures or offers any false or forged instrument to be filed, registered, or recorded, in any public office within this state, which instrument, if genuine, might be filed, or registered, or recorded under any law of this state or of the United States, is guilty of felony.

P.C. 475—*Passing or receiving forged bills or notes, etc., with unlawful intent: fraudulent possession of blank or unfinished bill or note or blank or unfinished check, etc.; punishment.* Every person who has in his possession, or receives from another person, any forged promissory note or bank bill, or bills, for the payment of money or property, with the intention to pass the same, or to permit, cause, or to procure the same to be uttered or passed, with the intention to defraud any person, knowing the same to be forged or counterfeited, or has or keeps in his possession any blank or unfinished note or bank bill made in the form or similitude of any promissory note or bill for payment of money or property, made to be issued by any incorporated bank or banking company, or any blank or unfinished check, money order, or traveler's check, made in the form or similitude of any check, money order, or traveler's check whether the parties thereto are real or fictitious, with intention to fill up and complete such blank and unfinished note or bill, check, money order, or traveler's check, or to permit, or cause, or procure the same to be filled up and completed in order to utter or pass the same, or to permit, or cause, or procure the same to be uttered or passed, to defraud any person, is punishable by imprisonment in the state prison for not less than one nor more than 14 years, or by imprisonment in the county jail for not more than one year.

P.C. 475a—*Fraudulent possession of completed check, money order, or traveler's check: punishment.* Every person who has in his possession a completed check, money order, or traveler's check, whether the parties thereto are real or fictitious, with intention to utter or pass the same, or to permit, cause, or procure the same to be uttered or passed, to defraud any person, is punishable by imprisonment in the state prison for not less than one nor more than 14 years, or by imprisonment in the county jail for not more than one year.

P.C. 132—*Offering false evidence.* Every person who upon any trial, proceeding, inquiry, or investigation whatever, authorized or permitted by law, offers in evidence, as genuine or true, any book, paper document, record, or other instrument in writing, knowing the same to have been forged or fraudulently altered or antedated, is guilty of felony.

(The above Penal Code sections establish crimes created by the use of a forged instrument. The following Code sections create offenses constituting the forgery of the records or documents shown.)

APPLICABLE STATUTES

Gov. Code 6200—*Theft, destruction, falsification, or removal by officer custodian.* Every officer having the custody of any record, map, or book, or of any paper or proceeding of any court, filed or deposited in any public office, or placed in his hands for any purpose, who is guilty of stealing, wilfully destroying, mutilating, defacing, altering or falsifying, removing or secreting the whole or any part of such record, map, book, paper, or proceeding, or who permits any other person to do so, is punishable by imprisonment in the state prison not less than one nor more than 14 years.

Gov. Code 6201—*Theft, destruction, falsification, or removal by person other than officer custodian.* Every person not an officer referred to in section 6200, who is guilty of any of the acts specified in that section, is punishable by imprisonment in the state prison not exceeding five years, or in a county jail not exceeding one year, or by a fine not exceeding one hundred dollars ($100) or by both such fine and imprisonment. Altering or falsifying government records.

H & S 2433—*Filing another's medical certificate as felony; punishment as forgery.* Every person filing for record, or attempting to file for record, the certificate issued to another, falsely claiming himself to be the person named in or entitled to the certificate, is guilty of a felony, and upon conviction thereof, shall be subject to such penalties as are provided by the laws of this state for the crime of forgery.

B & P 4390—*Forgery of prescription; offense; punishment.* Every person who signs the name of another, or of a fictitious person, or falsely makes, alters, forges, utters, publishes, passes, or attempts to pass, as genuine, any prescription for any drug is guilty of a forgery and upon conviction thereof shall be punished by imprisonment in the state prison for not less than 1 year nor more than 14 years, or by imprisonment in the county jail for not more than 1 year.

Every person who has in his possession any drugs secured by such forged prescription shall be punished by imprisonment in the state prison for not less than one year nor more than six years, or by imprisonment in the county jail for not more than one year.

B & P 20921—*Failure to keep or forgery of records or authorizations.* It is unlawful for any person to fail to keep in the form prescribed, or to forge or falsify, any records or authorizations provided for in *this article*, or knowingly to keep, use or display any such false or forged records. This article as used above includes all laws controlling the production, storage and sale of petroleum products. Records of sales of petroleum products.

Trademarks

B & P 14320—*Forged trademark; counterfeit trademark.* "Forged trademark" and "counterfeited trademark," as used in this article, include every alteration, imitation, copy or reproduction of any trademark so resembling the original as to be likely to deceive.

B & P 14321—*Forgery or counterfeiting; offense.* Every person who willfully forges or counterfeits, or procures to be forged or counterfeited, a trademark registered with the secretary of state or the commissioner of patents in the United States patent office, or who affixes such a forged or counterfeited trademark to goods of essentially the same descriptive qualities as those referred to in the registration of the trademark, with intent to pass off or assist any other person to pass off any goods to which the trademark is attached or applied as those of the registrant shall be punishable by imprisonment of not more than five years in the state prison or by not more than one year in the county jail.

P.C. 472—*Forgery of public and corporate seals.* Every person who, with intent to defraud another, forges, or counterfeits the seal of this state, the seal of any public officer authorized by law, the seal of any court of record, or the seal of any corporation, or any other public seal authorized or recognized by the laws of this state, or of any other state, government, or country, or who falsely makes, forges, or counterfeits any impression purporting to be an impression of any such seal, or who has in his possession any such counterfeited seal or impression thereof, knowing it to be counterfeited, and willfully conceals the same, is guilty of forgery.

P.C. 481—*Counterfeiting railroad or steamship tickets.* Every person who counterfeits, forges, or alters any ticket, check, order, coupon, receipt for fare, or pass, issued by any railroad or steamship company, or by any lessee or manager thereof, designed to entitle the holder to ride in the cars or vessels of such company, or who utters, publishes, or puts into circulation, any such counterfeit or altered ticket, check, or order, coupon, receipt for fare, or pass, with intent to defraud any such railroad or steamship company, or any lessee thereof, or any other person, is punishable by imprisonment in the state prison, or in the county jail, not exceeding one year, or by fine not exceeding one thousand dollars, or by both such imprisonment and fine.

P.C. 482—*Restoring canceled railroad or steamship tickets.* Every person who, for the purpose of restoring to its original appearance and nominal value in whole or in part, removes, conceals, fills up, or obliterates, the cuts, marks, punchholes, or other evidence of cancellation, from any ticket, check, order coupon, receipt for fare, or pass, issued by any railroad or steamship company, or any lessee or manager thereof, canceled in, whole or in part, with intent to dispose of by sale or gift, or to circulate the same, or with intent to defraud the railroad or steamship company, or lessee thereof, or any other person, or who, with like intent to defraud, offers for sale, or in payment of fare on the railroad or vessel of the company, such ticket, check, order, coupon, or pass, knowing the same to have been so restored, in whole or in part, is punishable by imprisonment in the county jail not exceeding six months, or by a fine not exceeding one thousand dollars, or by both such imprisonment and fine.

P.C. 471—*Making false entries in records or returns.* Every person who, with intent to defraud another, makes, forges, or alters any entry in any book of records, or any instrument purporting to be any record or return specified in the preceding section, is guilty of forgery.

P.C. 337.7—*Unlawful possession and use of credentials. Felony.* Any person other than the lawful holder thereof who has in his possession any credential or license issued by the California Horse Racing Board to licensees and any person who has a forged or simulated credential or license of said board in his possession, and who uses such credential or license for the purpose of misrepresentation, fraud or touting is guilty of a felony and shall be punished by a fine of five thousand dollars ($5,000) or by imprisonment in the state prison for not less than one year nor more than five years, or by both such fine and imprisonment. If he has previously been convicted of any offense under this chapter, he shall be imprisoned.

P.C. 337.8—*Unauthorized or forged credentials.* Any person who uses any credential, other than a credential or license issued by the California Horse Racing Board, for the purpose of touting is guilty of touting, and if the credential has been forged shall be imprisoned as provided in this chapter, whether the offense was committed on or off a race track.

Labor Code 1015—*Forgery; misdemeanor; penalty.* Any person who, without having an unrevoked written authority from such trade union, labor association or labor organization, willfully forges or procures to be forged such label or trademark, with intent to sell or assist other persons to sell, any goods to which such forged label is affixed as having been made, manufactured, or produced in whole or in part by labor, laborers, or employees who are members of, or allied or associated with, such trade union, labor association, or labor organization, is guilty of a misdemeanor, punishable by a fine of not more than five hundred dollars ($500) or imprisonment for not more than 90 days, or both.

Vehicle Code 4463—*False evidences of registration.* Every person who with intent to defraud, alters, forges, counterfeits, or falsifies any certificate of ownership, registration card, certificate, license or special plate or permit provided for by this code or any comparable certificate of ownership, registration card, certificate, license or special plate or permit relating to motor vehicles provided for by any foreign jurisdiction or who alters, forges, counterfeits, or falsifies any such document or plate with intent to represent the same as issued by the department or who alters, forges, counterfeits, or falsifies with fraudulent intent any endorsement of transfer on a certificate of ownership, or who with fraudulent intent displays or causes or permits to be displayed or have in his possession any canceled, suspended, revoked, altered, forged, counterfeit, or false certificate of ownership, registration card, certificate, license or special plate or permit or who utters, publishes, passes, or attempts to pass, as true and genuine, any of the above named false, altered, forged, or counterfeited matters knowing the same to be false, altered, forged, or counterfeited with intent to prejudice, damage, or defraud any person is guilty of a felony and upon conviction thereof shall be punished by imprisonment in the state prison for not less than one year or more than 14 years, or in the county jail for not more than one year.

Election Code 14691—Any person attempting to vote an absent voter's ballot by fraudulently signing the name of a regularly qualified voter is guilty of forgery.

Election Code 29100—*Forged or counterfeit election returns.* Every person is punishable by imprisonment in the state prison for not less than two nor more than seven years who:

(a)   forges or counterfeits returns of an election purported to have been held at a precinct where no election was in fact held.

(b)   willfully substitutes forged or counterfeit returns of election in the place of true returns for a precinct where an election was actually held.

Election Code 29101—*Altering returns.* Every person who willfully adds to or subtracts from the votes actually cast at an election, in any official or unofficial returns, or who alters the returns, is punishable by imprisonment in the state prison for not less than one year nor more than five years.

Election Code 29102—*Aiding or abetting offense.* Every person who aids or abets in the commission of any of the offenses mentioned in Sections 14431, 29100, 29101, or 29103 is punishable by imprisonment in the county jail for the period of six months or in the state prison not exceeding two years.

Election Code 29216—*Filing with false signature.* Every person is punishable by a fine not exceeding five thousand dollars ($5,000), or by imprisonment in the state prison not exceeding two years or in a county jail not exceeding one year, or by both such fine and imprisonment, who files in the office of the clerk or other officer designated by law to receive such filing, any initiative, referendum, or recall petition to which is attached, appended or subscribed any signature which the person filing the petition knows to be false or fraudulent or not the genuine signature of the person whose name it purports to be. Executing false initiatives, referendum recall or nominating petition or entry of a false or fictitious name thereon.

LEGAL DISCUSSION

The above-cited sections are not all-inclusive; before concluding that there is no crime, it is necessary to check with the city attorney to ascertain whether the forgery in question falls within a specific statute which enlarges the field over that described herein.

In general and aside from the specially created crimes (in Code sections cited above), the following elements must be considered. The document must be such that if genuine it would create a legal right or obligation of legal significance. The word "writing" includes typewriting, printing, and other related means of communication. The false document must have on its face the ability to injure. If on its face it is incapable of legal significance, there can be no forgery. On the other hand, if the invalidity is not apparent from the face of the document but must be established by extrinsic facts, there is no forgery.

Attention is directed to the above-cited statutes which not only extend to the mailing of false signatures but establish that a material alteration of the document or instrument is forgery. The materiality of the obligation is tested by the same test; viz, has the alteration changed legal rights and duties?

The use of a fictitious name and the use of one's own name when it is done with the knowledge that the name-signature will be treated as that of another is forgery. Similarly, where the obtaining of an actual signature is by fraud and subterfuge, the party committing this fraud and subterfuge is guilty of forgery although he does not make the spurious signature.

ENFORCEMENT ASPECTS

The false evidence sections (P.C. 115, 132, 134) may oftentimes be filed. Unfortunately many officers have overlooked these felony crimes. The act of filing a false instrument, preparing a false instrument, and introducing or offering a false instrument are offenses that usually occur when the defendant has been previously prosecuted. While they are infrequent, officers should be cognizant of these offenses.

Forgery of narcotic prescriptions usually involves joint violations and may also involve crimes under the Health and Safety Code discussed in Chapter 23.

The sections on possession of false documents, auto registration, etc., are of relevance to the officer as he may frequently have "probable cause" to arrest the defendant for violations of these sections.

Uttering is the offering for sale, the sale or otherwise passing, of a forged instrument with knowledge of the forgery and with the intent to defraud. Where the forger utters his own work, he may be charged jointly with forgery and uttering.

The offering or knowingly procuring the offering of a forged instrument for recording and/or filing in a public office is a crime. However, not all documents are instruments under this section. To be an instrument the document must transfer title *to* or create interests *in* real property or give a right to a debt or a duty;[5] a false affadavit of birth and parentage is not such an instrument;[6] a will is such an instrument;[7] a car dealer's report of sale and nonuse is not;[8] a permit to issue stock is not.[9]

P.C. 475—applies to possession of a completed or incompleted check, and whether parties are real or fictitious.[10]

Counterfeiting of currency, money, stamps, etc., is basically a federal crime.[11] However, there are also state statutes.

APPLICABLE STATUTES—COUNTERFEITING

P.C. 477—*Counterfeiting coin, bullion, etc.* Every person who counterfeits any of the species of gold or silver coin current in this state, or any kind of species of gold dust, gold or silver bullion, or bars, lumps, pieces, or nuggets, or who sells, passes, or gives in payment such counterfeit coin, dust, bullion, bars, lumps, pieces, or nuggets, or permits, causes, or procures the same to be sold, uttered, or passed, with intention to defraud any person knowing the same to be counterfeited, is guilty of counterfeiting.

P.C. 478—*Punishment of counterfeiting.* Counterfeiting is punishable by imprisonment in the state prison for not less than one nor more than fourteen years.

P.C. 479—*Possessing or receiving counterfeit coin, bullion, etc.* Every person who has in his possession, or receives for any other person, any counterfeit gold or silver coin of the species current in this state, or any counterfeit gold dust, gold or silver bullion or bars, lumps, pieces, or nuggets, with the intention to sell, utter, put off, or pass the same, or permits, causes or procures the same to be sold, uttered, or passed, with intention to defraud any person, knowing the same to be counterfeit, is punishable by imprisonment in the state prison not less than one nor more than fourteen years.

P.C. 480—*False personation in signing and sending letter to newspaper.* Every person who signs any letter addressed to a newspaper with the name of a person other than himself and sends such letter to the newspaper, or causes it to be sent to such newspaper, with intent to lead the newspaper to believe that such letter was written by the person whose name is signed thereto, is guilty of a misdemeanor.

P.C. 480—*Making or possessing counterfeit dies or plates.* Every person who makes, or knowingly has in his possession any die, plate, or any apparatus, paper, metal, machine, or other thing whatever, made use of in counterfeiting coin current in this state, or in counterfeiting gold dust, gold or silver bars, bullion, lumps, pieces, or nuggets, or in counterfeiting bank notes or bills, is punishable by imprisonment in the state prison not less than one nor more than fourteen years; and all such dies, plates, apparatus, paper, metal, or machine, intended for the purpose aforesaid, must be destroyed.

P.C. 540—*Counterfeiting of ration stamps, etc. Punishment.* Every person, who steals, or, without authority to do so, alters, forges, or counterfeits any coupon, stamp, token, certificate, or other ration evidence or document issued by the United States government or any agency thereof in furtherance of its rationing program, or forges, or alters, without authority, any ration check shall be punishable by imprisonment in the state prison not less than six months nor more than five years or in the county jail not exceeding six months, or by fine not exceeding five hundred dollars ($500), or by both such fine and imprisonment.

P.C. 640a—*Misuse of slot machines, etc.* 1.   Any person who shall knowingly and willfully operate, or cause to be operated, or who shall attempt to operate, or attempt to cause to be operated, any automatic vending machine, slot machine, or other receptacle designed to receive lawful coin of the United States of America in connection with the sale, use or enjoyment of property or service, by means of a slug or any false, counterfeited, mutilated, sweated or foreign coin, or by any means, method, trick or device whatsoever not lawfully authorized by the owner, lessee or licensee of such machine or receptacle, or who shall take, obtain or receive from or in connection with any automatic vending machine, slot machine, or other receptacle designed to receive lawful coin of the United States of America in connection with the sale, use or enjoyment of property or service, any goods, wares, merchandise, gas, electric current, article of value, or the use or enjoyment of any musical instrument, phonograph or other property, without depositing in and surrendering to such machine, or receptacle lawful coin of the United States of America to the amount required therefore by the owner, lessee or licensee of such machine or receptacle, shall be guilty of a misdemeanor.

2. Any person who, with intent to cheat or defraud the owner, lessee, licensee or other person entitled to the contents of any automatic vending machine, slot machine or other receptacle, depository or contrivance designed to receive lawful coin of the United States of America in connection with the sale, use or enjoyment of property or service, or who, knowing or having cause to believe that the same is intended for unlawful use, shall manufacture for sale, or sell or give away any slug, device or substance whatsoever intended or calculated to be placed or deposited in any such automatic vending machine, slot machine or other such receptacle, depository or contrivance, shall be guilty of a misdemeanor.

P.C. 648—*Issuing or circulating paper money.* Every person who makes, issues, or puts in circulation any bill, check, ticket, certificate, promissory note, or the paper of any bank, to circulate as money, except as authorized by the laws of the United States, for the first offense, is guilty of a misdemeanor, and for each and every subsequent offense, is guilty of felony.

P.C. 648a—*Slugs resembling coins of United States. Definitions. Exceptions.* Every person who has in his possession for any illegal purpose or who makes, sells, issues, or puts in circulation any slug or token of the size and shape or of a size and shape such that the radius, the diameter and the thickness thereof are each within six one-hundredths of an inch of that of any coin of the United States of America is guilty of a misdemeanor. The term "slug" and the term "token" as used herein, mean any piece of metal or other material not a coin of the United States or a foreign country. However, tokens sold by and accepted as fares by electric railways and lettered checks having a returnable trade value shall not be subject to the provisions of this act.

LEGAL DISCUSSION AND ENFORCEMENT ASPECTS

Most of the counterfeiting offenses as regards currency are under the district jurisdiction of the U.S. Treasury Department. They are the "watchdogs" of the American monetary system.

Frequently, however, there are cases of counterfeiting the purpose of which is to defraud the public. This offense has manifested itself in the counterfeiting of credit cards, airline tickets, tokens, and slugs which have activated parking control "arms." The state offenses enumerated may be of assistance to the enforcement officer and should be available for his reference.

DISCUSSION QUESTIONS

1. What are the elements of "straight forgery"?
2. Can a post-dated check be prosecuted under (P.C. 476a) N.S.F.?
3. Is the preparation and offering of false evidence a misdemeanor or a felony?
4. In prosecuting a defendant for falsifying a vehicle registration certificate is it necessary to prove an intent to defraud?
5. What codes contain statutes relating to forgery?

NOTES

[1]People v. Cortez, 290 P 1083; 108 CA 111.
[2]People v. Eppstein, 292 P 1054; 108 CA 72.
[3]People v. Kahn, 182 P 803; 41 CA 393.
[4]People v. Bowles, 108 CA 72; 290 P 1054.
[5]People v. Frasier, 23 CA 82; 137 P 276.
[6]In re Parker, 57 CA 2d 388; 134 P 2d 302.
[7]People v. Horowitz, 70 CA 2d 675; 161 P 2d 833.
[8]People v. Wood, 161 CA 2d 23; 325 P 2d 1014.
[9]People v. Olf, 195 CA 2d 97; 15 CR 1390.
[10]People v. Parks, 230 CA 2d 805; 41 CR 329.
[11]18 USC 471 et seq.
[12]People v. O'Brien, 96 C 171; 31 P 45.

10

Robbery
and Extortion

APPLICABLE STATUTES

P.C. 211—*Robbery defined.* Robbery is the felonious taking of personal property in the possession of another, from his person or immediate presence, and against his will, accomplished by means of force or fear.

P.C. 211a—*Degree of robbery.* All robbery which is perpetrated by torture or by a person being armed with a dangerous or deadly weapon, and the robbery of any person who is performing his duties as operator of any motor vehicle, streetcar, or trackless trolley used for the transportation of persons for hire, is robbery in the first degree. All other kinds of robbery are of the second degree.

P.C. 212—*What fear may be element in robbery.* The fear mentioned in section 211 may be either:
1. The fear of an unlawful injury to the person or property of the person robbed, or of any relative of his or member of his family; or,
2. The fear of an immediate and unlawful injury to the person or property of anyone in the company of the person robbed at the time of the robbery.

P.C. 213—*Punishment for robbery*. Robbery is punishable by imprisonment in the state prison as follows:

1. Robbery in the first degree for not less than five years.
2. Robbery in the second degree, for not less than one year. The preceding provisions of this section notwithstanding, in any case in which defendant committed robbery, and in the course of commission of the robbery, with the intent to inflict such injury, inflicted great bodily injury on the victim of the robbery, such fact shall be charged in the indictment or information and if found to be true by the jury, upon a jury trial, or if found to be true by the court, upon a court trial, or if admitted by the defendant, defendant shall suffer confinement in the state prison from 15 years to life.

P.C. 214—*Train robbery*. Every person who goes upon or boards any railroad train, car or engine, with the intention of robbing any passenger or other person on such train, car or engine, of any personal property thereon in the possession or care or under the control of any such passenger or other person, or who interferes in any manner with any switch, rail, sleeper, viaduct, culvert, embankment, structure or appliance pertaining to or connected with any railroad, or places any dynamite or other explosive substance or material upon or near the tract of any railroad, or who sets fire to any railroad bridge or trestle, or who shows, masks, extinguishes or alters any light or other signal, or exhibits or compels any other person to exhibit any false light or signal, or who stops any such train, car or engine, or slackens the speed thereof, or who compels or attempts to compel any person in charge or control thereof to stop any such train, car or engine, or slacken the speed thereof, with the intention of robbing any passenger or other person on such train, car or engine, or any personal property thereon in the possession or charge or under the control of any such passenger or other person, is guilty of a felony.

LEGAL DISCUSSION

The Penal Code is divided into crimes against property, persons, and public peace, and the crime of robbery traverses two of these areas. Robbery is a crime against the person *and* against property.

Robbery contains all the elements of theft, assault and/or battery. The specific intent to permanently deprive the person of his personal property is an element.[1] Asportation becomes important in robbery as it is in theft. The distinguishing characteristic in this regard is that the "taking" must be *from the person* or *his immediate presence*. This may be accomplished when the victim, by force or fear, is compelled to turn over property in his possession to the suspect or in fact to any other third party.

The circumstances of the robbery frequently make evident the intent to deprive the owner of his property. A claim of right or ownership by the suspect may invalidate the intent to steal. Also, if the "taking" is on a temporary basis, it does not constitute the offense.

"From the person" is an element of the felony of grand theft/person. Hence, robbery necessarily includes that crime. In addition it should be noted that "immediate presence" has been loosely construed by case decisions. Hence if a victim is tied up in one room and property is then taken in another, this is sufficient to be construed "in immediate presence."[2] Also, if the victim flees leaving the property, the taking is held to constitute robbery.[3]

It is also important to note that the property taken must be that belonging to a person other than the suspect. The victim need not be the sole or legal owner of the property; he need only have possession. Therefore, a domestic servant or office employee left in charge of a residence or business establishment may well be the victim of a robbery.[4] There is no restriction on the amount or value of this property. As long as the property taken has some value, no matter how slight, the crime of robbery is consummated.

The last element of this crime is most important and sometimes confused. Force *or* fear is required. Force must actually be applied and used; hence the term "strong-arm" robbery. This force must be more than casual. Frequently, this becomes a deciding element in the crime of grand theft/person. Surely force is used by a purse-snatcher. The victim may have had her handbag wrenched from her hands, or she may have been thrown to the pavement, or she may have participated in an actual tug-of-war with the suspect. The point where this crime becomes a robbery is moot. Reference to several leading cases is herewith suggested: People v. Jefferson, 31 Cal. App. 2d 562; People v. Church, 116 Cal. 300; People v. Clayton 89, Cal. App. 405. The use of this force is related to the suspect achieving the element of asportation of the property.

The alternative to force-fear is further defined in P.C. 212. Although this element of fear must be satisfied, the victim need not be turned into a "quivering tower of jello." Fear may be shown by the circumstances surrounding the transaction. A victim who is not afraid as long as he is complying with the suspect's demands and who complies because of some threatened injury which might be inflicted in case of noncompliance is in fear within the meaning of the crime of robbery.[5]

First-degree robbery is defined in P.C. 211a. No cases have been appealed under the torture area; hence the law here is still nebulous. However, the meaning of torture as it applies to murder would govern. The deadly or dangerous weapon is similar to that discussed under assault in Chapter 12. Robbery of a common carrier becomes first degree. This section was prompted after frequent robberies of taxicab operators and bus drivers took place.

As regards an unloaded firearm, there are many cases holding it to be a dangerous weapon within P.C. 211a. In the case of People v. Eagan the court stated:

> It is a matter of common knowledge that in committing robbery pistols are frequently used as bludgeons rather than as firearms. The fact, therefore, that a person perpetrating such crime is armed with a pistol is enough to justify the conclusion that the pistol is a dangerous weapon within the meaning of said section 211a of the penal code, even though it be not loaded.

In fact toy pistols have also been declared dangerous inasmuch as they can be used as a club. Other instruments that are used must be determined as a matter of fact by the jury.

ENFORCEMENT ASPECTS

Basic techniques of investigation should be employed by officers called upon to solve robberies. The most important aspect of this, however, should be the safety of the officers. Robbery suspects are usually armed and dangerous. Plans for apprehension should be carefully made so as to assure the safety of all parties.

There must be a victim of robbery, and this is the most important witness to interview. The victim probably saw and heard the suspect and should be able to give identification testimony. The property was taken from the victim's presence; hence, this witness should be able to describe and identify the "loot." This witness should also be able to give information on the suspect's methods of operation.

In the absence of physical evidence the modus operandi of the suspect becomes most important. This should include the type of robbery (messenger, store, professional persons, residence, business, etc.); method of attack (assault, threat, drugging, etc.); weapon used (firearm, knife, etc.); object of attack (money, merchandise, etc.); physical characteristics (voice, height, weight, etc.); vehicle used; other distinctive peculiarities.

The type of robbery may be in itself distinctive as in bank robbery. The Federal Bank Robbery Statute[6] provides a $5,000 maximum fine or twenty-year maximum sentence or both as a penalty. If during the commission of the offense a person's life is placed in jeopardy or an assault is committed, the penalty is raised to a $10,000 fine or twenty-five year sentence. This statute applies to member banks of the Federal Reserve System or Federal Deposit Insurance Corporation as well as all banks operated under the laws of the United States. Federal Savings and Loan associations and Federal Saving and Loan Corporation members are also included.

Primary jurisdiction for investigation of these crimes rests with the Federal Bureau of Investigation.

APPLICABLE STATUTES—EXTORTION

P.C. 518—*"Extortion" defined.* Extortion is the obtaining of property from another, with his consent, or the obtaining of an official act of a public officer, induced by a wrongful use of force or fear, or under color of official right.

P.C. 519—*What threats may constitute extortion.* Fear, such as will constitute extortion, may be induced by a threat, either:

1. To do an unlawful injury to the person or property of the individual threatened or of a third person; or,
2. To accuse the individual threatened, or any relative of his, or member of his family, of any crime; or,
3. To expose, or impute to him or them any deformity, disgrace or crime; or,
4. To expose any secret affecting him or them.

P.C. 520—*Punishment of extortion in certain cases.* Every person who extorts any money or other property from another, under circumstances not amounting to robbery, by means of force, or any threat, such as is mentioned in the preceding section, is punishable by imprisonment in the state prison for not less than one nor more than ten years.

P.C. 521—*Punishment of extortion committed under color of official right.* Every person who commits any extortion under color of official right, in cases for which a different punishment is not prescribed in this code, is guilty of a misdemeanor.

P.C. 522—*Obtaining signature by means of threats.* Every person who, by any extortionate means, obtains from another his signature to any paper or instrument, whereby, if such signature were freely given, any property would be transferred, or any debt, demand, charge, or right of action created, is punishable in the same manner as if the actual delivery of such debt, demand, charge, or right of action were obtained.

P.C. 523—*Sending threatening letters with intent to extort money, etc.* Every person who, with intent to extort any money or other property from another, sends or delivers to any person any letter or other writing, whether subscribed or not, expressing or implying or adapted to imply, any threat such as is specified in section 519, is punishable in the same manner as if such money or property were actually obtained by means of such threat.

P.C. 524—*Attempts to extort money or property*. Every person who attempts, by means of any threat, such as is specified in section 519 of this code, to extort money or other property from another is punishable by imprisonment in the county jail not longer than one year or in the state prison not exceeding five years, or by fine not exceeding five thousand dollars, or by both such fine and imprisonment.

P.C. 650—*Sending letters threatening to expose another*. Every person who knowingly and willfully sends or delivers to another any letter or writing, whether subscribed or not, threatening to accuse him or another of a crime, or to expose or publish any of his failings or infirmities, is guilty of a misdemeanor.

P.C. 660—*Criminal sending of letters; completion of offense*. In the various cases in which the sending of a letter is made criminal by this Code, the offense is deemed complete from the time when such letter is deposited in any post office or any other place, or delivered to any person, with intent that it shall be forwarded.

LEGAL DISCUSSION

The interpretations made by the courts for the "fear" required in extortion are clear. This fear must be the compelling or motivating reason causing the transfer of property. The injury or threat of injury by a third person is sufficient to constitute the fear. There is an implication of alternatives in the threat.

This leads to the element of "consent." If the force or fear were such as to *compel* the victim to part with his property, the crime would be robbery. Legally speaking, the victim of extortion is considered to be consenting to the giving of his property willfully, although this is done by the victim with the understanding that this act may save him injury or other calamity. Despite the mental protest existing, the victim has the alternative of accepting the act threatened. Therefore consent is willingly granted.

The property extorted may be real or personal. It makes no difference if the property is turned over directly to the defendant or a third party.

The term "threat" is specifically defined under P.C. 519.

ENFORCEMENT ASPECTS

This type of crime has an interesting aspect in that it is infrequently prosecuted as the completed act. Usually only the crime of attempted extortion prevails.

Most victims who are threatened will notify the police. In order to secure evidence the officers will request the victim to proceed with the demands of the suspect. When payment is made and possible surveillance, recordings, and other evidence are obtained, the police arrest the defendant. Since the threat or fear is not the compelling reason to give the property to the defendant but it is done instead at the request of the law enforcement agency, only an attempted extortion has been committed.

In order to prosecute for the crime of extortion the property must have changed hands prior to the police being called in. This usually occurs when the victim has made a small previous payoff and the defendant now feels he has a perpetual victim. After an investigation of the case the usual charge would be Count I Extortion (the first time) and Count II Attempted Extortion (using this to corroborate the first offense).

DISCUSSION QUESTIONS

1. What are the elements of the crime of robbery?
2. What acts constitute first-degree robbery?
3. What is the relationship of grand theft to robbery?
4. If a robbery is committed by a suspect using a toy pistol, what degree of the crime would exist?
5. What are the elements of the crime of extortion?
6. How does extortion differ from robbery?

NOTES

[1]People v. Morlock, 46 C 2d 141; 292 P 2d 897.
[2]People v. Deene, 66 CA 602; 226 P 943.
 People v. Hornes, 168 CA 2d 314; 335 P 2d 756.
[3]People v. Sylvis, 72 CA 632; 237 P 2d 802.
[4]People v. Downs, 114 CA 2d 758; 251 P 2d 369.
[5]People v. Barra, 123 CA 482; 11 P 2d 403.
 People v. Renteria, 61 C 2d 497; 393 P 2d 413.
[6]12 USC 558b.

MALICIOUS MISCHIEF
TRESPASS
PUBLIC NUISANCE
HIGHWAYS-TRESPASS AND MALICIOUS MISCHIEF
CREDIT CARDS
ENFORCEMENT ASPECTS

11

Malicious Mischief, Trespass, and Miscellaneous Crimes

MALICIOUS MISCHIEF—APPLICABLE STATUTES

P.C. 594—*Malicious mischief in general, defined.* Every person who maliciously injures or destroys any real or personal property not his own, in cases otherwise than such as are specified in this code, is guilty of a misdemeanor.

P.C. 600.5—*Burning, growing or standing grain, etc.* [See Chapter 7.]

P.C. 650½—*Injuring person or property of another.* A person who willfully and wrongfully commits any act which seriously injures the person or property of another, or which seriously disturbs or endangers the public peace or health, or which openly outrages public decency, or who willfully and wrongfully in any manner, verbal or written, uses another's name for accomplishing lewd or licentious purposes, whether such purposes are accomplished or not, or who willfully and wrongfully uses another's name in any manner that will affect, or have a tendency to affect, the moral reputation of the person whose name is used, generally, or in the estimation of the person or persons to whom it is so used, or who with intent of accomplishing any lewd or licentious purpose, whether

134

such purpose is accomplished or not, personifies any person other than himself, or who causes or procures any other person than himself, or who causes or procures any other person or persons to identify him, or to give assurance that he is any other person than himself to aid or assist him to accomplish any lewd or licentious purpose, for which no other punishment is expressly prescribed by this code, is guilty of a misdemeanor.

LEGAL DISCUSSION

The element of crime implied by the word "malice" in the foregoing is generally construed to mean more than "mere intentional harm" accompanied by a lack of justification or excuse. The law requires a wanton, willful, reckless disregard of the rights of others. Naturally, where any justification, excuse or mitigating circumstance exists, such malice cannot concurrently exist.

ENFORCEMENT ASPECTS

Recent court decisions have made this section (P.C. 650½) ineffective as regards the "outrage of public decency." Many of the topless entertainment nightclubs have placed large signs at entrances. The courts have held that the public is warned by the signs that they will see topless performers; therefore, there can be no "outrage" if they view what was announced.

APPLICABLE STATUTES—TRESPASS

P.C. 602—*Trespasses upon land enumerated: misdemeanor.* Every person who willfully commits any trespass by either:

   (a)   cutting down, destroying, or injuring any kind of wood or timber standing or growing upon the lands of another;
   (b)   carrying away any kind of wood or timber lying on such lands;
   (c)   maliciously injuring or severing from the freehold of another anything attached thereto, or the produce thereof;
   (d)   digging, taking, or carrying away from any lot situated within the limits of any incorporated city, without the license of the owner or legal occupant thereof, any earth, soil, or stone;
   (e)   digging, taking, or carrying away from land in any city or town laid down on the map or plan of such city, or otherwise recognized or established as a street, alley, avenue, or park, without the license of the proper authorities, any earth, soil, or stone;
   (f)   maliciously tearing down, damaging, mutilating, or destroying

any sign, signboard or notice placed upon, or affixed to, any property belonging to the state, or to any city, county, city and county, town, or village or upon any property of any person, by the state or by an automobile association, which sign, signboard or notice is intended to indicate or designate a road or roads, or a highway or highways, or is intended to direct travelers from one point to another, or relates to fires, fire control, or any other matter involving the protection of property, or putting up, affixing, fastening, printing, or painting upon any property belonging to the state, or to any city, county, town or village, or dedicated to the public, or upon any property of any person, without license from the owner, any notice, advertisement, or designation of, or any name for any commodity, whether for sale or otherwise, or any picture, sign, or device intended to call attention thereto;

(g) entering upon any lands owned by any other person whereon oysters or other shellfish are planted or growing; or injuring, gathering or carrying away any oysters or other shellfish planted, growing, or being on any such lands, whether covered by water or not, without the license of the owner or legal occupant thereof; or destroying or removing, or causing to be removed or destroyed, any stakes, marks, fences, or signs intended to designate the boundaries and limits of any such lands;

(h) willfully opening, tearing down, or otherwise destroying any fence on the enclosed land of another, or opening any gate, bar, or fence, of another and willfully leaving it open without the written permission of the owner, or maliciously tearing down, mutilating, or destroying any sign, signboard, or other notice forbidding shooting on private property; or

(j) entering any lands, whether unenclosed or enclosed by fence, for the purpose of injuring any property or property rights or with the intention of interfering with, obstructing, or injuring any lawful business or occupation carried on by the owner of such land, his agent or by the person in lawful possession; or

(k) entering any lands under cultivation or enclosed by fence, belonging to, or occupied by, another, or entering upon uncultivated or unenclosed lands where signs forbidding trespass are displayed at intervals not less than three to the mile along all exterior boundaries and at all roads and trails entering such lands without the written permission of the owner of such land, his agent or of the person in lawful possession, and

   (1) Refusing or failing to leave such lands immediately upon being requested by the owner of such land, his agent or by the person in lawful possession to leave such lands, or

   (2) tearing down, mutilating or destroying any sign, sign-

board, or notice forbidding trespass or hunting on such lands, or

(3) removing, injuring, unlocking, or tampering with any lock on any gate on or leading into such lands;

(4) discharging any firearm;

(1) entering and occupying real property or structures of any kind without the consent of the owner, his agent, or the person in lawful possession thereof;

(m) entering upon any lands declared closed to entry as provided in section 4126.5 of the public resources code, provided such closed areas shall have been posted with notices declaring such closure, at intervals not greater than one mile along the exterior boundaries or along roads and trails passing through such lands;

(n) refusing or failing to leave a public building of a public agency during those hours of the day or night when the building is regularly closed to the public upon being requested to do so by a regularly employed guard, watchman, or custodian of the public agency owning or maintaining the building or property, if the rounding circumstances are such as to indicate to a reasonable man that such person has no apparent lawful business to pursue; is guilty of a misdemeanor.

P.C. 607—*Destroying or injuring bridges, dams, levees, etc.* Every person who willfully and maliciously cuts, breaks, injures, or destroys any bridge, dam, canal, flume, aqueduct, levee, embankment, reservoir, or other structure erected to create hydraulic power, or to drain or reclaim any swamp, overflow, tide or marsh land, or to store or conduct water for mining, manufacturing, reclamation, or agricultural purposes, or for the supply of the inhabitants of any city or town, or any embankment necessary to the same, or either of them, or willfully or maliciously makes, or causes to be made, any aperture or plows up the bottom or sides in such dam, canal, flume, aqueduct, reservoir, embankment, levee, or structure, with intent to injure or destroy same; or draws up, cuts, or injures any piles fixed in the ground for the purpose of securing any seabank, or seawalls, or any dock, quay, or jetty, lock, or sea-wall; or who, between the first day of October and the fifteenth day of April of each year, plows up or loosens the soil in the bed or on the side of any natural watercourse, reclamation or drainage ditch, with an intent to destroy the same, without removing such soil within twenty-four hours from such watercourse, reclamation or drainage ditch; or who, between the fifteenth day of April and the first day of October of each year, shall plow up or loosen the soil in the bed or on the sides of such natural watercourse, reclamation or drainage ditch, with an intent to destroy the same, and shall not remove therefrom the soil so plowed up or loosened before the first day of October next thereafter, is guilty of a misdemeanor, and upon conviction, punishable by a fine of not exceeding one thousand dollars, or by imprisonment in a county jail, not exceeding one year, or by both such fine and imprisonment; provided, that nothing in this section shall be construed so as to in any manner prohibit any person from digging or removing soil from any such watercourse, reclamation or drainage ditch, for the purpose of mining.

P.C. 146—*Making arrests, etc., without lawful authority.* Every public officer, or person pretending to be a public officer, who, under the pretense or color of any process or other legal authority, arrests any person or detains him against his will, or seizes or levies upon any property, or dispossesses any one of any lands or tenements, without a regular process or other lawful authority therefor, is guilty of a misdemeanor.

P.C. 146a—*Impersonation of officers.* Any person who falsely represents himself to be a public officer, or investigator, inspector, deputy or clerk in any state department and in such assumed character arrests or detains or threatens to arrest or detain, or otherwise intimidates any person or searches the person, building, or other property of any person, or obtains money, or property, or other thing of value, shall be deemed guilty of a misdemeanor and upon conviction thereof shall be punished by a fine of not more than one thousand dollars ($1,000) or imprisonment for not more than one year or by both such fine and imprisonment.

P.C. 552—*Exceptions.* This article does not apply to any entry in the course of duty of any peace or police officer or other duly authorized public officer, nor does it apply to the lawful use of an established and existing right of way for public road purposes.

P.C. 556.3—*Public nuisance.* Any sign, picture, transparency, advertisement, or mechanical device placed on any property contrary to the provisions of section 556 and 556.1 is a public nuisance.

P.C. 593b—*Unauthorized climbing upon any electric transmission line.* Every person who shall, without the written permission of the owner, lessee, or person or corporation operating any electrical transmission line, distributing line or system, climb upon any pole, tower or other structure which is a part of such line or system and is supporting or is designed to support a wire or wires, cable or cables, for the transmission or distribution of electric energy, shall be deemed guilty of a misdemeanor; provided, that nothing herein shall apply to employees of either privately or publicly owned public utilities engaged in the performance of their duties.

P.C. 587b—*Trespassing on railroad trains.* Every person, who shall, without being thereunto authorized by the owner, lessee, person or corporation operating any railroad, enter into, climb upon, hold to, or in any manner attach himself to any locomotive, locomotive engine tender, freight or passenger car upon such railroad, or any portion of any train thereon, shall be deemed guilty of a misdemeanor, and, upon conviction thereof shall be punished by a fine not exceeding fifty dollars, or by imprisonment not exceeding thirty days, or by both such fine and imprisonment.

P.C. 591—*Injuring telegraph, telephone or other electric line: punishment.* A person who unlawfully and maliciously takes down, removes, injures or obstructs any line of telegraph or telephone, or any other line used to conduct electricity, or any part thereof, or appurtenances or apparatus connected therewith, or severs any wire thereof, or makes any unauthorized connection with any line, other than a telegraph or telephone line, used to conduct electricity, or any part thereof, or appurtenances or apparatus connected therewith, is punishable by imprisonment in the state prison not exceeding five years, or by a fine not exceeding five hundred dollars ($500), or imprisonment in the county jail not exceeding one year.

P.C. 600—*Burning structures, etc.* [See Chapter 7.]

P.C. 593—*Interference with electrical transmission lines.* Every person who unlawfully and maliciously takes down, removes, injures, interferes with, or obstructs any line erected or maintained by proper authority for the purpose of transmitting electricity for light, heat, or power, or any part thereof, or any insulator or cross-arm, appurtenance or apparatus connected therewith, or severs or in any way interferes with any wire, cable, or current thereof, is punishable by imprisonment in the state prison not exceeding five years, or by fine not exceeding five hundred dollars, or imprisonment in the county jail not exceeding one year.

P.C. 593c—*Interference with distribution of gas.* Every person who willfully and maliciously breaks, digs up, obstructs, interferes with, removes or injures any pipe or main erected, operated, or maintained by proper authority for the purpose of transporting, conveying or distributing gas for light, heat, power or any other purpose, or any part thereof, or any valve, meter, holder, compressor, machinery, appurtenance, equipment or apparatus connected with any such main or pipeline, or used in connection with or affecting the operation thereof or the conveying of gas therethrough, or shuts off, removes, obstructs, injures, or in any way interferes with any valve installed on, connected to or operated in connection with any such main or pipeline or controlling or affecting the flow of gas through any such main or pipeline, is guilty of a felony.

P.C. 624—*Breaking or obstructing water pipes.* Every person who willfully breaks, digs up, obstructs, or injures any pipe or main for conducting water, or any works erected for supplying buildings with water, or any appurtenances or appendages connected thereto, is guilty of a misdemeanor.

P.C. 625a—*Unlawful interference with fire-alarm apparatus; penalty.*

(1) Any person who willfully and maliciously tampers with, molests, injures, or breaks any public fire alarm apparatus, wire, or signal, or willfully and maliciously sends, gives, transmits, or sounds any false alarm of fire, by means of any public fire alarm system or signal or by any other means or methods, is guilty of a misdemeanor and upon conviction thereof shall be punishable by imprisonment in the county jail, not exceeding one year, or by a fine, not exceeding one thousand dollars ($1,000), or by both such fine and imprisonment.

(2) Any person who willfully and maliciously sends, gives, transmits, or sounds any false alarm of fire, by means of any public fire alarm system or signal, or by any other means or methods, and great bodily injury or death is sustained by any person as a result thereof, is guilty of a felony and upon conviction thereof shall be punishable by imprisonment in the state prison for not less than one year nor more than five years or by a fine of not less than five hundred dollars ($500) nor more than five thousand dollars ($5,000) or by both such fine and imprisonment.

P.C. 355—*Defacing marks upon wrecked property and destroying bills of lading.* Every person who defaces or obliterates the marks upon wrecked property, or in any manner disguises the appearance thereof, with intent to prevent the owner from discovering its identity, or who destroys or suppresses any invoice, bill of lading, or other document tending to show the ownership, is guilty of a misdemeanor.

Public nuisance—Although the elimination of a public nuisance is usually a matter for civil action, there are penal statutes affecting same.

APPLICABLE STATUTES

P.C. 370—*Public nuisances defined.* Anything which is injurious to health, or is indecent, or offensive to the senses, or an obstruction to the free use of property, so as to interfere with the comfortable enjoyment of life or property by an entire community or neighborhood, or by any considerable number of persons, or unlawfully obstructs the free passage or use, in the customary manner, of any navigable lake, or river, bay, stream, canal, or basin, or any public park, square, street, or highway is a public nuisance.

P.C. 372—*Maintaining a nuisance, a misdemeanor.* Every person who maintains or commits any public nuisance, the punishment for which is not otherwise prescribed, or who willfully omits to perform any legal duty relating to the removal of a public nuisance, is guilty of a misdemeanor.

P.C. 374b—*Placing or dumping offensive matter on highways.* It shall be unlawful to place, deposit or dump, or cause to be placed, deposited or dumped, any garbage, swill, cans, bottles, papers, ashes, refuse, carcass of any dead animal, offal, trash or rubbish or any noisome, nauseous or offensive matter in or upon any public or private highway or road, including any portion of the right-of-way thereof, or in or upon any private property into or upon which the public is admitted by easement or license, or upon any private property without the consent of the owner, or in or upon any public park or other public property other than property designated or set aside for such purpose by the governing board or body having charge thereof. It shall be unlawful to place, deposit, or dump, or cause to be placed, deposited or dumped, any rocks or dirt in or upon any private highway or road, including any portion of the right-of-way thereof, or any private property, without the consent of the owner, or in or upon any public park or other public property, without the consent of the state or local agency having jurisdiction over such highway, road, or property. Any person, firm or corporation violating the provisions of this section shall be guilty of a misdemeanor.

(No portion of this section shall be construed to restrict a private owner in the use of his own private property.)

P.C. 374d—*Carcass of dead animal on roadway.* Every person who knowingly allows the carcass of any dead animal which belonged to him at the time of its death to be put, or to remain, within 100 feet of any street, alley, public highway, or road in common use, and every person who puts the carcass of any dead animal within 100 feet of any street, alley, highway, or road in common use is guilty of a misdemeanor.

P.C. 375—*Offensive substances in places of assemblage. Penalty.*

(1) It shall be unlawful to throw, drop, pour, deposit, release, discharge or expose, or to attempt to throw, drop, pour, deposit, release, discharge or expose in, upon or about any theater, restaurant, place of business, place of amusement or any place of public assemblage, any liquid, gaseous or solid substance or matter of any kind which is injurious to person or property, or is nauseous, sickening, irritating or offensive to any of the senses.

(2) It shall be unlawful to manufacture or prepare, or to possess any liquid, gaseous, or solid substance or matter of any kind which is injurious to person or property, or is nauseous, sickening, irritating or offensive to any of the senses with intent to throw, drop, deposit, release, discharge or expose the same in, upon or about any theater, restaurant,

place of business, place of amusement, or any other place of public assemblage.

(3) Penalty. Any person violating any of the provisions hereof shall be punished by imprisonment in the county jail for not less than three months and not more than one year, or by a fine of not less than five hundred dollars and not more than two thousand dollars, or by both such fine and imprisonment.

(4) Any person who, in violating any of the provisions of subdivision (1) of this section, willfully employs or uses any liquid, gaseous or solid substance which may produce serious illness or permanent injury through being vaporized or otherwise disbursed in the air or who, in violating any of the provisions of subdivision (1) of this section, willfully employs or uses any tear gas, mustard gas or any of the combinations or compounds thereof, or willfully employs or uses acid or explosives, shall be guilty of a felony and shall be punished by imprisonment in the state prison for not less than one year and not more than five years.

P.C. 592—*Canals, ditches, etc., interfering with.* Every person who shall, without authority of the owner or managing agent, and with intent to defraud, take water from any canal, ditch, flume or reservoir used for the purpose of holding or conveying water for manufacturing, agricultural, mining, irrigating or generation of power, or domestic uses, or who shall without like authority, raise, lower or otherwise disturb any gate or other apparatus thereof, used for the control or measurement of water, or who shall empty or place, or cause to be emptied or placed, into any such canal, ditch, flume or reservoir, any rubbish, filth or obstruction to the free flow of the water, is guilty of a misdemeanor.

P.C. 384a—*Cutting, destroying or removing shrubs, etc., from highways and private property without written permit.* Every person who within the state of California willfully or negligently cuts, destroys, mutilates, or removes any tree or shrub, or fern or herb or bulb or cactus or flower, or huckleberry or redwood greens, or portion of any tree or shrub, or fern or herb or bulb or cactus or flower, or huckleberry or redwood greens, growing upon state or county highway rights-of-way, or who removes leaf mold thereon; provided, however, that the provisions of this section shall not be construed to apply to any employee of the state or of any political subdivision thereof engaged in work upon any state, county or public road or highway while performing such work under the supervision of the state or of any political subdivision thereof, and every person who willfully or negligently cuts, destroys, mutilates or removes any tree or shrub, or fern or herb or bulb or cactus or flower, or huckleberry or redwood greens, or portions of any tree or shrub, or fern or herb or bulb or cactus or flower, or huckleberry or redwood greens, growing upon public land or upon land not his own, or leaf mold on the surface of public land, or upon land not his own, without a written permit from the owner of the land signed by such owner or his authorized agent, and every person who knowingly sells, offers, or exposes for sale, or transports for sale, any tree or shrub, or fern or herb or bulb or cactus or flower, or huckleberry or redwood greens, or portion of any tree or shrub, or fern or herb or bulb or cactus or flower, or huckleberry or redwood greens, or leaf mold, so cut or removed from state or county highway rights-of-way, or removed from public land or from land not owned by the person who cut or removed the same without the written permit from the owner of the land, signed by such owner or his authorized agent, shall be guilty of a misdemeanor and upon conviction thereof shall be punished by a fine of not more than five hundred dollars ($500) or by imprisonment in a county jail for not more than six months or by both such fine and imprisonment.

(Requisites of permit)   The written permit required under this section shall be signed by the landowner, or his authorized agent, and acknowledged before a notary public, or other person authorized by law to take acknowledgments. The permit shall contain the number and species of trees and amount of shrubs or ferns or herbs or bulbs or cacti or flowers, or huckleberry or redwood greens, or portions of any tree or shrub and shall contain the legal description of the real property as usually found in deeds and conveyances of the land on which cutting or removal, or both, shall take place. One copy of such permit shall be filed in the office of the sheriff of the county in which the land described in the permit is located. The permit shall be filed prior to commencement of cutting of the trees or shrub or fern or herb or bulb or cactus or flower or huckleberry or redwood green or portions of any tree or shrub authorized by the permit. The permit required by this section need not be notarized or filed with the office of the sheriff of the county where trees are to be removed when 5 (five) or less trees or 5 (five) or less pounds of shrubs or boughs are to be cut or removed.

(Authority to enforce and confiscate)   Any county or state firewarden, or personnel of the California Division of Forestry as designated by the State Forester, and personnel of the United States Forest Service as designated by the regional forester, region 5, of the United States Forest Service, or any peace officer of the State of California, shall have full power to enforce the provisions hereof and to confiscate any and all such shrubs, trees, ferns or herbs or bulbs or cacti or flowers, or huckleberry or redwood greens or leaf mold, or parts thereof unlawfully cut or removed or knowingly sold, offered or exposed or transported for sale as hereinbefore provided.

(Application of Section: public nuisance)   The provisions of this section shall not be construed to apply to any tree or shrub, or fern or herb or bulb or cactus or flower, or greens declared by law to be a public nuisance.

(Same: cutting to protect public utility property)   The provisions of this section shall not be deemed to apply to the necessary cutting or trimming of any such trees, shrubs, or ferns or herbs or bulbs or cacti or flowers, or greens if done for the purpose of protecting or maintaining an electric power line or telephone line or other property of a public utility. (Same: Logging: Fire suppression) The provisions of this section do not apply to persons engaged in logging operations, or in suppressing fires.

Highways—Trespass and Malicious Mischief

A part of trespass and/or malicious mischief offenses involving highways are separately treated herein.

APPLICABLE STATUTES

Vehicle Code 23111—Outside of a business or residence district no person in any vehicle and no pedestrian shall willfully or negligently throw or discharge from or upon any road or highway or adjoining area, public or private, any lighted cigarette, cigar, ashes, or any other flaming or glowing substance.

Vehicle Code 23110—(a) Any person who throws any substance at a vehicle or any occupant thereof on a highway is guilty of a misdemeanor.

(b) Any person who with intent to do great bodily injury maliciously and willfully throws or projects any rock, brick, bottle, metal or other missile, or projects any other substance capable of doing serious bodily harm, or discharges a firearm at such vehicle or occupant thereof is guilty of a felony and upon conviction shall be punished by imprisonment for not less than one year or more than five years in the state prison.

Vehicle Code 21464—No person shall without lawful authority deface, injure, attach any material or substance to, knock down, or remove, nor shall any person shoot at, any official traffic control device, traffic guidepost, traffic signpost, or historical marker placed or erected as authorized or required by law, nor shall any person without such authority deface, injure, attach any material or substance to, or remove, nor shall any person shoot at, any inscription, shield, or insigne on any such device, guide, or marker.

Vehicle Code 21465—No person shall place, maintain, or display upon, or in view of, any highway any unofficial sign, signal, or device, or any sign, signal, or device which purports to be or is an imitation of, or resembles, an official traffic control device or which attempts to direct the movement of traffic or which hides from view any official traffic control device.

Vehicle Code 21466—No person shall place or maintain or display upon or in view of any highway any light of any color of such brilliance as to blind or dazzle the vision of drivers upon the highway nor shall any light be placed in such position as to prevent the driver of a vehicle from readily recognizing any official traffic control device.

P.C. 219.1—*Throwing missiles at vehicles.* Every person who unlawfully throws, hurls or projects at a vehicle operated by a common carrier, while such vehicle is either in motion or stationary, any rock, stone, brick, bottle, piece of wood or metal or any other missile of any kind or character, or does any lawful act, with the intention of wrecking such vehicle and doing bodily harm, and thus wrecks the same and causes bodily harm, is guilty of a felony and punishable by imprisonment in the state prison for not less than one nor more than 14 years.

P.C. 219.2—*Throwing or shooting at trains, etc.* Every person who willfully throws, hurls, or projects a stone or other hard substance, or shoots a missile, at a train, locomotive, railway car, caboose, cable railway car, street railway car, or bus or at a steam vessel or watercraft used for carrying passengers or freight on any of the waters within or bordering on this state, is punishable by imprisonment in the county jail not exceeding one year, or in a state prison not exceeding three years, or by fine not less than fifty dollars ($50) nor more than five hundred dollars ($500), or by both such fine and imprisonment.

P.C. 219.3—*Dropping or throwing from toll bridge.* Any person who willfully drops or throws any object or missile from any toll bridge is guilty of a misdemeanor.

P.C. 588—*Digging up or flooding highways.* Every person who negligently, willfully or maliciously digs up, removes, displaces, breaks down or otherwise injures or destroys any state or other public highway or bridge, or any private way, laid out by authority of law, or bridge upon any such highway or private way, or who negligently, willfully or maliciously sprinkles, drains, diverts or in any manner permits water from any sprinkler, ditch, canal, flume, or reservoir, to flow upon or saturate by seepage any public highway, which act tends to damage such highway or tends to be a hazard to traffic thereon, shall be guilty of a misdemeanor. This section shall not apply to the natural flow of surface or flood waters that are not diverted, accelerated or concentrated by such person.

P.C. 590—*Injuries to guide posts.* Every person who maliciously removes, destroys, injures, breaks or defaces any mile post, board or stone, or guide post erected on or near any highway, or any inscription thereon, is guilty of a misdemeanor.

APPLICABLE STATUTES—CREDIT CARDS

P.C. 484d—*Definitions.* As used in this section and sections 484e to 484i, inclusive.

(1) "Cardholder" means the person or organization identified on the

face of a credit card to whom or for whose benefit the credit card is issued by an issuer.

(2) "Credit Card" means an instrument or device, whether known as a credit card, credit plate, or by any other name, issued with or without fee by an issuer for the use of the cardholder in obtaining money, goods, services or anything else of value, either on credit or in consideration of an undertaking or guaranty by the issuer of the payment of a check drawn by the cardholder.

(3) "Expired Credit Card" means a credit card which shows on its face it has elapsed.

(4) "Issuer" means the business organization or financial institution which issues a credit or its duly authorized agent.

(5) "Participating Party" means business organization or financial institution which is obligated by contract to acquire from a merchant a sales slip or sales draft or instrument for payment of money.

(6) "Merchant" means every person who is authorized by an issuer or a participating party to furnish money, goods, services or anything else of value upon presentation of a credit card by a cardholder.

(7) A credit card is "incomplete" if part of the matter other than the signature of the cardholder which an issuer requires to appear on the credit card before it can be used by a cardholder has not been stamped, embossed, imprinted, or written on it.

(8) "Revoked credit card" means a credit card for which permission to use it has been suspended or terminated by the issuer and notice thereof has been given to the cardholder.

P.C. 484e—*Theft of credit card*

(1) Every person who acquires a credit card from another without the cardholder's or issuer's consent or who, with knowledge that it has been so acquired, acquires the credit card, with intent to use it or sell or transfer it to a person other than the issuer or the cardholder is guilty of petty theft.

(2) Every person who acquires a credit card that he knows to have been lost, mislaid, or delivered under a mistake as to the identity or address of the cardholder, and who retains possession with intent to use it or to sell it or to transfer it to a person other than the issuer or the cardholder is guilty of petty theft.

(3) Every person who sells, transfers, conveys or receives a credit card with the intent to defraud is guilty of petty theft.

(4) Every person other than the issuer, who within any consecutive 12 month period, acquires credit cards issued in the names of four or more persons which he has reason to know were taken or retained under circumstances which constitute a violation of subdivisions (1), (2), or (3) of this section is guilty of grand theft.

P.C. 484f—*Forgery of credit card*

(1) Every person who, with intent to defraud, makes, alters, or embosses a card purporting to be a credit card or utters such a card is guilty of forgery.

(2) A person other than the cardholder or a person authorized by him who, with intent to defraud, signs the name of another or of a fictitious person to a credit card, sales slip, sales draft, or instrument for the payment of money which evidences a credit card transaction, is guilty of forgery.

P.C. 484g—*Use of forged credit card: misrepresentation as to identity of card holder.* Every person, who with intent to defraud, (a) uses for the purpose of obtaining money, goods, services or anything else of value a credit card obtained or retained in violation of section 484e or a credit card which he knows is forged, expired, or revoked, or (b) obtains money, goods, services or anything else of value by representing without the consent of the cardholder that he is the holder of a credit card or by representing that he is the holder of a credit card and such card has not in fact been issued, is guilty of theft. If the value of all money, goods, services and other things of value obtained in violation of this section exceeds two hundred dollars ($200) in any consecutive six-month period, then the same shall constitute grand theft.

P.C. 484h—*Knowingly furnishing goods or services on forged credit card.* Every merchant who, with intent to defraud: (a) furnishes money, goods, services or anything else of value upon presentation of a credit card obtained or retained in violation of section 484e hereof or a credit card which he knows is forged, expired or revoked, and who receives any payment therefor, is guilty of theft. If the payment received by the merchant for all money, goods, services, and other things of value furnished in violation of this section exceeds two hundred dollars ($200) in any consecutive six-month period, then the same shall constitute grand theft.

(b) fails to furnish money, goods, services or anything else of value which he represents in writing to the issuer or a participating party that he has furnished, and who receives any payment therefor, is guilty of theft. If the difference between the value of all money, goods, services and anything else of value actually furnished and the payment or payments received by the merchant therefor upon such representation exceeds two hundred dollars ($200) in any consecutive six-month period, then the same shall constitute grand theft.

P.C. 484i—*Filling in incomplete card: counterfeit cards.* (a) Every person who possesses an incomplete credit card, with intent to complete them without the consent of the issuer is guilty of a misdemeanor.

(b)   Every person who with intent to defraud possesses, with knowledge of its character, machinery, plates or any other contrivance designed for, and made use of in, the reproduction of instruments purporting to be the credit cards of an issuer who has not consented to the preparation of such credit cards, is punishable by imprisonment in the state prison for not less than one, nor more than 14 years, or by imprisonment in the county jail for not more than one year.

LEGAL DISCUSSION

Section 8 of the act which amended the "credit card statute" provides:

This act shall not be construed to preclude the applicability of any other provision of the criminal law of this state which presently applies or may in the future apply to any transaction which violates this act.

Accordingly, where the criminal act committed violates other Penal Code sections which may provide felony penalties whereas the Credit Card act provides no more than misdemeanor penalties, the crime should be considered as the greater offense.

The widespread use of credit cards in recent years has created new types of offenses frequently distinguishable from larceny, false pretenses, forgery, trick and device, etc. Originally (1961) these were included in the "credit card statute" (P.C. 484a), which was repealed in 1967 and superseded by P.C. 484d-i, inclusive.

P.C. 484a provided that the wrongful use of a credit card for the procurement of goods of value of $50 or less would be theft (misdemeanor) whereas procurement of goods of value in excess of $50 would be a felony. Note that the 1967 amendment provides that the procurement of goods in a six-month period in excess of $200 is a felony; if the value is less than $200, it is a misdemeanor.

ENFORCEMENT ASPECTS

Law enforcement officials are receiving more and more complaints of stolen credit cards and related crimes. Therefore, it is necessary to emphasize crime prevention in this area. The companies that issue the credit cards require notification of loss or theft and hold the credit card holder responsible until such notice is given.

Credit card thieves, credit card counterfeiters, and those intending to use false or stolen credit cards normally are attracted to tourist areas. Method of operation is important in police investigation inasmuch as these criminals will maintain a pattern of use of credit cards.

The possibility of the case being one of theft or forgery is ever present.

A recent case involves an individual who forged a credit card bearing his own true name. The innkeeper viewed the credit card; the suspect signed the credit voucher; and the innkeeper ultimately was left "holding the bag." A crime of forgery based upon the voucher was difficult to sustain since the defendant used his true name (even with false address). The fact that a forged or counterfeit credit card was used is difficult to prove inasmuch as the credit card was probably shown to the victim and returned to the suspect and hence may be unavailable to the prosecution. Out of this transaction the most likely crime for prosecution would be theft by false pretenses (P.C. 484h).

GENERAL SUMMARY AND ENFORCEMENT ASPECTS

Most of the sections of this chapter concern misdemeanors. These offenses cause law enforcement officers the most concern. The working officer should attempt, whenever possible, to obtain a complaining witness. In the prosecution of the case it is always recommended that he locate the victim. With respect to many violations of the sections contained herein, the officer is often in a quandary as to whether to make an arrest. If the complainant demands police action but is unwilling to sign a complaint or in fact to prosecute in court, the law enforcement officer should not take any positive action. Many of the sections under malicious mischief and trespass require complete cooperation and participation by the citizen concerned; without this aid action by the law enforcement officer is ineffective.

DISCUSSION QUESTIONS

1. Define the crime of malicious mischief.
2. List five examples of acts enumerated under trespass.
3. Can the former owner of a dead animal be prosecuted if the body is left on a public highway? If so, under what section?
4. Can a person throwing a cigarette butt out of the window of a moving car be prosecuted? If so, what offense will be charged?
5. Define "credit card."
6. If a person takes someone's credit card but doesn't use it, has a crime been committed? If so, what crime? Discuss fully.

IIB

CRIMES AGAINST PERSONS

*Crimes against persons are violations
of the individual's personal rights: the right to freedom
from fear, from injury to life or limb,
from undesirable invasions of his privacy and peace of
mind, and most of all, the right to have
helpless children protected from predatory individuals.
Here again there is some overlap between
crimes against the person and crimes against the public, as in
prostitution, pimping, pandering, statutory rape, etc.*

12

Assaults

APPLICABLE STATUTES

P.C. 240—*Assault defined.* An assault is an unlawful attempt, coupled with a present ability, to commit a violent injury on the person of another.

P.C. 241—*Punishment of assault: assault against person of peace officer: "peace officer" defined.* An assault is punishable by fine not exceeding five hundred dollars ($500), or by imprisonment in the county jail not exceeding six months, or by both. When it is committed against the person of a peace officer or fireman, and the person committing the offense knows or reasonably should know that such victim is a peace officer or fireman engaged in the performance of his duties, and such peace officer or fireman is engaged in the performance of his duties, the offense shall be punished by imprisonment in the state prison not exceeding two years.

As used in this section, "peace officer" refers to any person designated as a peace officer in the first paragraph of Section 817, as well as any inspector or investigator regularly employed as such in the Office of the District Attorney, any member of the California Highway Patrol, any member of the California State Police, any policeman of the San Francisco Port Authority, each member of an Arson Investigating Unit of an organized Fire Department, and each deputized law enforcement member of the Wildlife Protection Branch of the Department of Fish and Game.

153

LEGAL DISCUSSION

By usage the term "simple assault" is synonymous with "assault" as defined under P.C. 240. Inasmuch as assault is an attempt, the rules of attempts in general apply. The elements of this misdemeanor are:

1. *Unlawful attempt*—It must not be consented to nor can it disturb the peace (a violation of P.C. 415). This then excludes medical operations, athletic contests, lawful corporal punishments, self-defense, force used in making arrests, and lawful celebrations.

   As regards the attempt there must be intent and an overt act.[1] This must be more than a mere threat. Thus, for example, the firing of a pistol without aiming or menacing would not constitute the attempt; actual violence or action must have been initiated. Being thwarted by a third person or object does not lessen the attempted act. Successful completion of the attempt is not necessary; if it is completed, a battery may be committed. Usually the attempt is evident; and when there appears a clear intent to cause injury, the assault is complete.

2. *Present Ability*—This is an essential element of the crime; and the ability must be *actual*, not *apparent*. Therefore, the pointing of an *unloaded* gun with threats to shoot does not constitute an assault from a distance,[2] although it may constitute a violation of P.C. 417 (drawing, exhibiting, or using a firearm or other deadly weapon in a threatening manner). It is up to the trier of the facts to decide whether the circumstances are such that the person attempting the injury has the actual present ability. Thus a person throwing a stone or missile with the intent to injure someone must be within reasonable striking range. If the intended victim were a mile away, there would be no actual present ability and therefore no crime, no matter how strong the intent.

3. *Violent Injury*—This term does not mean that the injury attempted must be severe or cause great pain. The unlawful application of any kind of physical force upon the person of another suffices. Attempting to kiss a female (against her will), turning a water hose on someone (within range of the water stream), or spitting at a person all qualify as violent injuries.

Thus section 240 establishes the crime of simple assault, a misdemeanor. The first meeting of the 1965 legislature after the Watts riots, where police and fire personnel were attacked, resulted in the passage of P.C. 241.

The important element here, making the crime felonious, is *knowledge* on the part of the suspect that the intended victim is a police officer or fireman.

ENFORCEMENT ASPECTS

Officers should not overestimate the "protection" afforded under the felonious assault section. The legislature certainly manifested its concern by enacting this provision. It is, however, necessary to prove that the suspect knew or reasonably should have known that the person attacked was a peace officer or fireman carrying out his duties. Hence, an officer must be in uniform or properly identified for this section to be applicable. Unfortunately, convictions have been all too infrequent, and the authors hope that this trend will change. It is relevant to note that in England the assault on an officer requires a mandatory minimum sentence of five years.

APPLICABLE STATUTES—BATTERY

P.C. 242—*Battery defined.* A battery is any willful and unlawful use of force or violence upon the person of another.

P.C. 243—*Punishment of battery: commitment of battery against peace officer: "peace officer" defined.* A battery is punishable by fine not exceeding one thousand dollars ($1,000), or by imprisonment in the county jail not exceeding six months, or by both. When it is committed against the person of a peace officer or fireman, and the person committing the offense knows or reasonably should know that such victim is a peace officer or fireman engaged in the performance of his duties, and such peace officer or fireman is engaged in the performance of his duties, the offense shall be punished by imprisonment in the state prison for not less than one nor more than ten years.

As used in this Section, "peace officer" refers to any person designated as a peace officer in the first paragraph of Section 817, as well as any inspector or investigator regularly employed as such in the Office of a District Attorney, any member of the California Highway Patrol, any member of the California State Police, any policeman of the San Francisco Port Authority, each member of an Arson Investigating Unit of an organized Fire Department, and each deputized law enforcement member of the Wildlife Protection Branch of the Department of Fish and Game.

LEGAL DISCUSSION

Actually this crime is a "completed assault." It could even be stated, for explanatory purposes, that an attempted battery is an assault. Every assault need not result in a battery; however, every battery includes an assault and is the greater offense.[3]

The elements of battery include:

1. *Willful and unlawful*—Here, as in assault, there must be intent and act. General or constructive intent suffices. Gross negligence, constituting a reckless disregard for other persons, would also suffice.[4]

2. *Use of force or violence*—The amount of force or degree of injury is immaterial. Any force applied that is unlawful is sufficient. The significant element is the unlawfulness of the act rather than the seriousness. It can be caused by a third person or agent; for example, provoking a dog to bite the victim or whipping a horse so as to cause the victim (rider) to fall.

ENFORCEMENT ASPECTS

Felonious battery against peace officers and firemen requires proof similar to that in felonious assault (P.C. 241).

Lawful Use of Force

Battery, like assault, can be consented to and may be justified. This would include self-defense so long as the force used is reasonable. The law does not condone or justify the use of greater force than is reasonably necessary.[5]

Lawful Resistance, by Whom Made. Lawful resistance to the commission of a public offense may be made:
1. By the party about to be injured;
2. By other parties.[6]

By the Party, in What Cases and to What Extent. Resistance sufficient to prevent the offense may be made by the party about to be injured:
1. To prevent an offense against his person, or his family, or some member thereof.
2. To prevent an illegal attempt, by force, to take or injure property in his lawful possession.[7]

By other parties, in what cases. Any other person, in aid or defense of the person about to be injured, may make resistance sufficient to prevent the offense.[8]

A public officer in the interest of public safety and justice is justified in using force while

1. Executing criminals—by court order under capital punishment
2. Making arrests
3. Preventing escapes
4. Preserving the peace and preventing crime
5. Quelling riots and crime disorders

There are certain cases where the use of force is lawful as long as the act is reasonable and the punishment moderate. This applies to specific relationships such as that between parent and child; guardian and ward; teacher and pupil; master of a ship at sea and crew. Guards or private patrolmen may eject persons who disturb the peace or safety of others in railroad stations, common carriers, theaters, and other public places. The force must be limited to what is reasonable under the circumstances.

APPLICABLE STATUTES—FELONIOUS ASSAULTS

P.C. 216—*Administering poison.* Every person who, with intent to kill, administers, or causes or procures to be administered, to another, any poison, or other noxious or destructive substance or liquid, but by which death is not caused, is punishable by imprisonment in the state prison not less than ten years.

P.C. 217—*Assault with intent to commit murder.* Every person who assaults another with intent to commit murder, is punishable by imprisonment in the state prison not less than one nor more than fourteen years.

P.C. 220—*Assault with intent to commit rape, robbery, etc.* Every person who assaults another with intent to commit rape, the infamous crime against nature, mayhem, robbery, or grand larceny, is punishable by imprisonment in the state prison not less than one nor more than twenty years.

P.C. 221—*Other assaults: punishment.* Every person who is guilty of an assault, with intent to commit any felony, except an assault with intent to commit murder, the punishment for which assault is not prescribed by the preceding Section, is punishable by imprisonment in the state prison not exceeding fifteen years, or in a county jail not exceeding one year, or by fine not exceeding five hundred dollars ($500), or by both.

P.C. 222—*Administering stupefying drugs.* Every person guilty of administering to another any chloroform, ether, laudanum, or other narcotic, anaesthetic, or intoxicating agent, with intent thereby to enable or assist himself or any other person to commit a felony, is guilty of felony.

P.C. 244—*Assault with caustic chemicals.* Every person who willfully and maliciously places or throws, or causes to be placed or thrown, upon the person of another, any vitriol, corrosive acid, or caustic chemical of any nature, with the intent to injure the flesh or disfigure the body of such person, is punishable by imprisonment in the state prison not less than one nor more than fourteen years.

P.C. 246—*Assault with firearms on inhabited dwelling or occupied building.* Any person who shall maliciously and willfully discharge a firearm at an inhabited dwelling house or occupied building, is guilty of a felony, and upon conviction shall be punished by imprisonment in the state prison for not less than one or more than five years or by imprisonment in the county jail not exceeding one year.

Vehicle Code 23110—*Throwing Substance at Vehicles.* [See Chapter 11.]

P.C. 4500—*Aggravated assault: by life prisoner: punishment: discretion to sentence for life instead of ordering death penalty where victim does not die within year: computation of period between assault and victim's death.* Every person undergoing a life sentence in a state prison of this State, who with malice aforethought, commits an assault upon the person of another, other than another inmate, with a deadly weapon or instrument, or by any means of force likely to produce great bodily injury is punishable with death; however, in cases in which the person subjected to such assault does not die within a year and a day after such assault as a proximate result thereof, or the person so assaulted is another inmate, the punishment shall be death or imprisonment in the state prison for life without possibility of parole for nine years, at the discretion of the court or jury trying the same, and the matter of punishment shall be determined as provided in Section 190.1 of the Penal Code. For the purpose of computing the days elapsed between the commission of the assault and the death of the person assaulted, the whole of the day on which the assault was committed shall be counted as the first day.

Any person who, under this Section, is punished by imprisonment rather than death, shall be required to serve his sentence consecutively to any sentence he is presently serving.

P.C. 4501—*Aggravated assault by prisoner serving sentence of less than life.* Every person confined in a state prison of this State except one undergoing a life sentence who commits an assault upon the person of another with a deadly weapon or instrument, or by any means of force likely to produce great bodily injury, shall be guilty of a felony and shall be imprisoned in the state prison not less than three years.

P.C. 671—*Imprisonment for life.* Whenever any person is declared punishable for a crime by imprisonment in the state prison for a term not less than any specified number of years, and no limit to the duration of such imprisonment is declared, punishment for such offender shall be imprisonment during his natural life subject to the provisions of part three of this Code.

LEGAL DISCUSSION

These sections cover specific felonious assaults. They require the element of specific intent; e.g., to commit murder (P.C. 217). Assaults with specific intent to commit the felonies listed in P.C. 220 carry a more severe punishment than do the unspecified felonious assaults referred to in P.C. 221.

As regards the assault by a life termer or other convict, it is not necessary that the assault be with intent to kill. The malice, purpose, and design of the assaulting party precludes a determination of accident or misfortune.[9] This crime, of course, requires the defendant to be a convict as part of the corpus delicti.

It should be noted that, once an assault with specific intent is committed, it is no less a crime though the suspect be thwarted or change his mind. Once consummated, the assault cannot legally be abandoned.[10]

As regards the assault with intent to commit rape, it must be shown that it can be accomplished. Thus an attack on a man dressed as a woman would be a simple assault as it would also be if the facts are negative to proving the intent to rape.[11] If the victim is under the age of 18, she is incapable of consenting to an act of intercourse with a man not her husband; hence she is also incapable of consenting to an assault with intent to commit rape.[12]

As regards the administering of poison with intent to kill (P.C. 216), the definition of "poison" includes any substance or liquid which, when applied to the human body externally or in any way introduced into the human system, without acting mechanically but by its own inherent qualities, is capable of destroying life. This statute provides punishment for attempts to kill; hence, the means used must be capable of destroying life.

Under the caustic chemical section (P.C. 244) there must be more than a mere assault. It must be shown that the chemical actually touched the intended victim. The crime is complete if any quantity of acid, no matter how small or weak, touches the victim with specific intent to injure the flesh or to disfigure.[13]

APPLICABLE STATUTES—WIFE AND CHILD BEATING

P.C. 273d—*Infliction of traumatic injury upon wife or child.* [Quoted in Chapter 15.]

LEGAL DISCUSSION

As regards "wife or child beating" (P.C. 273d), the term "traumatic injury" means bodily injury caused by the application of force.[14]

ENFORCEMENT ASPECTS

There are several problems to be considered in investigating violations of this section. As regards section 273d, there must be evidence of traumatic injury to the wife or child. It is recommended that color photographs of the injured area be taken. It is also necessary to make certain that the wife wants to prosecute; too often she will appear the next day to request that her husband be released so that he can return to gainful employment. The Saturday night wife beating followed by the Monday morning "kiss and make-up" is a common frustration for the policeman. The child victim, on the other hand, is more tragic. The need for evidence of traumatic injury in order to obtain a conviction often permits serious injustices. A child who is starved does not show traumatic injury. So too, one who is chained or tied to a bed for days may not suffer traumatic injury. Hence, these types of investigations often result in child neglect charges rather than assaults.

APPLICABLE STATUTES—ASSAULT WITH A DEADLY WEAPON

P.C. 245—*Assault with deadly weapon: punishment.* (a)   Every person who commits an assault upon the person of another with a deadly weapon or instrument or by any means of force likely to produce great bodily injury is punishable by imprisonment in the state prison not exceeding ten years, or in a county jail not exceeding one year, or by fine not exceeding five thousand dollars ($5,000), or by both such fine and imprisonment. When a person is convicted of a violation of this Section, in a case involving use of a deadly weapon or instrument, and such weapon or instrument is owned by such person, the court may, in its discretion, order that the weapon or instrument be deemed a nuisance and shall be confiscated and destroyed in the manner provided by Section P.C. 12028.

(b)   Every person who commits an assault with a deadly weapon or instrument or by any means likely to produce great bodily injury upon the person of a peace officer or fireman, and who knows or reasonably should know that such victim is a peace officer or fireman engaged in the performance of his duties, when such peace officer or fireman is engaged in the performance of his duties shall be punished by imprisonment in the state prison not exceeding fifteen years: provided, that if such person has previously been convicted of an offense under the laws of any other state or of the United States which, if committed in this State, would have been punishable as a felony, he shall be punished by imprisonment in the state prison for five years to life.

As used in this subdivision, "peace officer" refers to any person designated as a peace officer in the first paragraph of Section 817, as well as any inspector or investigator regularly employed as such in the Office of a District Attorney, any member of the California Highway Patrol, any member of the California State Police, any policeman of the San Francisco Port Authority, each member of an Arson Investigating Unit of an organized Fire Department, and each deputized law enforcement member of the Wildlife Protection Branch of the Department of Fish and Game.

LEGAL DISCUSSION

The assault with a deadly weapon (hereafter called ADW) section (P.C. 245) has two basic components. The first depends on the definition of deadly weapon or instrument. The courts have held that the most important criterion is the *use* of the instrument. The object or instrument is a deadly weapon depending not upon the use for which it was intended but upon whether it was used in a manner to create injury or death. A chair used as a club; a hat pin used as a dagger; an unloaded gun or a toy gun used as a club; a broken bottle used to stab; an automobile used to strike; a nail file used to stab; all are examples of instruments whose use constitutes them as deadly weapons. (Note that P.C. 3024f, which defines deadly weapons, does not affect ADW but is restricted to the Deadly Weapons Control Law.[15])

The crime of ADW does not require specific intent or malice. Injury to the victim is not necessary. The main element of the crime is the unlawful attempt to commit a violent injury with a deadly weapon on the person of another. If the victim is injured, then the injury may be considered in determining the means used and the manner in which the victim received the injury.

The second phase of section 245 covers assaults by means of force likely to produce great bodily harm or injury. To commit this type of assault, it is not necessary that a weapon or instrument be used in the assault but only that violence and the likelihood of causing great bodily injury exist. Hence, throwing a person from a fifth-story window would be an ADW/GBI (assault with great bodily injury) felony whether or not the victim were injured. The force of a five-story fall would reasonably cause great bodily injury, and if the victim were protected by a canopy breaking his fall the crime would still be complete. The hands, knees, or feet may be used to inflict the injury. It is the actual injury that oftentimes proves that the force used must have been such as to create great bodily injury, since the injury was in fact sustained. The question of how much or what force is likely to produce great bodily injury is a question to be determined by the trial court or the jury.

ENFORCEMENT ASPECTS

The ADW section covering deadly weapons is fairly easy to establish as long as the instrument is available and introduced into evidence. However, the weapon frequently is not available, and in absence of testimony or other evidence proving that there was a deadly instrument used, you must look to the extent of injury. Most prosecutors will want to see medical reports showing that at least five stitches were taken in cases of cuttings or knifings. Broken bones or other traumatic injury will also suffice for a charge of assault with intent to commit great bodily harm. To some extent the nature and seriousness of the injury attests to the amount of force that must have been used. So in fact one must work backward in terms of proving the case. It is, therefore, most important to always include evidence and details of the injury in all crime reports of this offense.

APPLICABLE STATUTES—MAYHEM

P.C. 203—*Mayhem defined.* Every person who unlawfully and maliciously deprives a human being of a member of his body, or disables, disfigures, or renders it useless, or who cuts or disables the tongue, puts out an eye, slits the nose, ear, or lip, is guilty of mayhem.

P.C. 204—*Mayhem, how punishable.* Mayhem is punishable by imprisonment in the state prison not exceeding fourteen years.

LEGAL DISCUSSION

This is a type of assault, and every crime of mayhem must necessarily include an assault.[16] A necessary element of this crime is that the act shall have been done maliciously (includes "a wish to vex, annoy or injure another person, or an intent to do a wrongful Act").[17] The intent of this statute (P.C. 203) is to prevent brutality. If one person attacks another unlawfully and maliciously and causes one of the specified injuries, regardless of his intent to commit the injury, the crime of mayhem is committed. Even if, say, only a part of a person's ear is destroyed, it is sufficient to constitute the specified injury.

ENFORCEMENT ASPECTS

The greatest problem the officer faces in the investigation of this offense is proof of the element of "willful and malicious." The injury is usually proven easily by medical testimony. But more than intent is required. There must be a *malicious* intent to disfigure or disable; and the desire to maim the victim must be shown. In the absence of such proof, the charge is most logically assault with intent to do great bodily injury—a felony. A charge of mayhem should not be considered unless the ultimate extent of the injuries is material, namely the loss of an eye, finger, breaking of a bone or serious disfigurement.

DISCUSSION QUESTIONS

1. What are the elements of assault?
2. Give an example of a lawful use of force.
3. Explain the corpus delicti of battery as compared with assault.
4. What are the elements of assault with a deadly weapon?
5. Define the terms "present ability," "violent injury," and "traumatic injury."
6. List and explain other types of felonious assaults.
7. What are the elements of mayhem?

NOTES

[1]General, specific or transferred intent is sufficient.
[2]People v. Sylva, 143 C 62; 76 P 814.
[3]People v. Hebling, 61 C 620.
[4]People v. Vasquez, 85 CA 575; 259 P 1005.
[5]People v. Alexandra, 1 CA 2d 570; 37 P 2d 125.
[6]P.C. 692.
[7]P.C. 693.
[8]P.C. 694.
[9]People v. McNabb, 3 C 2d 441; 45 P 2d 334.
[10]People v. Steward, 97 C 238; 82 P 8.
[11]People v. Manchengo, 80 C 306; 22 P 223.
[12]People v. Gordon, 70 C 467; 11 P 762.
[13]People v. Day, 199 C 78; 248 P 250.
[14]People v. Burns, 88 CA 2d 867; 200 P 2d 134.
[15]People v. Calvera, 104 CA 414; 286 P 176.
[16]People v. Defoor, 100 C 150; 34 P 642.
[17]P.C. 7(4).

13

Homicide — Murder—Manslaughter

The term "homicide" refers to the killing of a human being by human act or agency. It may be felonious as in the case of murder and manslaughter, or nonfelonious as in the case of justifiable or excusable homicide. Of the two kinds of felonious homicide, murder is the more serious crime; manslaughter the less serious.

APPLICABLE STATUTES—MURDER

P.C. 187—*Murder defined.* Murder is the unlawful killing of a human being, with malice aforethought.

P.C. 188—*Malice defined.* Such malice may be expressed or implied. It is expressed when there is manifested a deliberate intention unlawfully to take away the life of a fellow creature. It is implied, when no considerable provocation appears, or when the circumstances attending the killing show an abandoned and malignant heart.

P.C. 189—*Degrees of murder.* All Murder which is perpetrated by means of poison, or lying in wait, torture, or by any other kind of willful,

164

deliberate, and premeditated killing, or which is committed in the perpetration or attempt to perpetrate arson, rape, robbery, or mayhem, or any act punishable under Section 288, is Murder of the first degree; and all other kinds of Murders are of the second degree.

P.C. 190—*Punishment for murder.* Every person guilty of Murder in the first degree shall suffer death, or confinement in the state prison for life, at the discretion of the court or jury trying the same, and the matter of punishment shall be determined as provided in Section 190.1, and every person guilty of Murder in the second degree is punishable by imprisonment in the state prison from five years to life.

P.C. 190.1—*Punishment for offenses for which penalty is death or life imprisonment.* The guilt or innocence of every person charged with an offense for which the penalty is in the alternative death or imprisonment for life shall first be determined, without a finding as to penalty. If such person has been found guilty of an offense punishable by life imprisonment or death, and has been found sane on any plea of not guilty by reason of insanity, there shall thereupon be further proceedings on the issue of penalty, and the trier of fact shall fix the penalty. Evidence may be presented at the further proceedings on the issue of penalty, of the circumstances surrounding the crime, of the defendant's background and history, and of any facts in aggravation or mitigation of the penalty. The determination of the penalty of life imprisonment or death shall be in the discretion of the court or jury trying the issue of fact on the evidence presented, and the penalty fixed shall be expressly stated in the decision or verdict. The death penalty shall not be imposed, however, upon any person who was under the age of 18 years at the time of the commission of the crime. The burden of proof as to the age of said person shall be upon the defendant.

If the defendant was convicted by the court sitting without a jury, the trier of fact shall be the court. If the defendant was convicted by a plea of guilty, the trier of fact shall be a jury unless a jury is waived. If the defendant was convicted by a jury, the trier of fact shall be the same jury unless, for good cause shown, the court discharges that jury in which case a new jury shall be drawn to determine the issue of penalty.

In any case in which defendant has been found guilty by a jury, and the same or another jury, trying the issue of penalty, is unable to reach a unanimous verdict on the issue of penalty, the court shall dismiss the jury and either impose the punishment for life in lieu of ordering a new trial on the issue of penalty, or order a new jury impaneled to try the issue of penalty, but the issue of guilt shall not be retried by such jury.

P.C. 194—*Death must occur within a year and a day.* To make the killing either Murder or Manslaughter, it is requisite that the party die within a year and a day after the stroke received or the cause of death administered; in the computation of which the whole of the day on which the act was done shall be reckoned the first.

LEGAL DISCUSSION

The first element is proof of the prior existence of a live human being. By legal definition, a live human being possesses an *independent circulatory system*. The fact that a child is still attached to his mother by the umbilical cord is not determinative in itself. The child's circulatory system must be complete and independent; the lungs must be able to oxygenate and the heart must be able to circulate blood. Mere proof of a dead body or a cadaver would not establish the corpus delicti.[1]

Medical testimony may prove a person to have been alive. If the child was born alive, even though injury was received in the mother's womb, there may be a prosecutable homicide. But a fetus that was killed in the mother's womb does not constitute a homicide as the fetus was never legally alive. Hence abortion is not a homicide of the fetus.

Once the existence of a live human being has been proven, the method of killing becomes important. The proximate cause of death must be proven. This act may be overt and positive or it may be a failure to act. For negligence to be considered criminal negligence, it must amount to a course of conduct which so departs from the conduct of an ordinarily prudent or careful man under the same circumstances as to be incompatible with a proper regard for human life. The facts must be such that the fatal consequences of the careless or negligent act could reasonably have been foreseen. The death must not appear to be by misadventure but must be a natural and probable result of a reckless or culpably negligent act.

Criminal negligence may also constitute the necessary proximate cause. The act or failure to act need not be the sole cause of death but a contributing proximate cause. Thus persons who are mortally wounded or persons dying of incurable diseases may be killed. If the act or failure to act hastens their demise, they are victims even though their death was inescapable. These types of homicides are often publicized as "mercy killings" but are, nonetheless, murder.

For the act to be considered murder, the death of the victim must occur within the time limits set by P.C. 194. If the blow or act does not cause death within the statutory period and the person dies thereafter, it is held not to have been from the proximate cause of the injury. In computing the statutory period the whole day on which the act was committed is counted as the first day. The statute tolls at midnight one calendar year later.

If the victim is injured and requires an operation, blood transfusion, or other medical treatment and then succumbs, the act has been held proximate cause.[2] The necessity for treatment or operation would not exist were it not for the act of the defendant. Blood poisoning or secondary infection causing death would justify prosecution if caused by the defendant's actions and the inflicting of wounds.

Proof of Death

Proof of death is necessary to establish the corpus delicti of homicide. The body, however, need not be produced. Proof of death by an unlawful act or criminal agency is all that is required for a felonious homicide. This may be proven circumstantially.[3] Thus, parts of a body, testimony of witnesses, unusual circumstances surrounding disappearance, and actions of the defendant may suffice to prove the crime.

Malice

Malice is a necessary element for the crime of murder.[4] A pre-existing hatred or malicious feeling is not necessary or implied. Malice aforethought is generally manifested by the intentional commission of a felonious act without legal reason or excuse. First-degree murder is usually committed with expressed malice; second-degree murder is committed with implied malice; manslaughter is committed with no malice. Often the degree of malice may be used to establish the gravity of the charge. Malice is more than specific intent to kill. While a specific intent to kill formed during deliberation and premeditation constitutes first-degree murder, it is not absolutely required. The shooting into a crowd of people with the subsequent death of some is first-degree murder by virtue of the implication of malice.[5]

First-Degree Murder

First-degree murder is divided into three groups, two of which are similar.[6] Killings by poison, torture, and lying in wait are by the very method of the crime declared first degree. All other killings committed willfully, deliberately, and premeditatedly are also first degree. This then is an extension and may include numerous methods of killing. As long as the death is caused by a willful, deliberate and premeditated act, we have a first-degree murder charge.

When poison is used, it can only be first-degree murder. The poison need not have caused death; if the victim is incapacitated by the poison and is killed by subsequent actions, this is sufficient to hold the poison as the proximate cause.[7]

Killing by torture requires more than the inflicting of pain. If, after injuries have been inflicted, the victim is abandoned to die without medical aid or other assistance, this is murder by torture.[8] Physical suffering is not sufficient in itself to show murder by torture. There must be an intent that the victim suffer. This may be inferred from the condition of the body or the method of creating the injury.

Lying in wait means that the perpetrator places himself in a position to wait and watch for the victim with the intent of killing or of inflicting injury likely to produce death. The period of lying in wait need not extend over any particular time; it is only necessary that the act which is the proximate cause of death be preceded by and be the outgrowth of lying in wait.

The third method of committing first-degree murder is that the killing take place during the attempt or commission of burglary, arson, rape, robbery, mayhem, and child molesting (P.C. 288). This is referred to as statutory first-degree murder inasmuch as the killing is declared automatically by statute to be first degree. The charge is valid whether the killing was intentional or unintentional or even accidental. The courts have held that a killing occurring in the attempt or actual commission of the specified felony is first-degree murder. Flight and fresh pursuit after the crime is also included in the time period of "in the perpetration." A co-principal, intended victim, innocent third party, or police officer may be a victim of first-degree murder. The defendant is entitled, upon request, to a specific jury instruction pointing out the necessity of proving the specific felony beyond a reasonable doubt. This is over and above the general instruction for guilt beyond reasonable doubt.

Second-Degree Murder

Second-degree murder requires implied malice. Any death occurring in the commission of any felony not declared first degree is by statute second degree. Thus a woman who dies during an abortion attempt permits a charge of second-degree murder against the person committing the abortion.

If a killing occurs during the commission of an unlawful act intentionally performed, the natural consequences of which are dangerous to human life, the crime is second-degree murder.[9] There is no deliberate premeditation in second-degree murder, but there is still an implied malice aforethought. Where there is no specific intent to kill and the killing does not constitute first-degree murder and the circumstances show an "abandoned and malignant heart," the killing is second-degree murder.[10]

Burden of Proof

Burden of proof in murder is most important and is covered in P.C. 1105, which states:

When burden of proof shifts in trials for murder. Upon a trial for murder, the commission of the homicide by the defendant being proved, the burden of proving circumstances of mitigation, or that justify or excuse it, devolves upon him, unless the proof on the part of the prosecution tends to show that the crime committed only amounts to manslaughter, or that the defendant was justifiable or excusable.

The effect of this section is that after the prosecution proves that the defendant killed the deceased and there is no evidence as to the circumstances of the killing from which it can be determined that the killing was felonious or nonfelonious, the burden of proof shifts to the defendant. In the absence of proof on his part, the killing amounts to murder. This legal theory applies only on murder charges.[11]

ENFORCEMENT ASPECTS

Police officers should adhere closely to all departmental regulations involving possible homicide cases. In California police officers in most metropolitan law enforcement agencies do not pronounce a person dead. Most areas can be reached by ambulance or medical personnel within minutes, and they are the persons authorized and qualified to pronounce death. Most deaths other than by natural causes, which are usually attested to by a physician, are handled by coroner personnel. The coroner has prime jurisdiction over cause of death, personal identification, notification of kin, and autopsy proceedings. The coroner also conducts an inquest when he feels that the facts warrant it. The current trend is toward having as a coroner a qualified legal medical examiner, a medical doctor who has studied or has experience in pathology. A close relationship should exist between this office and the law enforcement agency.

APPLICABLE STATUTES—MANSLAUGHTER

P.C. 192—*Manslaughter defined: voluntary and involuntary manslaughter.* Manslaughter is the unlawful killing of a human being, without malice. It is of three kinds:

1. Voluntary—upon a sudden quarrel or heat of passion.
2. Involuntary—in the commission of an unlawful act, not amounting to felony; or in the commission of a lawful act which might produce death, in an unlawful manner, or without due caution and circumspection; provided that this subdivision shall not apply to acts committed in the driving of a vehicle.
3. In the Driving of a Vehicle—
   a) In the commission of an unlawful act, not amounting to felony, with gross negligence; or in the commission of a lawful act

which might produce death, in an unlawful manner, and with gross negligence.

b)   In the commission of an unlawful act, not amounting to felony, without gross negligence; or in the commission of a lawful act which might produce death, in an unlawful manner, but without gross negligence.

(This Section shall not be construed as making any homicide in the Driving of a Vehicle punishable which is not a proximate result of the commission of an unlawful act, not amounting to a felony, or of the commission of a lawful act which might produce death, in an unlawful manner.)

P.C. 193—*Punishment of manslaughter.* Manslaughter is punishable by imprisonment in the state prison for not exceeding 15 years except that a violation of Subsection 3 of Section 192 of this code is punishable as follows: in the case of a violation of Subdivision (a) of said Subsection 3 the punishment shall be either imprisonment in the county jail for not more than one year or in the state prison for not more than five years, and in such case the jury may recommend by their verdict that the punishment shall be by imprisonment in the county jail; in the case of a violation of Subdivision (b) of said Subsection 3, the punishment shall be by imprisonment in the county jail for not more than one year. In cases where, as authorized in this Section, the jury recommends by their verdict that the punishment shall be by imprisonment in the county jail, the court shall not have authority to sentence the defendant to imprisonment in the state prison, but may nevertheless place the defendant on probation as provided in this code.

LEGAL DISCUSSION

The very important element of malice aforethought for murder is absent in manslaughter. There is neither expressed nor implied malice in manslaughter.[12] The intent to kill is not the determining factor. The method of killing is equally nondeterminative.

Voluntary Manslaughter

Voluntary manslaughter is the killing under "heat of passion" and may be brought about by words of abuse or reproach.[13] This "heat of passion" must be the result of sufficient and reasonable provocation. "Irresistible passion" or "irresistible compulsion" may be taken into consideration. The circumstances surrounding a sudden quarrel or "heat of passion" may be such as to constitute a crime less serious than murder. The basic consideration is whether or not the perpetrator's reason was obscured by passion; not necessarily fear, but not revenge, lust, or desire.[14]

Not only must the act have been perpetrated in the "heat of passion," but the killing must have occurred while the perpetrator was under the direct and immediate influence of the circumstances. If the effect of the "heat of passion" or sudden quarrel had ceased to obscure the mind of the accused and sufficient time had passed so that the angry passion cooled, then murder could not be mitigated to manslaughter. This "cooling off" period may vary; but the test applied is the period of time in which an average or ordinarily reasonable person would have regained his reason.

The provocation is a question for the trier of the facts. The total circumstances must be taken into consideration to determine whether the provocation was such as to make the perpetrator react under "heat of passion."

A clear interpretation of voluntary manslaughter is contained in the opinion found in *People* v. *Bridgehouse*, 47 Cal. 2d 406:

> Voluntary Manslaughter is a willful act, characterized by the presence of an intent to kill, engendered by sufficient provocation and the absence of premeditation, deliberation and (by presumption of law) malice aforethought. To be sufficient to reduce a homicide to Manslaughter the "heat of passion" must be such as would naturally be aroused in the mind of an ordinary, reasonable person, under the given facts and circumstances or in the mind of a person of ordinary self-control.

Involuntary Manslaughter

Involuntary manslaughter, on the other hand, is specified in P.C. 192. There is frequently a nebulous overlap between this offense and second-degree murder. If the killing occurs during the commission of an unlawful act, not amounting to a felony, the crime is involuntary manslaughter. Any act which violates a law designated to protect life or prevent injury (including misdemeanors) and which causes death constitutes a violation of section 192. Thus, when an unlicensed cosmetologist uses a phenol solution on the face of a customer and thereby causes death, a charge of involuntary manslaughter is appropriate.[15]

Simply stated, involuntary manslaughter is a homicide unintentionally caused, without malice, by an unlawful act not a felony. Remember, of course, that there must be a causal connection between the unlawful act and the death.

The other theory of involuntary manslaughter revolves around a lawful act which might produce death in an unlawful manner or without due caution and circumspection. The "due caution" is that which a reasonable and prudent man would be expected to observe to prevent injury. The lack of "due caution" may be a failure to act when required under a doctrine of criminal negligence. In all cases, however, criminal liability cannot be predicated upon every careless act that results in injury or death. The act must be one which has apparent potential to cause injury or death. It is the quality of an act that makes criminal prosecution possible rather than mere intent or mistake of judgment from which a death may occur.

When a duty is imposed by law upon a person and his failure to comply causes the death of a human being, he is chargeable with manslaughter; if malice is present, it becomes murder. Some examples are parents who fail to furnish food or medical aid to their children; an employer who fails to protect his employee when required by law; a practical nurse under contract to care for a patient who fails to administer such care. Basically it is a question of whether there is a legal duty which, if left unperformed, would cause or accelerate death.

Civil negligence alone would not be sufficient to sustain a conviction. To constitute criminal negligence, this must be aggravated, culpable, gross, or reckless.

The conduct must so deviate from what an ordinarily reasonable man would do under similar circumstances as to be incompatible with regard to life or limb. The fatal consequences should have been reasonably foreseen. Thus, recklessly playing with a firearm which discharges causing death becomes involuntary manslaughter. There is negligence when one handles or points a firearm at another without first checking to see if it is loaded. This is also true if the weapon is discharged in an area likely to injure someone.

On occasion a possible defense of imminent peril may be valid to justify an act causing death. Such peril, however, must be without negligence and must arise suddenly and unexpectedly. The reasonableness of the actions stimulated by the facts must be taken into consideration.

Vehicular Manslaughter

Vehicular manslaughter is included in section 192 and provides the charge when death occurs due to the operation of a motor vehicle with or without gross negligence. The element of gross negligence determines whether the crime is a felony or a misdemeanor. If gross negligence is not present, the crime is punishable as a misdemeanor.

Gross negligence is not specifically defined by statute; hence, it is necessary to report the court interpretations. It has generally been defined as being such a degree of negligence or carelessness as to amount to a wanton failure to exercise care even to so slight a degree as to indicate a complete indifference for the safety or property of individuals.

There being no extenuating circumstances where an individual swerved his auto and crossed a safety zone thereby killing a pedestrian in the marked safety zone, a manslaughter charge with gross negligence was held.[16]

Passing through a stop sign which results in a collision that kills another person is sufficient to constitute gross negligence.

Death which results where a driver is blinded by the approaching lights of another vehicle and, as a result of his impaired visibility, strikes and kills a pedestrian in a crosswalk is manslaughter by motor vehicle without gross negligence.[17]

In cases of negligence the possible contributory negligence of a third party or of the victim is no defense to the criminal charge. The victim is the state, and contributory negligence on the part of the victim does not comprise a criminal defense. There may, however, be civil considerations.

ENFORCEMENT ASPECTS

The decision to file a charge of second-degree murder or involuntary manslaughter should be left to the prosecuting attorney. The officer may arrest for the more serious offense, keeping in mind that murder necessarily includes the lesser offense of manslaughter.

An essential consideration in voluntary manslaughter is the "cooling off" period; many cases involve this issue. Basically, the officer must decide whether the suspect's thought processes were operating. Generally, acts committed in the "heat of passion" are committed without thought. The elements of the crime require that a death occur. The laws of arrest normally permit the officer to make a valid arrest, even if, after additional investigation, it appears that there may be a lesser violation or no violation at all.

As regards the area of vehicular manslaughter, the term "misdemeanor manslaughter" may often be seen on the disposition or arrest record of a suspect. The crime of felony drunk driving is a more serious offense than the crime of manslaughter by motor vehicle. If both charges are possible, only the more serious charge (felony drunk driving) should stand.

APPLICABLE STATUTES—NONFELONIOUS HOMICIDES

P.C. 199—*Justifiable and excusable homicide not punishable.* The homicide appearing to be justifiable or excusable, the person indicted must, upon his trial, be fully acquitted and discharged.

P.C. 195—*Excusable homicide.* Homicide is excusable in the following cases:

1. When committed by accident and misfortune, in lawfully correcting a child or servant, or in doing any other lawful act by lawful means,

with usual and ordinary caution, and without any unlawful intent.

2. When committed by accident and misfortune, in the "heat of passion," upon any sudden and sufficient provocation, or upon a sudden combat, when no undue advantage is taken, nor any dangerous weapon used, and when the killing is not done in a cruel or unusual manner.

P.C. 196—*Justifiable homicide by public officers.* Homicide is justifiable when committed by public officers and those acting by their command in their aid and assistance, either:

1. In obedience to any judgment of a competent court; or,

2. When necessarily committed in overcoming actual resistance to the execution of some legal process, or in the discharge of any other legal duty; or,

3. When necessarily committed in retaking felons who have been rescued or have escaped, or when necessarily committed in arresting persons charged with felony, and who are fleeing from justice or resisting such arrest.

P.C. 197—*Justifiable homicide.* Homicide is also justifiable when committed by any person in any of the following cases:

1. When resisting any attempt to Murder any person, or to commit a felony, or to do some great bodily injury upon any person; or,

2. When committed in defense of habitation, property, or person, against one who manifestly intends or endeavors, by violence or surprise, to commit a felony, or against one who manifestly intends and endeavors, in a violent, riotous or tumultuous manner, to enter the habitation of another for the purpose of offering violence to any person therein; or,

3. When committed in the lawful defense of such person, or of a wife or husband, parent, child, master, mistress, or servant of such person, when there is reasonable ground to apprehend a design to commit a felony or to do some great bodily injury, and imminent danger of such design being accomplished; but such person, or the person in whose behalf the defense was made, if he was the assailant or engaged in mutual combat, must really and in good faith have endeavored to decline any further struggle before the Homicide was committed; or,

4. When necessarily committed in attempting, by lawful ways and means, to apprehend any person for any felony committed, or in lawfully suppressing any riot, or in lawfully keeping and preserving the peace.

P.C. 198—*Bare fear not to justify killing.* A bare fear of the commission of any of the offenses mentioned in Subdivisions 2 and 3 of the preceding Section, to prevent which Homicide may be lawfully committed, is not sufficient to justify it. But the circumstances must be sufficient to excite the fears of a reasonable person, and the party killing must have acted under the influence of such fears alone.

LEGAL DISCUSSION

Excusable Homicide

Excusable homicide is distinguishable from felonious homicide primarily in the existence of a concurrence of both accident and misfortune. On the other hand, when all the elements of a felonious homicide are present and the victim died unexpectedly or by accident, no defense is possible.[18] It is necessary that the person who causes the death be doing a lawful act in an entirely lawful manner and that death be caused by accident or misfortune.

A nebulous area exists between voluntary manslaughter and subdivision 2 of section 195. In excusable homicide, however, the intent to kill must be absent, and the homicide must be by accident or misfortune upon provocation both sudden and sufficient or upon a sudden quarrel. In addition, there must have been no unfair advantage taken nor any dangerous weapon used, and the killing must not have been committed cruelly or in an unusual manner. The killing will not be excused if it was caused by an unlawful act or by a lawful act causing death in an unlawful manner or without due caution or circumspection. This is true notwithstanding that the death may have been accidental or by misfortune.[19]

When a lawfully permitted punishment is administered and death by accident or misfortune occurs, there is no crime. Examples of lawful use of force include:

1. Parent—child
2. Teacher—pupil
3. Guardian—ward
4. Ship's captain–crew—while at sea
5. Guards and security personnel in public places or areas open to the public, e.g., theaters, common carriers, stations.

Justifiable Homicide

Justifiable homicide is the result of an intentional act likely to cause death, or even of an intent to kill, when the law justifies the killing as a means of protecting and enforcing the rights of the individual or society.

Subdivision 1 of section 196 grants justification to a public officer where a death sentence is carried out under a valid warrant and in a lawful manner. This covers executions at San Quentin of persons under death sentence.

Subdivision 2 of section 196 grants justification for homicides committed by public officers while attempting or carrying out their legal duties when they are met with such actual resistance as to require the act. There must be, or appear to be, a very real necessity; for if the duty could have been performed without such killing, no justification may be taken.

Subdivision 3 of section 196 deals specifically with a peace officer making a lawful arrest in a lawful manner or while retaking a *felon*. The officer is justified in using deadly force to compel submission to an arrest for a *felony* as long as such force appears *reasonably necessary* to accomplish the arrest.[20] If, however, the circumstances when viewed by an ordinarily reasonable and prudent man do not appear to warrant the homicide, it is not justifiable. Keep in mind the discussion in Chapter 5 on arrests that deadly force is *never* authorized or justified in apprehending a misdemeanant.[21] A peace officer, however, does not lose his right to self-defense when performing his duties. Therefore, if the officer is assaulted by the suspect, the officer's actions will be considered under the law of self-defense rather than under subdivision 3 of P.C. 196. A peace officer need not retreat, and his authority under self-defense is covered under section 197.

In the prevention of a felony under section 197, the force authorized is only allowable when necessary and when other means of preventing the felony would probably fail. Here too, when resisting the commission of a felony, one is not required to retreat and force may be used even though safety may have been accomplished by flight.[22] The law, however, does not justify the killing of a suspect who has abandoned his attempt and fled.[23]

Under subdivision 2 of section 197, whenever it appears necessary or is actually necessary, deadly force may be justified in defense of one's habitation. If a person appears, or manifestly intends by violence or surprise, to commit a felony against the habitation, property, or person of another and there appears no other reasonable way to stop the perpetrator, the killing is justified. This does not apply to a trespasser. Force may be used to remove an intruder, but mere intrusion does not constitute sufficient provocation for a killing in defense of habitation. The perpetrator must manifest an intent to do violence to a party within the house, and his tumultuous and violent entry may be sufficient to presume it.

Subdivision 3 of section 197 is directed toward defense of persons. There must be reasonable ground to find a design to commit a felony or to do some great bodily injury. This must exist at the time of the killing. Anyone viewing a violent felony being committed or attempted is justified in using violence to prevent it.

Subdivision 4 of section 197 is clear and relatively self-explanatory. It excuses and justifies peace officers whose acts cause death while in lawful performance of their duties.

Self-Defense

Self-defense is founded upon necessity. To justify the taking of a life, it must appear to the person, as a reasonable and prudent man, not only that he has reason to believe and does believe that he is in danger of great bodily injury but that the only way to prevent the injury is by the exercise of force.

The force, then, is self-defense. Fear of injury is covered in section 198. A person cannot set up his own standards of fear and belief of danger threatened. He who acts in self-defense does so at his own peril. The act will be judged in light of what the ordinarily careful and prudent man would reasonably do. The right of self-defense, however, is not available to one who has sought a quarrel with the idea of forcing a deadly issue and through his fraud creates a real or apparent necessity for a felonious assault. This would be committed by a person who entices or by fraud "invites" an assault so that he may use self-defense as a justification for killing. The degree of resistance must always be in proportion to the injury threatened.

ENFORCEMENT ASPECTS

The officer investigating possible manslaughter crimes should use the same diligence as if he were investigating a murder. The officer may arrive at the scene of the crime prior to the victim's death. Care for the victim is most important, but too often the crime scene is forgotten. Much evidence corroborating or negating self-defense theories is lost or destroyed by emergency aid personnel.

SUMMARY OF HOMICIDE—*Killing of a human being by human act or agency (not a crime)*

FELONIOUS—MURDER	FELONIOUS—MANSLAUGHTER	NONFELONIOUS
First Degree (Expressed Malice)	*Voluntary Manslaughter (No Malice)*	*Justifiable Homicide*
1. Poison, lying in wait, torture	1. Heat of passion	1. By public officers:
2. Willful, deliberate, lying in wait	2. Sudden quarrel	a. pursuant to court order
3. During commission of:	3. Lack of thought	b. overcoming actual resistance
Burglary	4. No "cooling off"	c. retaking or arresting felons
Arson		
Rape	*Involuntary Manslaughter (No Malice)*	2. By private persons:
Robbery	1. During commission of an un-	a. preventing murder, a felony,
Mayhem	lawful act not amounting to a	or great bodily harm
Child molesting (288 P.C.)	felony	b. defending person, property
	2. During commission of a lawful	or habitation
	act which produces death in an	
	unlawful manner or without	

Second Degree (Implied Malice)

1. In course of any other felony not first degree

2. With malice (implied) aforethought but with no deliberation or premeditation

3. During commission of any unlawful act dangerous to life, even if only amounting to a misdemeanor

due caution or circumspection (excludes by motor vehicle)

Vehicular Manslaughter (No Malice)

While driving a vehicle and:

1. In the commission of an unlawful act, not amounting to felony, with gross negligence; or in the commission of a lawful act which might produce death, in an unlawful manner, and with gross negligence

2. In the commission of an unlawful act, not amounting to felony, without gross negligence; or in the commission of a lawful act which might produce death, in an unlawful manner, but without gross negligence

c. defending person related (refer P.C. 197)

d. preventing riot or apprehending felons

Excusable Homicide

1. By accident or misfortune during commission of a lawful act with no unlawful intent

2. By accident or misfortune, in heat of passion, upon provocation, with no undue advantage, no use of dangerous weapons, and death not in a cruel or unusual manner

DISCUSSION QUESTIONS

1. Discuss the point at which a human being is alive.
2. Define malice and explain its applicability to murder and manslaughter.
3. What are the elements of murder?
4. Define statutory first-degree murder.
5. Compare second-degree murder and involuntary manslaughter.
6. Explain justifiable and excusable homicide and give examples of each.

NOTES

[1] People v. Simonsen, 107 C 345; 40 P 440.
[2] People v. Frendenberg, 121 CA 2d 564; 263 P 2d 875.
[3] People v. Scott, 176 CA 2d 458; 1 CR 600.
[4] P.C. 188.
[5] People v. Stein, 23 CA 108; 137 P 271.
[6] P.C. 189.
[7] People v. Cobler, 2 CA 2d 375; 37 P 2d 869.
[8] People v. Kerr, 37 C 2d 11; 229 P 2d 777.
[9] People v. Copley, 32 CA 2d 74; 89 P 2d 160.
[10] People v. Hubbard, 64 CA 27; 220 P 315.
[11] People v. Turner, 93 CA 133; 269 P 204.
[12] People v. Samsels, 66 C 99; 4 P 1061.
[13] People v. Valentine, 28 C 2d 121; 169 P 2d 1.
[14] People v. Valentine, 28 C 2d 121; 169 P 2d 1.
[15] People v. Penny, 44 C 2d 861; 282 P 2d 879.
[16] People v. Leitgeb, 77 CA 2d 764; 176 P 2d 384.
[17] People v. Lett, 77 CA 2d 917; 177 P 2d 47.
[18] People v. Kerrick, 86 CA 542; 261 P 756.
[19] People v. Attema, 75 CA 642; 243 P 461.
[20] People v. Brite, 9 C 2d 666; 72 P 2d 122.
[21] People v. Wilson, 36 CA 589; 172 P 1116.
[22] People v. Collins, 189 CA 2d 575; 11 CR 504.
[23] People v. Conklin, 111 C 616; 44 P 314.

14

Crimes of Restraint

APPLICABLE STATUTES—FALSE IMPRISONMENT

P.C. 236—*False imprisonment defined.* False imprisonment is the unlawful violation of the personal liberty of another.

P.C. 237—*False imprisonment, punishment for.* False imprisonment is punishable by fine not exceeding five hundred dollars, or by imprisonment in the county jail not more than one year, or by both. If such false imprisonment be effected by violence, menace, fraud, or deceit, it shall be punishable by imprisonment in the state prison for not less than one nor more than ten years.

In addition to the foregoing there is:

P.C. 146—*Making arrests, etc., without lawful authority.* [Quoted in Chapter 11.]

P.C. 146a—*Impersonation of officers.* [Quoted in Chapter 11.]

P.C. 363—*Reconfining persons discharged upon writ of habeas corpus.* Every person who, either solely or as a member of a court, knowingly

181

and unlawfully recommits, imprisons, or restrains of his liberty, for the same cause, any person who has been discharged upon a writ of habeas corpus, is guilty of a misdemeanor.

P.C. 364—*Concealing persons entitled to benefit of habeas corpus.* Every person having in his custody, or under his restraint or power, any person for whose relief a writ of habeas corpus has been issued, who, with the intent to elude the service of such writ or to avoid the effect thereof, transfers such person to the custody of another, or places him under the power or control of another, or conceals or changes the place of his confinement or restraint, or removes him without the jurisdiction of the court or judge issuing the writ, is guilty of a misdemeanor.

V.C. 22516—*Locked Vehicle.* No person shall leave standing a locked vehicle in which there is any person who cannot readily escape therefrom.

LEGAL DISCUSSION

The "confinement" consists primarily of restraint: (1) detention or forcing a person to go to a particular place; (2) preventing someone from departing from a certain place or locale. "Lock-out" or preventing access to a particular place without restricting movement to other places is not confinement. The confinement may be physical by means of walls, fences, bonds, etc., or it may be created by threats or apprehension of harm; the threat of force may be expressed or implied; its effect is to compel the victim to stay where he doesn't want to stay or go where he doesn't want to go, or to refrain from going where he wants to go.

The detention is not unlawful if it is privileged. A lawful arrest is privileged. An unlawful arrest by a peace officer is not privileged. Unreasonable detention following a lawful arrest is not privileged.

ENFORCEMENT ASPECTS

This offense can be criminal or civil in nature. Usually the violations of the above sections will result in a civil suit for damages. Most police personnel carry false arrest insurance. City and county counsels will represent the officers, the chief of police, or the municipal entity who tend to be the defendants in the civil suit.

Occasionally there are criminal violations of these sections, involving severe and unusual circumstances. Recently, a Chicago bail bondsman took custody of one of his defendants who had fled the state. He did this lawfully and, in fact, with the aid of local police in Los Angeles county. The defendant was a strong man and known to be dangerous, while the bondsman was frail and rather meek. In order to transport his "prisoner" the bondsman placed him in the trunk compartment of his car.

The custody and restraint of the defendant was lawful and privileged. However, the locking of the defendant in the trunk was an aggravated and unusual circumstance. In fact, when the bondsman was stopped several hundred miles away, the defendant was nearly asphyxiated in the trunk. The bondsman was charged with false imprisonment and assault.

APPLICABLE STATUTES—ABDUCTION

P.C. 265—*Abduction for marriage or defilement.* Every person who takes any woman unlawfully, against her will, and by force, menace, or duress, compels her to marry him, or to marry any other person, or to be defiled, is punishable by imprisonment in the state prison not less than two nor more than fourteen years.

P.C. 266—*Enticing of unmarried female.* Every person who inveigles or entices any unmarried female, of previous chaste character, under the age of eighteen years, into any house of ill-fame, or of assignation, or elsewhere, for the purpose of prostitution, or to have illicit carnal connection with any man; and every person who aids or assists in such inveiglement or enticement; and every person who, by any false pretenses, false representation, or other fraudulent means procures any female to have illicit carnal connection with any man, is punishable by imprisonment in the state prison not exceeding five years, or by imprisonment in a county jail not exceeding one year, or by a fine not exceeding one thousand dollars, or by both such fine and imprisonment.

P.C. 267—*Abduction of female under 18.* Every person who takes away any female under the age of eighteen years from her father, mother, guardian, or other person having the legal charge of her person, without their consent, for the purpose of prostitution, is punishable by imprisonment in the state prison not exceeding five years, and a fine not exceeding one thousand dollars.

LEGAL DISCUSSION

An old English law, abduction, was directed at the man who by abduction and marriage sought to obtain the property of his heiress. Modern California statutes broaden the area of crime and include defilement as well as marriage and invasion of the lawful custody of a parent or guardian.

Note that P.C. 265 does not require a particular intent.

Under P.C. 267 the female's consent is not a defense.[1] The taking must be from the lawful custody or control of a parent or guardian. Where the female is not under such lawful custody, the crime falls under P.C. 266 (seduction for prostitution). There is no requirement under P.C. 267 that the female be chaste or unmarried, and a mistake in the age of the female is not a defense. The "purpose of prostitution" required may be inferred from all of the circumstances, and there need be no placement in prostitution so long as the taking was with that purpose.

APPLICABLE STATUTES—KIDNAPPING

P.C. 207—*Kidnaping defined.* Every person who forcibly steals, takes, or arrests any person in this State, and carries him into another country, state or county, or into another part of the same county, or who forcibly takes or arrests any person, with a design to take him out of this State, without having established a claim according to the laws of the United States, or of this State, or who hires, persuades, entices, decoys, or seduces by false promises, misrepresentations, or the like, any person to go out of this State, or to be taken or removed therefrom, for the purpose and with the intent to sell such person into slavery or involuntary servitude, or otherwise to employ him for his own use, or to the use of another, without the free will and consent of such persuaded person; and every person who, being out of this State, abducts or takes by force or fraud any person contrary to the law of the place where such act is committed, and brings, sends, or conveys such person within the limits of this State, and is afterwards found within the limits thereof, is guilty of kidnaping.

P.C. 208—*Punishment of kidnaping.* Kidnaping is punishable by imprisonment in the state prison not less than one nor more than twenty-five years.

P.C. 209—*Punishment of kidnaping for ransom, reward.* Any person who seizes, confines, inveigles, entices, decoys, abducts, conceals, kidnaps, or carries away any individual by any means whatsoever with intent to hold or detain, or who holds or detains such individual for ransom, reward or to commit extortion or to exact from relatives or friends of such person any money or valuable thing, any person who kidnaps or carries away any individual to commit robbery, or any person who aids or abets any such act, is guilty of a felony and upon conviction thereof shall suffer death or shall be punished by imprisonment in the state prison for life without possibility of parole, at the discretion of the jury trying the same, in cases in which the person or persons subjected to such kidnaping suffers or suffer bodily harm, or shall be punished by imprisonment in the state prison for life with possibility of parole in cases where such person or persons do not suffer bodily harm.

Any person serving a sentence of imprisonment for life without possibility of parole following a conviction under this section as it read prior to the effective date of this act shall be eligible for a release on parole as if he had been sentenced to imprisonment for life with possibility of parole.

P.C. 210—*Extortion by posing as kidnaper; penalty and exception.* Every person who for the purpose of obtaining any ransom or reward, or to extort or exact from any person any money or thing of value, poses as, or in any manner represents himself to be a person who has seized, confined, inveigled, enticed, decoyed, abducted, concealed, kidnaped or carried away any person, or who poses as, or in any manner represents himself to be a person who holds or detains such person, or who poses as, or in any manner represents himself to be a person who has aided or abetted any such act, or who poses as or in any manner represents himself to be a person who has the influence, power, or ability, to obtain the release of such person so seized, confined, inveigled, enticed, decoyed, abducted, concealed, kidnaped or carried away, is guilty of a felony and upon conviction thereof shall be punished by imprisonment in a state prison during his natural life, or for any number of years not less than five.

Nothing in this section prohibits any person who, in good faith, believes that he can rescue any person who has been seized, confined, inveigled, enticed, decoyed, abducted, concealed, kidnaped or carried away, and who has had no part in, or connection with, such confinement, inveigling, decoying, abducting, concealing, kidnaping or carrying away, from offering to rescue or obtain the release of such person for a monetary consideration or other thing of value.

LEGAL DISCUSSION

In general, restraint during or after abduction suffices. A person may voluntarily accompany the kidnappers and be restrained at a later time. Although there is no requirement for secrecy, there must be an "asportation" or carrying away. It is the fact of moving a person against his will which constitutes the offense—not the moving of a certain distance or over certain boundaries without regard to distance, route taken, or area covered.

The asportation in kidnapping cases under P.C. 209 has often involved movement over very short distances: In Chessman[2] a movement of 22 feet; in Wein[3] a movement from one room to another; in O'Farrel[4] a movement within the same building; in Enriques,[5] 6 feet; in Mark,[6] 6 to 8 feet.

Note that simple kidnapping (P.C. 207) does not require proof of a specific intent, except where the victim is incapable of consenting (immature or incompetent).[7] Examples cited by the Supreme Court are (1) a young child lost on the highway or near a lake or precipice, and (2) a helpless drunk.[8] In such cases an evil intent must be proved to establish the crime.

P.C. 209 couples kidnapping with the offenses of "extortion," "ransom," and "robbery." The distinction in sentences rests on whether the victim suffered bodily harm.

Bodily harm has consisted of rape of a woman; binding with wire and burning; indecent assault. On the other hand, bonds impairing circulation have been held not to constitute bodily harm. Where the bodily harm results from efforts to escape under threat of rape, it has been held that the proximate cause of the harm was the threat of rape even though the defendant never touched the victim.

In fact, detention without asportation has been held to constitute kidnapping when coupled with another offense where another individual was kidnapped or carried away.

P.C. 210 makes it a felony to pose as a kidnapper, or one acting with a kidnapper or able to influence him. It is directed at anyone who seeks to profit by the kidnapping and of course excludes the person who has no part in the crime but "offers for a consideration to rescue or obtain release of the kidnaper."

APPLICABLE STATUTES—CHILD STEALING

P.C. 278—*Child stealing; penalty*. Every person who maliciously, forcibly, or fraudulently takes or entices away any minor child with intent to detain and conceal such child from its parent, guardian, or other person having the lawful charge of such child, is punishable by imprisonment in the state prison not exceeding twenty years.

P.C. 279—*Custody of child; concealment or removal without consent; penalty*. (a)   Every person who has actually physical control of a child for a limited period of time in the exercise of the right to visit with, or to be visited by, such child, or the right to limited custody of such child, pursuant to an order, judgment or decree of any court, which order, judgment or decree grants custody of such child to another, and who, without good cause and with intent to detain or conceal such child, keeps said child in this State after the expiration of such period without the consent of the person or persons entitled to custody of such child, violates this Section.

(b)   Every person who has custody of a child pursuant to an order, judgment or decree of any court, which order, judgment or decree grants another person limited rights to custody of such child or the right to visit with, or to be visited by, such child, and who conceals such child in this State without good cause and with intent to deprive such other person of such right of limited custody or visitation, violates this Section.

(c)   In any case in which a parent of a child has, pursuant to an order, judgment or decree of any court, a right of custody to the child equal to that of the other parent or, pursuant to an order, judgment or decree of any court, has no right of custody to the child, and removes the child without the consent of the other parent, from the place where the child is then residing or staying and conceals the child in this State from such other parent without good cause and with intent to prevent the other parent from exercising rights of custody to the child, he violates this Section.

(d)   Every person who violates this section is guilty of a misdemeanor and is punishable as prescribed by Section 19 of the Penal Code.

LEGAL DISCUSSION

Note:

(1)   Consent of child is not a defense.

(2)   Crime is against the parent or custodian, not the child.

(3)   The double specific intent is:
    (a)   to detain, and
    (b)   to conceal.

(4)   The taking does not require physical force. There may be enticement or fraud.

The specific intent is usually inferred from the facts of concealment and detention; however, such concealment and detention need not be accomplished if the intent can be inferred from other conduct, admissions, or statements.

ENFORCEMENT ASPECTS

Kidnapping investigation follows standard procedures with possible emphasis on the safety of the victim. It is generally agreed among police authorities that the payment of the ransom does not increase the chances of safe return of the victim. Payment will, of course, tend to "reward" the perpetrator and possibly encourage more offenses.

The California kidnapping law is similar to the federal statute. The federal law is referred to as the "Lindbergh Law," as it was enacted by Congress after that notorious case. The federal offense is under the enforcement jurisdiction of the Federal Bureau of Investigation. The F.B.I. are able to assist in any state kidnapping as long as:

1.   Twenty-four hours have elapsed, after which it is presumed that the suspects have probably had time to cross state or national boundaries.

2.   There is evidence or strong circumstances at the time of the kidnapping or within twenty-four hours that the victim or suspects have passed state boundaries.

During the Frank Sinatra, Jr., kidnapping from the Lake Tahoe area in California, there was much jurisdictional concern. El Dorado County (where the crime originated) and Los Angeles County (where the victim was released) had possible jurisdiction for prosecution. The Federal Bureau of Investigation entered the case almost immediately, because the kidnapping took place so near the state line. They conducted the investigation. It would have been most interesting if after apprehension it had been found that the suspects and victim had not passed state lines.

As regards the crime of child stealing, it must be noted that numerous complaints and charges are made to the police involving possible violations. Generally speaking, when a natural parent takes the child there is usually no danger to the child but rather an intent to annoy and upset the spouse. With the high divorce rate it is most common now to have custody orders with visitation rights enumerated. Many irate parents call the police agencies for a criminal complaint. Generally the response is civil—a contempt of court; P.C. 279 now prescribes it a misdemeanor.

The district attorney will generally consider issuance of a child stealing complaint only when there is definite evidence of the child being in serious danger. Only when there are indications of mental unbalance on the part of the suspect or a specific intent to permanently retain custody of the child does the prosecutor consider a child stealing violation. The great majority of these complaints must be referred to the victim's private attorney who may have handled the divorce settlement.

DISCUSSION QUESTIONS

1. What are the elements of kidnapping?
2. How far does the victim have to be moved to constitute kidnapping?
3. Define "confinement."
4. Explain the differences between kidnapping under P.C. 207 and kidnapping under P.C. 209.
5. How does child stealing differ from kidnapping?
6. Under what conditions can the Federal Bureau of Investigation enter the investigation of a kidnapping in California?

NOTES

[1] People v. Marshall, 59 C 386.
 People v. Demonsett, 71 C 611; 12 P 788.
[2] People v. Chessman, 38 C 2d 166; 238 P 1001.
[3] People v. Wein, 50 C 2d 383; 326 P 2d 457.
[4] People v. O'Farrel, 161 CA 2d 13; 325 P 2d 1002.
[5] People v. Enriques, 190 CA 2d 481; 11 CR 889.
[6] People v. Mark, 56 C 2d 288; 14 CR 633.
[7] People v. Oliver, 55 C 2d 761; 12 CR 865.
[8] People v. Oliver, supra.

CHILD MOLESTING

RAPE

INCEST

SEDUCTION—SOLICITING—PIMPING AND

PANDERING—PROSTITUTION

SEX PERVERSION

BIGAMY

ABORTION

ENFORCEMENT ASPECTS

15

Sex Offenses

APPLICABLE STATUTES—CHILD MOLESTATION

P.C. 647a—*Annoying or molesting children.* (1) Every person who annoys or molests any child under the age of 18 is a vagrant and is punishable upon first conviction by a fine not exceeding five hundred dollars ($500) or by imprisonment in the county jail for not exceeding six months or by both such fine and imprisonment and is punishable upon the second and each subsequent conviction or upon the first conviction after a previous conviction, under Section 288 of this code by imprisonment in the State Prison for not less than one year.

P.C. 288—*Crimes against children, a felony.* Any person who shall willfully and lewdly commit any lewd or lascivious act including any of the acts constituting other crimes provided for in part one of this code upon or with the body, or any part or member thereof, of a child under the age of fourteen years, with the intent of arousing, appealing to, or gratifying the lust or passions or sexual desires of such person or of such child, shall be guilty of a felony and shall be imprisoned in the State prison for a term of from one year to life.

LEGAL DISCUSSION

The object of these provisions is clear: to protect children from sex offenders and to facilitate the recognition, arrest, and segregation of such offenders.

The acts which constitute a violation hereof are very difficult to describe. The court in the Pallares case[1] attempted to define the acts hereby proscribed as follows:

> *People* v. *Pallares*—[11] When the words "annoy" or "molest" are used in reference to offenses against children, there is a connotation of abnormal sexual motivation on the part of the offender. Although no specific intent is prescribed as an element of this particular offense, a reading of the section as a whole in the light of the evident purpose of this and similar legislation enacted in this state indicates that the acts forbidden are those motivated by an unnatural or abnormal sexual interest or intent with respect to children. It should be noted further that the section must be construed reasonable as setting up an objective test for annoyance or molestation; a childish and wholly unreasonable subjective annoyance, arising, for example, from a child's dislike for proper correction by a teacher, is not covered by the section. The annoyance or molestation which is forbidden is in no sense a purely subjective state on the part of the child. The objectionable acts of a defendant constitute the annoyance or molestation contemplated by the Statute. See *State* v. *Chaplinsky*, 91 N.H. 310, 18 A 2d 754.

Note that the absence of specific intent and of "sex motivation" of the defendant are not essential to the crime. Moreover, the state of mind of the child-victim is immaterial; the act need not be repugnant or offensive to the child so long as it is such that the normal person would unhesitatingly be annoyed or repulsed by same.

The acts required to constitute a violation of P.C. 288 need not be obviously sexual or obscene of themselves. If the intent is established, an otherwise innocent touching, fondling, rubbing, or feeling of a part of the child's body through his clothing will suffice.[2]

First offenders are misdemeanants, but a second offender or one previously convicted of indecent acts with a child (P.C. 288) is a felon.

The words "willfully" and "lewdly" here have their usual meaning; "willfully" means intentionally, not through accident or inadvertence, and "lewdly" means with a *lascivious intent*, viz., to arouse prurient desires or thoughts in one's own or another person's mind.

The usual act of molestation is a violation of P.C. 314 and P.C. 647a concurrently.

It should be noted that a person loitering near a school or public place where children congregate is punishable as a vagrant.

ENFORCEMENT ASPECTS

This type of crime usually attracts a great deal of public attention. The person who commits these offenses must be prosecuted vigorously; however, police officers should investigate this type of case very carefully to avoid possible false accusations.

The victim (child) should be interviewed outside the presence of his parents. The parents may, by virtue of their deep concern, direct the child's testimony. An interview with a female child may best be conducted by a policewoman. It must be remembered that the child will be the most important witness in the prosecution, and the manner of testimony may be evaluated by the officer.

Even after initial investigation and possible arrest of a suspect, parents often have second thoughts about subjecting their children to a courtroom "drama." It is therefore necessary for the investigator to maintain contact with the victim and his parents.

APPLICABLE STATUTES—RAPE

P.C. 261—*Rape defined.* Rape is an act of sexual intercourse, accomplished with a female not the wife of the perpetrator, under either of the following circumstances:

1. Where the female is under the age of eighteen years;
2. Where she is incapable, through lunacy or other unsoundness of mind, whether temporary or permanent, of giving legal consent;
3. Where she resists, but her resistance is overcome by force or violence;
4. Where she is prevented from resisting by threats of great and immediate bodily harm, accompanied by apparent power of execution, or by any intoxicating narcotic, or anaesthetic substance, administered by or with the privity of the accused;
5. Where she is at the time unconscious of the nature of the act, and this is known to the accused;
6. Where she submits under the belief that the person committing the act is her husband, and this belief is induced by any artifice, pretense, or concealment practiced by the accused, with intent to induce such belief.

P.C. 262—*When physical ability must be proved.* No conviction for rape can be had against one who was under the age of fourteen years at the time of the act alleged, unless his physical ability to accomplish penetration is proved as an independent fact, and beyond a reasonable doubt.

P.C. 263—*Penetration sufficient.* The essential guilt of rape consists in the outrage to the person and feelings of the female. Any sexual penetration, however slight, is sufficient to complete the crime.

LEGAL DISCUSSION

The crime of rape is accomplished by mere penetration of the female's vagina; in fact, so long as no consent is involved, the penetration of the sexual organ can be accomplished by objects other than the phallus. There is no requirement for emission or sexual satisfaction. Any penetration, no matter how slight, will suffice.

Since the marital relation presupposes consent to intercourse, a husband cannot rape his wife. But he can be guilty of her rape if he aids and abets a third person in raping her; or if the force used suffices, he may be guilty of a battery.

There is no requirement that the female be of previous chaste character; hence, it is possible to rape a common prostitute. However, consent may be inferred from prior unchastity.

The resistance must constitute resistance in fact. It must be sufficient to manifest the female's refusal or lack of consent but need not be resistance "to the uttermost" nor "extraordinary resistance," and she need not resist under circumstances where resistance would be futile so long as lack of consent or refusal is clearly manifested by her conduct. The required force may consist of threats and intimidation expressed by conduct as well as by words.

The lack of consent essential to rape may exist where consent was obtained by fraud, or where the female is incapacitated. The following are examples of fraud: when the defendant impersonates the husband; or the act is committed under the pretense that it is a medical treatment; or the female submits in the belief that a sham marriage was in fact a genuine ceremony.

There can be no consent where the female is unconscious or under the influence of narcotics, intoxicants or hypnotic drug administered by a third party who acted with the knowledge and consent, actual or implied, of the defendant.

Where the lack of consent arises from the immaturity of the female, the offense is commonly referred to as statutory rape. This offense includes not only females "under the age of consent" but also females who through idiocy, lunacy, or other unsoundness of mind, whether permanent or temporary, are incapable of giving their consent.

When the female has been married before the age of eighteen, intercourse with her by a male *other* than her husband is statutory rape.[3] Ignorance of the age of the female is not an excuse; in fact, her admitted manifestations, acts and statements to the effect that she is of age *are not a defense.* The prior conduct or unchastity of the female is not a defense.

Where the defendant is accused of raping an unconscious female, it must be proved that he knew she was unconscious. Note that the requirement of knowledge is not contained in the other subsections of P.C. 261.

ENFORCEMENT ASPECTS

In prosecutions where the victim is sixteen or seventeen years of age and the suspect is only three or four years older, unique circumstances may dictate a particular courtroom solution. When the victim and the defendant are "sweethearts," the parents are usually the most vociferous. It is not unusual for the parents to want to drop the charges a month or two after signing the complaint. Sometimes the victim and suspect plan to marry; or the feared pregnancy, which may have instigated the parents to take criminal action, does not materialize; or the parents may decide that they would rather forget the matter than have their daughter go through a courtroom trial.

In some cases of rape by force or fear the victim may be under eighteen years of age, and the prosecution could take place under P.C. 261(1) or (3). Defense attorneys who are looking for a compromise plea will often recommend that their client plead to a statutory rape (261(1)). This benefits their client in that the conviction will not be as stigmatic. Justice is served in that the court has complete latitude to sentence the defendant up to fifty years in the state prison based upon its evaluation of the probation report. The prosecution is satisfied in that a conviction has been sustained for which the defendant is subject to sentencing, and trial in court has been held to a minimum. On occasion, the police officer may need to explain to indignant parents of the victim the legal ramifications which make the plea acceptable. Most parents feel that a statutory rape charge indicates that the female submitted voluntarily; and hence, in contrast to forcible rape, it is a reflection on her character. This is an important area in which a police officer can exercise skill in human relations.

It must be remembered that women are often motivated by revenge, jealousy, and anger. Detailed questioning of the victim is necessary, and should include the time, place, and description of the act in detail.

As in most sex offenses the fact of prompt and fresh complaint by the victim prosecutrix lends credence to her story. This is particularly true in rape cases. A delayed complaint raises substantial doubt unless good reasons for the delay are furnished. All too frequently a belated complaint of rape is prompted by the defendant's failure to respond to extortion or undue influence.

APPLICABLE STATUTES—ADULTERY

Code Civil Procedure 93—*Adultery defined.* Adultery is the voluntary sexual intercourse of a married person with a person other than the offender's husband or wife.

P.C. 269a—*Adultery.* Every person who lives in a state of cohabitation and adultery is guilty of a misdemeanor and punishable by a fine not exceeding one thousand dollars, or by imprisonment in the county jail not exceeding one year, or by both.

P.C. 269b—*Adultery of married persons.* If two persons, each being married to another, live together in a state of cohabitation and adultery, each is guilty of a misdemeanor. A recorded certificate of marriage or a certified copy thereof, there being no interlocutory decree of divorce, proves the marriage of a person for the purpose of this section.

LEGAL DISCUSSION

Fornication—illicit sexual intercourse by an unmarried person—is not a crime in California.[4] An unmarried defendant having illicit sex relations with a married person commits no crime.[5] This is true as long as no other crime is committed, such as incest, seduction, or contributing to delinquency of a minor.

Note that the statutes require more than occasional, isolated acts of copulation. There must be a "living in a state of cohabitation and adultery," an "adulterous cohabitation." This is true whether one party or both parties are married.

The fact of marriage can be proved by the introduction of a marriage certificate and reasonable search for an interlocutory decree of divorce.

APPLICABLE STATUTES—SEDUCTION

P.C. 268—*Seduction; penalty.* Every person who, under promise of marriage, seduces and has sexual intercourse with an unmarried female of previous chaste character, is punishable by imprisonment in the state prison for not more than five years, or by a fine of not more than five thousand dollars, or by both such fine and imprisonment.

P.C. 269—*Intermarriage, when a bar to prosecution.* The intermarriage of the parties subsequent to the commission of the offense is a bar to a prosecution for a violation of the last section; provided, such marriage take place prior to the finding of an indictment or the filing of an information charging such offense.

P.C. 266—*Enticing, etc. of unmarried female.* [Quoted in Chapter 14.]

P.C. 1108—*Abortion and seduction, evidence upon a trial for.* Upon a trial for procuring or attempting to procure an abortion, or aiding or assisting therein, or for inveigling, enticing, or taking away an unmarried female of previous chaste character, under the age of eighteen years, for the purpose of prostitution, or aiding or assisting therein, the defendant cannot be convicted upon the testimony of the woman upon or with whom the offense was committed, unless she is corroborated by other evidence.

LEGAL DISCUSSION

There must be testimony in addition to that of the prosecutrix for conviction under P.C. 266 but not under P.C. 268.

The elements of the crime of seduction include proof of fact:

1. The woman was of previous chaste character.
2. The woman was unmarried.
3. She submitted to intercourse as a result of an unconditional promise to marry.

The promise to marry

1. Need not be legally enforceable.
2. May be made in good faith but never carried out.
3. Is not unconditional if:
   a. The female knows the male is married (conditioned on death or divorce).
   b. Marriage is to take place *if* pregnancy results.

It must be shown that the female relied on the promise as a condition of her submission to intercourse.

Note: Subsequent marriage (P.C. 269) absolves the crime.

APPLICABLE STATUTES—INCEST

P.C. 285—*Penalty for incest.* Persons being within the degrees of consanguinity within which marriages are declared by law to be incestuous and void, who intermarry with each other, or who commit fornication or adultery with each other, are punishable by imprisonment in the state prison not less than one year nor more than fifty years.

Civil Code 59—*Incompetency of parties; incest. Incompetency of parties:* Marriages between parents and children, ancestors and descendants of every degree, and between brothers and sisters of the half as well as the whole blood, and between uncles and nieces or aunts and nephews, are incestuous, and void from the beginning, whether the relationship is legitimate or illegitimate.

LEGAL DISCUSSION

The crime of incest originates from the consanguinity of the parties; i.e., their relationship. It can exist coupled with rape (forcible or statutory), adultery, fornication, or marital intercourse. Although the statute does not contain the word "knowing" or "knowingly," the courts have held that the parties must know of the relationship to constitute the crime and have even conjectured that where only one party knew of the relationship he alone would be guilty of incest. Honest mistake is a good defense.[6]

ENFORCEMENT ASPECTS

It should be noted that prosecutions for seduction, incest, and adultery are relatively infrequent. For sociological reasons complaints are very rare, but the police officer should be aware nevertheless of these areas for possible enforcement.

APPLICABLE STATUTES

P.C. 315—*Keeping or residing in house of ill-fame; proof.* Every person who keeps a house of ill-fame in this state, resorted to for the purposes of prostitution or lewdness, or who willfully resides in such house, is guilty of a misdemeanor; and in all prosecutions for keeping or resorting to such a house common repute may be received as competent evidence of the character of the house, the purpose for which it is kept or used, and the character of the women inhabiting or resorting to it.

P.C. 316—*Keeping disorderly houses, etc.* Every person who keeps any disorderly house, or any house for the purpose of assignation or prostitution, or any house of public resort, by which the peace, comfort, or decency of the immediate neighborhood is habitually disturbed, or who keeps any inn in a disorderly manner; and every person who lets any apartment or tenement, knowing that it is to be used for the purpose of assignation or prostitution, is guilty of a misdemeanor.

P.C. 318—*Prevailing upon person to visit a place kept for gambling or prostitution.* Whoever, through invitation or device prevails upon any person to visit any room, building, or other places kept for the purpose of gambling or prostitution, is guilty of a misdemeanor, and, upon conviction thereof, shall be confined in the county jail not exceeding six months, or fined not exceeding five hundred dollars, or be punished by both such fine and imprisonment.

P.C. 309—*Admitting minors to houses of prostitution a misdemeanor.* Any proprietor, keeper, manager, conductor, or person having the control of any house of prostitution or any house or room resorted to for the purpose of prostitution, who shall admit or keep any minor of either sex therein; or any parent or guardian of any such minor, who shall admit or keep such minor, or sanction, or connive at the admission or keeping thereof, into, or in any such house, or room, shall be guilty of a misdemeanor.

P.C. 273e—*Minor not to deliver messages, etc., to certain places.* Every telephone, special delivery company or association, and every other corporation or person engaged in the delivery of packages, letters, notes, messages, or other matter, and every manager, superintendent, or other agent of such person, corporation, or association, who sends any minor in the employ or under the control of any such person, corporation, association, or agent, to the keeper of any house of prostitution, variety theater, or other place of questionable repute, or to any person connected with, or any inmate of, such house, theater, or other place, or who permits such minor to enter such house, theater, or other place, is guilty of a misdemeanor.

P.C. 273f—*Sending children to immoral places.* Any person, whether as parent, guardian, employer, or otherwise, and any firm or corporation, who as employer or otherwise, shall send, direct, or cause to be sent or directed to any saloon, gambling house, house of prostitution or other immoral place, any minor under the age of eighteen, is guilty of a misdemeanor.

Business and Professions Code 25601—*Disorderly houses; places of disturbance, etc.* Every licensee, or agent or employee of a licensee, who keeps, permits to be used, or suffers to be used, in conjunction with a licensed premise, any disorderly house or place in which people abide or to which people resort, to the disturbance of the neighborhood, or in which people abide or to which people resort for purposes which are injurious to the public morals, health, convenience, or safety, is guilty of a misdemeanor.

Business and Professions Code 9979—*Referral of applicant to place adversely affecting health, safety, welfare or morals.* No employment agency shall send or cause to be sent any applicant to any place where the health, safety, welfare or morals of the applicant could be adversely affected, the character of which places the agency could have ascertained upon reasonable inquiry.

P.C. 266a—*Taking female for purpose of prostitution.* Every person who, within this state, takes any female against her will and without her consent, or with her consent procured by fraudulent inducement or misrepresentation, for the purpose of prostitution, is punishable by imprisonment in the state prison not exceeding five years, and a fine not exceeding one thousand dollars.

P.C. 266b—*Taking a female by force, duress, etc., to live in an illicit relation.* Every person who takes any female person unlawfully, and against her will, and by force, menace, or duress, compels her to live with him in an illicit relation, against her consent, or to so live with any other person, is punishable by imprisonment in the state prison not less than two nor more than four years.

P.C. 266c—*Importing Chinese or Japanese women for purpose of selling.* Every person bringing to, or landing within this state, any female person born in the Empire of China or the Empire of Japan, or the Islands adjacent thereto, with intent to place her in charge or custody of any other person, and against her will to compel her to reside with him, or for the purpose of selling her to any person whomsoever, is punishable by a fine of not less than one nor more than five thousand dollars, or by imprisonment in the county jail not less than six nor more than twelve months.

P.C. 266d—*Placing female in custody for the purpose of cohabitation.* Any person who receives any money or other valuable thing for or on account of his placing in custody any female for the purpose of causing her to cohabit with any male to whom she is not married, is guilty of a felony.

P.C. 266e—*Purchasing female for the purpose of prostitution.* Every person who purchases, or pays any money or other valuable thing for any female person for the purpose of prostitution, or for the purpose of placing her, for immoral purposes, in any house or place against her will, is guilty of a felony.

P.C. 266f—*Selling female for immoral purpose.* Every person who sells any female person or receives any money or other valuable thing for or on account of his placing in custody, for immoral purposes, any female person, whether with or without her consent, is guilty of a felony.

P.C. 266g—*Placing of one's wife in house of prostitution.* Every man who, by force, intimidation, threats, persuasion, promises, or any other means, places or leaves, or procures any other person or persons to place or leave, his wife in a house of prostitution, or connives at or consents to, or permits, the placing or leaving of his wife in a house of prostitution, or allows or permits her to remain therein, is guilty of a felony and punishable by imprisonment in the state prison for not less than three nor more than ten years; and in all prosecutions under this section a wife is a competent witness against her husband.

LEGAL DISCUSSION

Prostitution is the practice by a woman of engaging in common, indiscriminate sexual intercourse for hire. "Common" and "indiscriminate" mean available to any male who meets other conditions precedent, without the existence of a compelling *sex* drive. "For hire" means for remuneration whether in the form of social position, privilege, immunities, or monetary gain. Prostitution is frequently referred to as the world's "oldest profession." Crimes relating to prostitution are seldom directed at the prostitute, who is generally considered the victim, but rather at those who create the condition. In California the act of prostitution itself is a form of disorderly conduct (formerly of vagrancy).[7]

The principal proscriptions aimed at elimination of prostitution are directed at commercialized vice rather than at the simple act itself.

Historically, the Mann Act, more commonly known as the White Slave Act, makes it a federal crime to transport a woman over state lines "for an immoral purpose."

California law directs itself toward the suppression of places for assignation or prostitution.

In those crimes involving prostitution of wives there must be shown to exist a valid existing marriage.

An interesting and ludicrous picture is presented where it is contended that the wife was employed as cook or seamstress[8] in a brothel, inasmuch as the court seeks to protect all women from such exposure (temptations) and looks askance at such defenses.[9]

P.C. 266g goes much further and makes it a crime for a man who knows of his wife's condition and servitude to allow her to so remain—particularly where he enjoyed the fruits of her *labor*,[10] and even where she conducts her business of prostitution in the residence jointly occupied by the couple.[11]

The fact that the wife was a prostitute when the husband married her is not a defense.[12]

ENFORCEMENT ASPECTS

Entrapment is a major investigative problem when working on prostitution cases. When officers are engaged in undercover assignments, i.e., attempting to gather evidence on a female who is involved in prostitution, they must be careful not to act erroneously so as to allow a defense of entrapment to future prosecution (see Chapter 4).

Officers, while acting as feigned accomplices, must be very careful to secure admissible evidence showing the intent of the act. Tape recorders and other witnesses are usually needed to establish the promise and intent of the female prostitute. Experienced officers are usually required to testify to the meaning of vernacular terms, e.g., "turn a trick."

Officers should always be alert to the possibility that other crimes, such as narcotics, may be instigating the acts of prostitution.

APPLICABLE STATUTES—PIMPING OR PANDERING

P.C. 266h—*Soliciting or deriving support from prostitute.* Any male person who, knowing a female person is a prostitute, lives or derives support or maintenance in whole or in part from the earnings or proceeds of her prostitution, or from money loaned or advanced to or charged against her by any keeper or manager or inmate of a house or other place where prostitution is practiced or allowed, or who solicits or receives compensation for soliciting for her, is guilty of pimping, a felony, and is punishable by imprisonment in the state prison for not less than one year nor more than ten (10) years.

Any female person referred to in this section is a competent witness in any prosecution hereunder to testify for or against the accused as to any transaction or as to any conversation with the accused or by him with another person or persons in her presence, notwithstanding her having married the accused before or after the violation of any of the provisions of this section, whether called as a witness during the existence of the marriage or after its dissolution.

P.C. 266i—*Procuring female: competent witness.* Any person who: (a) procures a female inmate for a house of prostitution; or (b) by promises, threats, violence, or by any device or scheme, causes, induces, persuades or encourages a female person to become an inmate of a house of prostitution; or (c) procures for a female person a place as inmate in a house of prostitution or as an inmate of any place in which prostitution is encouraged or allowed within this state; or (d) by promises, threats, violence or by any device or scheme, causes, induces, persuades or encourages an inmate of a house of prostitution, or any other place in which prostitution is encouraged or allowed, to remain therein as an inmate; or (e) by fraud or artifice, or by duress of person or goods, or by abuse of any position of confidence or authority, procures any female person to become an inmate of a house of ill-fame, or to enter any place in which prostitution is encouraged or allowed within this state, or to come into this state or leave this state for the purpose of prostitution; or (f) receives or gives, or agrees to receive or give, any money or thing of value for procuring, or attempting to procure, any female person to become an inmate of a house of ill-fame within this state, or to come into this state or leave this state for the purpose of prostitution, is guilty of pandering, a felony, and is punishable by imprisonment in the state prison for not less than one year nor more than 10 years.

Any female person referred to in this section is a competent witness in any prosecution hereunder to testify for or against the accused as to any transaction or as to any conversation with the accused or by him with another person or persons in her presence, notwithstanding her having married the accused before or after the violation of any of the provisions of this section, whether called as a witness during the existence of the marriage or after its dissolution.

LEGAL DISCUSSION

In ordinary usage the words "pimping" and "pandering" are almost interchangeable. The statute makes a clear distinction.

Pimping (P.C. 266h) is commercial exploitation of a prostitute, i.e., making money from prostitution, whereas *pandering* (P.C. 266i) is procuring the prostitute, or a place for her to prostitute herself.

Pimping consists of a male person receiving money (1) from a prostitute's earnings whether paid by the prostitute, her "customer" or her employer or madam; or (2) for soliciting customers for her.

A female pimp acting alone without a male accomplice is not guilty of violation of 266h.[13] However, the wife of a pimp who lives on his earnings as such and participates by making assignations for the prostitute is guilty of violating P.C. 266h.[14]

A male person who sold narcotics to a prostitute and received her earnings in exchange therefore violated P.C. 266h, and his conviction thereof was sustained despite his contention that he was only guilty of selling narcotics.[15]

It is not necessary that the male person be dependent on the prostitute's earnings. He may even have other substantial income in which case the court has held his conduct to be more odious than in the case of one who relied on the prostitute's earnings in order to live.[16]

There is no requirement that the money be received directly from the prostitute herself. On the other hand, mere solicitation without compensation or expectation thereof does not violate the statute.[17]

There is no limitation to a "male person"; the offense of pimping or pandering consists of inducing or encouraging a woman to remain in or to enter into a house of prostitution. The inducement can be by promise, threat, violence, device or scheme, etc.

The courts have held that the acts can overlap the various distinctions of the statute and need not fit neatly into any one distinction in particular.[18]

Proof that the house was a brothel or house of prostitution can be by reputation[19] or by the fact of frequent nocturnal visits by men and the presence of strange women who engage in copulation.[20] The word "house" is used in its generic sense. It includes an apartment, or several apartments, taxicab, cabin, flatboat, tent, hotel or steamship room, etc.

Note that the statute uses the word "procurement" and does not require the existence of an intent. This does not eliminate the requirement that the defendant's acts must be knowingly made. He must know that the place is a brothel and that the woman intends or is intended to engage in illicit copulation. In other words, it is intended that she become an inmate. The act is complete without the female having engaged in prostitution.

The operator of the brothel can be guilty as a joint procurer, or as one who aids and abets the procurement.[21]

The woman's consent to enter prostitution is not a defense. In fact, she may importune the defendant to get her such a position. It is immaterial whether the prostitute is a young and innocent girl or a hardened whore of long experience.[22]

ENFORCEMENT ASPECTS

Prostitutes who work for a pimp or panderer are accomplices, and accordingly corroboration of their testimony is needed for prosecution of the panderer. Without the cooperation of at least one of the prostitutes it is usually impossible to convict the procurer. Frequent suspects for this type of crime are bartenders, bellhops, taxi-drivers, etc. Pimping and pandering are prevalent in organized crime and among minority groups.

APPLICABLE STATUTES—SEX PERVERSION

P.C. 314—*Indecent exposure*. Every person who willfully and lewdly, either

1. Exposes his person, or the private parts thereof, in any public place, or in any place where there are present other persons to be offended or annoyed thereby; or,

2. Procures, counsels, or assists any person so to expose himself or take any part in any model artists exhibition, or to make any other exhibition of himself to public view, or the view of any number of persons, such as is offensive to decency, or is adapted to excite to vicious or lewd thoughts or acts, is guilty of a misdemeanor.

Upon the second and each subsequent conviction under sub-division of this section, or upon a first conviction under sub-division 1 of this section after a previous conviction under Section 288 of this Code, every person so convicted is guilty of a felony, and is punishable by imprisonment in state prison for not less than one year.

P.C. 272—*Contributing to delinquency of a minor; penalty.* Every person who commits any act or omits the performance of any duty, which act or omission causes or tends to cause or encourage any person under the age of 21 years to come within the provisions of Sections 600, 601, or 602 of the Welfare and Institutions Code or which act or omission contributes thereto, or any person who, by any act or omission, or by threats, commands, or persuasion, induces or endeavors to induce any person under the age of 21 years or any ward or dependent child of the Juvenile Court to fail or refuse to conform to a lawful order of the Juvenile Court, or to do or to perform any act or to follow any course of conduct or to so live as would cause or manifestly tend to cause any such person to become or to remain a person within the provisions of Sections 600, 601 or 602 of the Welfare and Institutions Code, is guilty of a misdemeanor and upon conviction thereof shall be punished by a fine not exceeding one thousand dollars ($1,000), or by imprisonment in the county jail for not more than one year, or by both such fine and imprisonment in a county jail, or may be released on probation for a period not exceeding five years. The District Attorney shall prosecute all violations charged under this section.

P.C. 273d—*Infliction of traumatic injury upon wife or child.* Any husband who willfully inflicts upon his wife corporal injury resulting in a traumatic condition, and any person who willfully inflicts upon any child any cruel or inhuman corporal punishment or injury resulting in a traumatic condition, is guilty of a felony, and upon conviction thereof shall be punished by imprisonment in the State Prison for not more than 10 years or in the county jail for not more than one year.

P.C. 286—*Crimes against nature; punishment.* Every person who is guilty of the infamous crime against nature, committed with mankind, or with animal, is punishable by imprisonment in the state prison not less than one year.

P.C. 288a—*Sex perversions.* Any person participating in the act of copulating the mouth of one person with the sexual organ of another is punishable by imprisonment in the state prison for not exceeding fifteen years, or, by imprisonment in the county jail not to exceed one year; provided, however, whenever any person is found guilty of the offense specified herein, and it is charged and admitted or found to be true that he is more than 10 years older than his coparticipant in such an act, which coparticipant is under the age of 14, or that he has compelled the other's participation in such an act by force, violence, duress, menace, or threat of great bodily harm, he shall be punished by imprisonment in the state prison for not less than three years. The order of commitment shall expressly state whether a person convicted hereunder is more than 10 years older than his coparticipant and whether such coparticipant is under the age of 14. The order shall also state whether a person convicted hereunder has compelled coparticipation in his act by force, violence, duress, menace, or threat of great bodily harm.

LEGAL DISCUSSION

Perversion is frequently referred to as proscribed acts "other than those constituting other sex crimes." However, the courts have uniformly held that this crime did not merge with other crimes and would stand regardless of completion of more serious crimes.[23]

A child, as the term is used herein, may be of either sex so long as it is proven that the child is under fourteen years of age. (Note that since the child must be under fourteen he or she, as the case may be, is not an accomplice.)

Three principles of law should be kept in mind: (1) Consent of the child is *not* a defense. (2) Even though his or her tender years may render the child unable to testify or incompetent as a witness, the fact of the child's voluntary complaint to a person who can testify is admissible and can be offered in evidence to prove commission of the act.[24, 25] (3) If the child qualifies and testifies, her testimony does not require corroboration to sustain conviction.[26]

P.C. 314 requires a specific intent to arouse the passions of the *defendant* or *of the child*. That such passions are in fact aroused or gratified is not required but if proved will establish intent.

The intent may be established by proof of the acts and words of the defendant or by circumstantial evidence.[27] Attempts to induce the child victim to conceal or suppress defendant's conduct is a circumstantial element.

The crime proscribed by 288a PC is committed by copulating the sex organ of a male (fellatio) or of a female (cunnilingus) by the mouth of another person of either sex. Note that the gravity of the offense is augmented by disparity in the age of the participants and by the use of force or threat.

Both participants, if capable of consent, are guilty. Hence, the testimony of one participant, like that of an accomplice, must be corroborated to establish a conviction. Specific intent is not required, and intoxication is not a defense.

The term "copulation" implies some kind of sexual stimulation or satisfaction from the contact between mouth and sex organ. The decisions are in confusion as to whether penetration is required. However, the later cases seem to indicate that there is no requirement of penetration so long as mouth contact with the genital region of another is established.[28]

The term "sodomy" usually connotes (a) *buggery* (copulation per anus) and (b) *bestiality* (copulation with an animal). It has also been used to include fellatio and cunnilingus heretofore described.

The statute requires the copulation to be "per anus" or rectally. Any penetration, no matter how slight, is sufficient; there is no requirement that there be orgasm or emission.

The parties are described as the "active" party and the passive party or "victim"; however, both parties are equally guilty, and consent is not a defense. The testimony of one party against the other is that of an accomplice and requires corroboration. However, a child under fourteen cannot be an accomplice in the absence of a showing that the child had sufficient mental capacity to understand the character of his wrongful act.

ENFORCEMENT ASPECTS

Sex perversion is for the most part thought to be homosexuality; in fact, it covers several offenses. In certain states and countries homosexuality is no longer a crime but merely a social condition. In general, homosexuals are not inclined to be violent or to commit violent crimes. Disturbances and violence between homosexuals are usually "lovers' " arguments. Police problems are mainly restricted to maintaining the peace in places frequented by homosexuals. Homosexuals of both sexes are usually clannish and tend to remain aloof from the general public.

As regards contributing to the delinquency of minors and child beating, this is a type of perversion in many cases, and manifests itself through the violations of the sections. Police officers should realize that they have the authority and the duty to investigate complaints of this type. A common pitfall in investigative techniques occurs when an officer receives information of possible child neglect or injury and contacts the child in the presence of the parents. The parents may well deny all allegations and further indicate that the child has sustained no major injury. Police officers should be sure that they inspect the child before they discontinue their investigation. Should a body inspection of a female need to be conducted, a policewoman should be called if possible. The determination of the seriousness of the injury should be done by law enforcement officers and not necessarily by the parents.

APPLICABLE STATUTES—OBSCENITY

P.C. 311—*Definitions.* As used in this chapter: (a) "Obscene" means that to the average person, applying contemporary standards, the predominant appeal of the matter, taken as a whole, is to prurient interest, i.e., a shameful or morbid interest in nudity, sex, or excretion, which goes substantially beyond customary limits of candor in description or representation of such matters and is matter which is utterly without redeeming social importance.

(b) "Matter" means any book, magazine, newspaper, or other printed or written material or any picture, drawing, photograph, motion picture, or other pictorial representation or any statue or other figure, or any recording, transcription or mechanical, chemical or electrical reproduction or any other articles, equipment, machines or materials.

(c) "Person" means any individual, partnership, firm, association, corporation, or other legal entity.

(d) "Distribute" means to transfer possession of, whether with or without consideration.

(e) "Knowingly" means having knowledge that the matter is obscene.

P.C. 311.2—*Penalty for sending, selling, distributing, publishing, displaying obscene matter.* Every person who knowingly sends or causes to be sent, or brings or causes to be brought, into this state for sale or distribution, or in this state prepares, publishes, prints, exhibits, distributes, or offers to distribute, or has in his possession with intent to distribute or to exhibit or offer to distribute, any obscene matter is guilty of a misdemeanor.[29]

P.C. 311.9—*Penalties; prior conviction.* (a) Every person who violates section 311.2 is punishable by fine of not more than one thousand dollars ($1,000) plus five dollars ($5) for each additional unit of material coming within the provisions of this chapter, which is involved in the offense, not to exceed ten thousand dollars ($10,000), or by imprisonment in the county jail for not more than six months plus one day for each additional unit of material coming within the provision of this chapter, and which is involved in the offense, such basic maximum and additional days not to exceed 360 days in the county jail, or by both such fine and imprisonment. If such person has previously been convicted of a violation of Section 311.2, he is punishable by fine of not more than two thousand dollars ($2,000) plus five dollars ($5) for each additional unit of material coming within the provisions of this chapter, which is involved in the offense, not to exceed twenty-five thousand dollars ($25,000), or by imprisonment in the county jail for not more than one year, or by both such fine and such imprisonment. If such person has been twice convicted of a violation of this chapter, a violation of Section 311.2 is punishable as a felony.

(b) Every person who violates Sections 311.3 and 311.4 is punishable by fine of not more than two thousand dollars ($2,000) or by imprisonment in the county jail for not more than one year, or by both such fine and such imprisonment. If such person has been previously convicted of a violation of Section 311.3 or Section 311.4, he is punishable by imprisonment in the state prison not exceeding five years.

(c) Every person who violates Section 311.7 is punishable by fine of not more than one thousand dollars ($1,000) or by imprisonment in the county jail for not more than six months, or by both such fine and imprisonment. For a second and subsequent offense he shall be punished by a fine of not more than two thousand dollars ($2,000), or by imprisonment in the county jail for not more than one year, or by both such fine and imprisonment. If such person has been twice convicted of a violation of this chapter, a violation of Section 311.7 is punishable as a felony.

P.C. 311.5—*Advertising and promotion a misdemeanor.* Every person who writes or creates advertising or solicits anyone to publish such advertising or otherwise promote the sale or distribution of matter represented or held out by him to be obscene, is guilty of a misdemeanor.

Business and Professions Code §601—*Advertisements relating to abortion or contraception as felony.* Every person who willfully writes, composes or publishes any notice or advertisement of any medicine or means for producing or facilitating a miscarriage or abortion, or for the prevention of conception, or who offers his services by any notice, advertisement, or otherwise, to assist in the accomplishment of any such purpose is guilty of a felony and shall be punished as provided in the Penal Code. *It shall not, however, be unlawful for information about the prevention of conception to be disseminated for purposes of public health education by any person who is not commercially interested, directly or indirectly, in the sale of any medicine or means which may be used for the prevention of conception.*

Business and Professions Code §5290—*Indecency or immorality.* No person shall display or cause or permit to be displayed upon any advertising structure or sign any statements or words of an obscene, indecent or immoral character, or any picture or illustration of any human figure in such detail as to offend public morals or decency, or any other matter or thing of an obscene, indecent or immoral character.

Business and Professions Code §5311—*Violation creating nuisance.* All advertising displays which are placed or which exist in violation of the provisions of this chapter are public nuisances and may be removed by any public employee as further provided in this chapter.

Business and Professions Code §5313—*Violation as misdemeanor*. Every person as principal, agent, or employee, violating any of the provisions of this chapter is guilty of a misdemeanor.

P.C. 311.7—*Requiring purchase or consignment of obscene matter a misdemeanor*. Every person who, knowingly, as a condition to a sale, allocation, consignment, or delivery for resale of any paper, magazine, book, periodical, publication or other merchandise, requires that the purchaser or consignee receive any obscene matter or who denies or threatens to deny a franchise, revokes or threatens to revoke, or imposes any penalty, financial or otherwise, by reason of the failure of any person to accept obscene matter, or by reason of the return of such obscene matter, is guilty of a misdemeanor.

P.C. 311.3—*Distributing obscene matter to minors; misdemeanor*. Every person who, with knowledge that a person is a minor under 18 years of age, or who, while in possession of such facts that he should reasonably know that such person is a minor under 18 years of age, knowingly distributes to, or sends or causes to be sent to, or exhibits to or offers to distribute any obscene matter to a minor under 18 years of age, is guilty of a misdemeanor.

P.C. 311.4—*Hiring of a minor is misdemeanor*. Every person who, with knowledge that a person is a minor, or who, while in possession of such facts that he should reasonably know that such person is a minor, hires, employs, or uses such minor to do or assist in doing any of the acts described in Section 311.2, is guilty of a misdemeanor.

LEGAL DISCUSSION AND ENFORCEMENT ASPECTS

The law on obscenity and pornography is under direct attack and is subject to constant revision. Some definitions are in order.

For a discussion of "average person," "predominant appeal," "customary limits of candor," and "contemporary standards," see *Harvard Law Review*, Vol. 76, page 1498.

Matter refers to any book, magazine, newspaper, or other printed or written material or any picture, drawing, photograph, motion picture, statue, or other pictorial representation or any recording, transcription or mechanical, chemical or electrical reproduction.

Defense of legitimate purpose:[30] Supreme Court decisions have indicated that obscenity is primarily determined by the intent and purpose of the material. With books, magazines, etc., frequently the method of advertising and the advertising literature itself have been used to determine the intent. Court decisions have maintained that material which has "literary" value does not violate the obscenity laws. However, should the predominant appeal be to prurient interests, it may be in violation.

In the initial phases of investigation close liaison between police officers and the prosecuting attorney is highly desirable.

APPLICABLE STATUTES—BIGAMY

P.C. 281—*Bigamy defined.* Every person having a husband or wife living, who marries any other person, except in the cases specified in the next section, is guilty of bigamy.

P.C. 282—*Exceptions.* The last section does not extend—

1. To any person by reason of any former marriage, whose husband or wife by such marriage has been absent for five successive years without being known to such person within that time to be living; nor,
2. To any person by reason of any former marriage which has been pronounced void, annulled, or dissolved by the judgment of a competent court.

P.C. 283—*Bigamy, punishment of.* Bigamy is punishable by a fine not exceeding five thousand dollars ($5,000) or by imprisonment in a county jail not exceeding one year or in the state prison not exceeding ten years.

P.C. 1106—*Evidence on a trial for bigamy.* Upon a trial for bigamy, it is not necessary to prove either of the marriages by the register, certificate, or other record evidence thereof, but the same may be proved by such evidence as is admissible to prove a marriage in other cases; and when the second marriage took place out of this state, proof of that fact, accompanied with proof of cohabitation thereafter in this state, is sufficient to sustain the charge.

Civil Code §61—*Bigamous and polygamous marriages; exceptions; absentees.* A subsequent marriage contracted by any person during the life of a former husband or wife of such person, with any person other than such former husband or wife, is illegal and void from the beginning, unless:

1. The former marriage has been annulled or dissolved, *and in the case of dissolution by divorce obtained in this state, at least one year has elapsed from the date of service of a copy of summons and complaint upon, or appearance by, the defendant spouse in the former proceeding for such divorce.*

2. Unless such former husband or wife is absent, and not known to such person to be living for the space of five successive years immediately preceding such subsequent marriage, or is generally reputed or believed by such person to be dead at the time such subsequent marriage was contracted. In either of which cases the subsequent marriage is valid until its nullity is adjudged by a competent tribunal.

LEGAL DISCUSSION

The validity of a marriage is determined by the law of the state where the marriage took place. Ordinarily jurisdiction to punish bigamy lies in the state where the second marriage occurred. However, the California statute punishes out-of-state bigamy if there is cohabitation in this state.

The prior marriage can be proved by (1) the register, certificate or other record of the first marriage; (2) testimony of former spouse; (3) admission of defendant, or (4) evidence of cohabitation and repute. If defendant has entered into several bigamous marriages, proof of any prior marriage will suffice.

The second marriage can be proved by any of the aforesaid methods.

There must be proof that the former spouse is living. This must be proved. Reliance on the presumption of continued life will not suffice.

When the prosecution makes out a prima facie case as heretofore described, defendant must prove his defense if he can. Such defenses are:

1. *Spouse absent for five years.* This does not apply if defendant deserted his spouse, and there must have been no report to show or indicate the absent spouse was still living.

2. *Prior marriage invalid or dissolved.* The annulment decree or other resolution must be by judgment of a competent court. An exception to this rule is where defendant is accused of a bigamous marriage to A based on his prior marriage to B and he defends on the grounds that his marriage to B was invalid because bigamous in that he was married to A. This is overcome by charging the prior marriage in general terms and accepting proof of *any* prior marriage.

3. *Honest mistake of fact—as in C.C. §61.* Any marriage which is valid civilly as based on former spouse's death, reputed or believed, would not sustain a conviction for bigamy.

Although the statute does not recite a requirement that there be a specific intent, the courts have imposed such requirement but have placed the burden on defendant to show lack of intent rather than on the prosecution to show its existence in this particular crime.[31]

ENFORCEMENT ASPECTS

The proof of marriage is oftentimes an investigative problem. A certified copy of a marriage certificate, divorce decree, etc., will be needed for court proceedings. Frequently, officers will find it difficult to prove the prior marriage if the suspect is currently living happily with the present wife. Bigamy prosecution usually requires at least two "irate" victims.

It is always necessary to establish a valid marriage for the defendant prior to proving the bigamous marriage. This often requires considerable effort on the part of the investigator. In the case of a suspect who had recently married, the officer could have procured a certified copy of the marriage certificate of a previous marriage, thereby believing that he had a prima facie case of bigamy. But he would not have proceeded far enough: it must be shown that the previous marriage is still legal. If the suspect had married again prior to his divorce becoming final, this would void the second marriage. If shortly after the second marriage his divorce was granted, it would allow him to enter into a valid third marriage—one which would appear at first glance to be bigamous.

Social conditions have been reflected in court decisions, and in several instances the courts have alluded to the knowledge and intent of the defendant in bigamy cases. It has been suggested that if the suspect thought that he had been divorced by his spouse and then remarried, this would be a valid defense in a bigamy charge. Therefore, investigation should attempt to establish the intent and state of mind of the suspect at the time of the alleged bigamous marriage.

APPLICABLE STATUTES—ABORTION

P.C. 274—*Administering drugs, etc., with intent to procure miscarriage.* Every person who provides, supplies, or administers to any woman, or procures any woman to take any medicine, drug or substance, or uses or employs any instrument or other means whatever, with intent thereby to procure the miscarriage of such woman, except as provided in the Therapeutic Abortion Act, Chapter 11 (commencing with Section 25950) of Division 20 of the Health and Safety Code, is punishable by imprisonment in the state prison not less than two nor more than five years.

P.C. 275—*Submitting to an attempt to produce miscarriage.* Every woman who solicits of any person any medicine, drug, or substance whatever, and takes the same, or who submits to any operation, or to the use of any means whatever, with intent thereby to procure a miscarriage, except as provided in the Therapeutic Abortion Act, Chapter 11 (commencing with

Section 25950) of Division 20 of the Health and Safety Code, is punishable by imprisonment in the state prison not less than one nor more than five years.

P.C. 276—*Abortion: solicitation for; penalty.* Every person who solicits any woman to submit to any operation, or to the use of any means whatever, to procure a miscarriage, except as provided in the Therapeutic Abortion Act, Chapter 11 (commencing with Section 25950) of Division 20 of the Health and Safety Code, is punishable by imprisonment in the county jail not longer than one year or in the state prison not longer than five years, or by fine of not more than five thousand dollars ($5,000). Such offense must be proved by the testimony of two witnesses, or of one witness and corroborating circumstances.

H. & S. 25951—*Authority to perform or to aid or assist or attempt abortion; requirements.* A holder of the physician's and surgeon's certificate, as defined in the Business and Professions Code, is authorized to perform an abortion or aid or assist or attempt an abortion, only if each of the following requirements is met:

(a)   The abortion takes place in a hospital which is accredited by the Joint Commission on Accreditation of Hospitals.

(b)   The abortion is approved in advance by a committee of the medical staff of the hospital, which committee is established and maintained in accordance with standards promulgated by the Joint Commission on Accreditation of Hospitals. In any case in which the committee of the medical staff consists of no more than three licensed physicians and surgeons, the unanimous consent of all committee members shall be required in order to approve the abortion.

(c)   The Committee of the Medical Staff finds that one or more of the following conditions exist:

(1)   There is substantial risk that continuance of the pregnancy would gravely impair the physical or mental health of the mother;

(2)   The pregnancy resulted from rape or incest.

H. & S. 25952—*Pregnancy resulting from rape or incest; procedure.* The Committee of the Medical Staff shall not approve the performance of an abortion on the ground that the pregnancy resulted from rape or incest except in accordance with the following procedure:

(a)   Upon receipt of an application for an abortion on the grounds that the pregnancy resulted from rape or incest, the committee shall immediately notify the district attorney of the county in which the alleged rape or incest occurred of the application, and transmit to the district attorney the affidavit of the applicant attesting to the facts establishing the alleged rape or incest. If the district attorney informs the committee that there is probable cause to believe that the pregnancy resulted from a violation of Section 261 or Section 285 of the Penal Code, the committee may approve the abortion. If, within five days after the committee has notified the district attorney of the application, the committee does not receive a reply from the district attorney, it may approve the abortion. If the district attorney informs the committee that there is no probable cause to believe the alleged violation did occur, the committee shall not approve the abortion, except as provided in subdivision (b) of this section;

(b)   If the district attorney informs the committee that there is no probable cause to believe the alleged violation did occur, the person who applied for the abortion may petition the superior court of the county in which the alleged rape or incest occurred, to determine whether the pregnancy resulted from a violation of Section 261 or Section 285 of the Penal Code. Hearing on the petition shall be set for a date no later than one week after the date of filing of the petition.

The district attorney shall file an affidavit with the court stating the reasons for his conclusion that the alleged violation did not occur, and this affidavit shall be received in evidence. The district attorney may appear at the hearing to offer further evidence or to examine witnesses.

If the court finds that it has been proved, by a preponderance of the evidence, that the pregnancy did result from a violation of Section 261 or Section 285 of the Penal Code, it shall issue an order so declaring and the committee may approve the abortion. Any hearing granted under this section may, at the court's discretion, be held in chambers. The testimony, findings, conclusions or determinations of the court in a proceeding under this section shall be inadmissible as evidence in any other action or proceeding, although nothing herein shall be construed to prevent the appearance of any witness who testified at a proceeding under this section, or to prevent the introduction of any evidence that may have been introduced at a proceeding under this section, in any other action or proceeding.

(c)   Notwithstanding any other provision of this section, an abortion shall be approved on the ground of a violation of subdivision 1 of Section 261 of the Penal Code only when the woman at the time of the alleged violation, was below the age of 15 years.

(d)   Notwithstanding any other provision of this section, the testimony of any witness in a proceeding under this section shall be admissible as evidence in any prosecution of that witness for perjury.

H. & S. 25953—*Medical staff committee; number of members required.* The committee of the medical staff referred to in Section 25951 must, in all instances, consist of not less than two licensed physicians and surgeons, and if the proposed termination of pregnancy will occur after the 13th week of pregnancy, the committee must consist of at least three such licensed physicians and surgeons. In no event shall the termination be approved after the 20th week of pregnancy.

H. & S. 25954—*Mental health defined.* The term "mental health" as used in Section 25951 means mental illness to the extent that the woman is dangerous to herself or to the person or property of others or is in need of supervision or restraint.

LEGAL DISCUSSION

Medically, the term "abortion" includes accidental as well as induced miscarriage. Legally, the term applies to the unlawful use of drugs, instruments, or other means of causing a miscarriage.

The statute is directed at the abortionist. The loss of life, whether that of the fetus or of the mother, is considered under homicide (Chapter 13).

The elements of the offense are (1) the act, (2) the specific intent, (3) the lack of necessity. It is not a defense that (1) the victim was not pregnant; (2) the pregnancy was not advanced (medical theory that miscarriage cannot occur until the third month is not accepted); (3) the victim attempted to abort herself or was in the process of aborting when the act was committed; or (4) no miscarriage resulted (see attempted abortions below).

Proof of the crime requires the testimony of two witnesses or of one witness with corroborating circumstances. Testimony of the victim alone and unsupported will not suffice.

Circumstantial evidence can be used to establish intent.

Lack of necessity

See the Therapeutic Abortion Statute above (H. & S. 29951).

Note that necessity is not a defense. Lack of necessity is an essential element of the crime; in fact, a part of the corpus delicti.[32] Lack of necessity can be proved by circumstantial evidence (woman's health).

Soliciting or submitting to abortion is a separate crime (P.C. 275 and 276).

Death from abortion; unlawful abortion or attempted abortion

Felony murder doctrine applies. The crime is second-degree murder.[33]

Lawful abortion negligently performed

In the absence of malice aforethought, the negligence amounting to criminal negligence, the crime is involuntary manslaughter.[34]

ENFORCEMENT ASPECTS

There is little case law to amplify the Therapeutic Abortion Statute. In general, circumstantial evidence in abortion may be proven by:

1. Illicit relationship between abortee and defendant
2. Appearance of symptoms of pregnancy
3. Strong intent to conceal pregnancy
4. Purchase of drugs thought to be abortificants
5. Medical evidence of partial or complete abortion
6. Payment of money to a party known or believed to be an abortionist

The victim of an abortion is the accomplice, and accordingly corroboration is required for conviction. This is frequently provided by the testimony of the "boy friend" or the person who provided the transportation for the woman to the suspect's place of operation. Many abortion victims are identified and referred to police authorities by hospitals and ethical doctors. Frequently, the victims are in critical condition, and investigations of these complaints sometimes result in second-degree murder prosecutions.

GENERAL SUMMARY AND ENFORCEMENT ASPECTS

One of the most significant overall results of many of the sex crimes discussed herein has been the requirement for sex registration.[35] Persons who have been convicted of the following crimes are required to register with the chief of police or the sheriff of the county in which they reside: P.C. 220—assault with intent to commit rape; P.C. 266 (a through i), including pimping and pandering; P.C. 267—induction; P.C. 268—seduction; P.C. 285—incest; P.C. 286—crimes against nature; P.C. 288—child molesting; P.C. 288a—sex perversion; P.C. 647a(1)—vagrancy, lewd; and P.C. 314(1) and (2)—indecent exposure.

A person who has been convicted of crimes requiring registration must notify the law enforcement agency within ten days in writing, giving his address, fingerprints, and photograph.

Many defense attorneys are very conscious of the requirements of this section, and often attempt to plead their clients to a charge that does not require registration: for example, since a charge of 647a(1)—vagrancy, lewd—requires a registration, they will plead instead to P.C. 415—disturbing the peace.

DISCUSSION QUESTIONS

1. What are the elements of child molesting?
2. Can the victim of child molesting be of either sex?
3. What is meant by "statutory rape"?

4. Can a man married to the victim be charged with her rape? Explain.
5. How does incest differ from seduction?
6. What is a "pimp" or "panderer"?
7. Define "obscene."
8. What are the elements of bigamy?
9. What are the requirements for a legal therapeutic abortion?

NOTES

[1]People v. Pallares, 112 CA 2d Supp 895; 246 P 2d 173.

[2]People v. Dabner, 25 CA 630; 144 P 975;
People v. Hobbs, 109 CA 2d 189; 240 P 2d 411;
People v. Pollock, 61 CA 2d 213; 142 P 2d 328;
Compare People v. Webb, 158 CA 2d 537; 323 P 2d 141.

[3]People v. Courtney, 180 CA 2d 61; 4 CR 274.

[4]People v. Hopwood, 130 CA 168; 19 P 2d 824.

[5]Ex Parte Sullivan, 17 CA 278; 119 P 526.

[6]People v. Koller, 142 C 621; 76 P 500;
People v. Patterson, 102 C 239; 36 P 436.

[7]P.C. 647b.

[8]People v. Mock Yick Gar, 14 CA 324; 111 P 1039.

[9]People v. Conners, 150 C 114; 88 P 821.

[10]People v. Coronado, 57 CA 2d 805; 135 P 2d 647.

[11]People v. Stein, 55 CA 2d 417; 130 P 2d 750.

[12]People v. Duncan, 22 CA 430; 134 P 797;
People v. Head, 146 CA 2d 744; 304 P 2d 761.

[13]People v. Smith, 44 C 2d 77; 279 P 2d 33.

[14]People v. Courtney, 176 CA 2d 731; 1 CR 789.

[15]People v. Yipton, 124 CA 2d 213; 268 P 2d 196.

[16]People v. Coronado, 90 CA 2d 762; 203 P 2d 862;
People v. Jackson, 128 CA 2d 506; 275 P 2d 802.

[17]P.C. 266;
People v. Smith, 44 C 2d 77; 279 P 2d 33.

[18]People v. Montgomery, 47 CA 2d 1; 117 P 2d 437;
People v. Cimar, 127 CA 9; 15 P 2d 166 and 16 P 2d 139.

[19]People v. DeMartini, 25 CA 9; 142 P 898.

[20]People v. Mitchell, 91 CA 2d 214; 205 P 2d 101.

[21]People v. Van Way, 108 CA 2d 129; 238 P 2d 56.

[22]People v. Montgomery, 47 CA 2d 1; 117 P 2d 437.

[23]People v. Lind, 68 CA 575; 229 P 990;
People v. Bronson, 69 CA 83; 230 P 213;
People v. Parker, 74 CA 540; 241 P 401;
People v. Hunt, 17 CA 2d 284; 61 P 2d 1208.

[24]People v. Burton, 55 C 2d 328; 11 CR 65.

[25]See Witkins California Evidence, 2d Edition §543.

[26]People v. Rickout, 154 CA 2d 669; 316 P 2d 396;
People v. Jaquish, 170 CA 2d 376; 338 P 2d 974.

[27]People v. Hyche, 52 CA 2d 661; 126 P 2d 885.

[28]People v. Stewart, 109 CA 2d 334; 240 P 2d 704;
People v. Bennett, 119 CA 2d 224; 259 P 2d 476;
People v. Harris, 108 CA 2d 84; 238 P 2d 158.

[29]In re Harris, 56 C 2d 879; 16 CR 889;
People v. Williamson, 207 CA 2d 839; 24 CR 734.

[30]76 Harvard Law Review 1498.

[31]People v. Marler, 199 CA 2d Supp 889; 218 CR 923;
Zeitlion v. Arreberger, 59 C 2d 901; 31 CR 800.

[32]People v. Vogel, 46 C 2d 798; 299 P 2d 850;
People v. Bolland, 167 CA 2d 803; 335 P 2d 204.

[33]People v. Balkwell, 143 C 259; 76 P 1017;
People v. Hickock, 23 CA 2d 574; 83 P 2d 39;
People v. Powell, 34 C 2d 196; 208 P 2d 974;
People v. Hawkins, 177 CA 2d 714; 2 CR 524.

[34]People v. Hunt, 26 CA 514; 147 P 476;
People v. Mount, 93 CA 81; 269 P 177.

[35]P.C. 290—Sex registration.

IIC

CRIMES AGAINST PUBLIC PEACE AND SAFETY

*Crimes against public peace and safety
are enacted by the elected representatives for the benefit
of the public or society in general. The
complexity of our civilization requires more of these types
of laws, even though their effect may be
to whittle away the individual's rights. As Justice Oliver
Wendell Holmes justly observed, a person
has the right to shout "Fire" in the middle of an empty field,
but he violates the rights of others by
shouting "Fire" in a crowded theater. Again, some
of the crimes included in this chapter
could just as well have been classified as crimes against
the person or crimes against property.*

16

Perjury

APPLICABLE STATUTES—PERJURY

P.C. 118—*Perjury defined*. Every person who, having taken an oath that he will testify, declare, depose, or certify truly before any competent tribunal, officer, or person in any of the cases in which such an oath may by law be administered, willfully and contrary to such oath, states as true any material matter which he knows to be false and every person who testifies, declares, deposes, or certifies "under penalty of perjury" in any of the cases in which such testimony, declarations, depositions, or certification is permitted by law under "penalty of perjury" and willfully states as true any material matter which he knows to be false, is guilty of perjury.

Government Code #1094—*Accounts; certificate as prerequisite to allowance*. Every officer whose duty is to audit and allow the accounts of other state, county, or city officers shall, before allowing such accounts, require each of such officers to make and file with him an affidavit or certificate under penalty of perjury that he has not violated any of the provisions of this article, and any individual who willfully makes and subscribes such certificate to an account which he knows to be false as to any material matter shall be guilty of a felony and upon conviction thereof shall be subject to the penalties prescribed for perjury by the penal code of this state.

Government Code #1368—*Perjury*. Every person who, while taking and subscribing to the oath of affirmation required by this chapter, states as true any material matter which he knows to be false, is guilty of perjury, and is punishable by imprisonment in the state prison not less than one nor more than fourteen years.

Government Code #3108—*False statement as perjury*. Every person who, while taking and subscribing to the oath or affirmation required by this chapter, states as true any material matter which he knows to be false, is guilty of perjury, and is punishable by imprisonment in the state prison not less than one nor more than 14 years.

Welfare and Institutions Code #11054—Any person signing a statement containing such declaration, who willfully and knowingly with intent to deceive states as true any material matter which he knows to be false, is subject to the penalty prescribed for perjury in the penal code.

Welfare and Institutions Code #12103—*Written statements of information; perjury*. Written statements of information required from responsible relatives of applicants need not be under oath, but shall contain a written declaration that they are made under the penalties of perjury, and any person so signing such statements who willfully states therein as true any material matter which he knows to be false, is subject to the penalties prescribed for perjury in the penal code.

Welfare and Institutions Code #12850—*Perjury; restitution; preference for civil remedies*. Any person who, in order to secure for himself or another to the aid provided in this chapter or Chapter 5 of this part, makes a false statement under oath, shall be deemed guilty of perjury. Whenever any person has, by means of false statement or representation or by impersonation or other fraudulent device, obtained aid under this chapter or Chapter 5 of this part, he shall make restitution and all actions necessary to secure restitution may be brought against him.

It is the intent of the legislature that restitution shall be sought by request, civil action, or other suitable means prior to the bringing of a criminal action.

Welfare and Institutions Code #11265—Any person signing such certificate (i.e. a certificate applying for aid for needy children) who willfully states therein any material matter which he knows to be false is guilty of a misdemeanor.

Welfare and Institutions Code #11353—*Statement of parent's current monthly income and expenses; penalty*. Any parent in the state whose absence is the basis upon which an application is filed for aid in behalf of a child shall be required to complete a statement of his current monthly income, his total income over the past twelve months, the number of dependents for whom he is providing support, the amount he is contributing regularly toward the support of all children for whom application for aid is made under this chapter, his current monthly living expenses and such other information as is pertinent to determining his ability to support his children.

Violation of this section constitutes a misdemeanor.

Code of Civil Procedure #446—*Subscription; necessity of verification; contents of affidavit; persons who may verify; answer by state, political subdivision, etc.; verification under penalty of perjury.* Every pleading (except in justice courts when the pleadings are oral) shall be subscribed by the party or his attorney. When the state, any county thereof, city, school district, *district, public agency, or public corporation,* or any officer of the state, or of any county thereof, city, school district, *public agency, or public corporation,* in his official capacity, is plaintiff, the answer shall be verified, unless an admission of the truth of the complaint might subject the party to a criminal prosecution, or, unless a county thereof, city, school district, *district, public agency, public corporation,* or an officer of the state, or of any county, city, school district, *district, public agency, or public corporation,* in his official capacity, is defendant. Except in justice courts, when the complaint is verified, the answer shall be verified. In all cases of a verification of a pleadings, the affidavit of the party shall state that the same is true of his own knowledge, except as to the matters which are therein stated on his information, or belief and as to those matters that he believes it to be true; and where a pleading is verified, it shall be by the affidavit of a party, unless the parties are absent from the county where the attorney has his office, or from some cause unable to verify it, or the facts within the knowledge of his attorney or other person verifying the same. When the pleading is verified by the attorney, or any other person except one of the parties, he shall set forth in the affidavit the reasons why it is not made by one of the parties.

When a corporation is a party, the verification may be made by any officer thereof. When the state, any county thereof, city, school district, *district, public agency, or public corporation,* or an officer of the state, or of any county thereof, city, school district, *district, public agency, or public corporation,* in his official capacity is plaintiff, the complaint need not be verified; and if the state, any county thereof, city, school district, *district, public agency, or public corporation,* or an officer of such state, county, city, school district, *district, public agency, or public corporation,* in his official capacity is defendant, its or his answer need not be verified.

When verification is made by the attorney for the reason that the parties are absent from the county where he has his office, or from some other cause are unable to verify it, or when the verification is made on behalf of a corporation or public agency by an officer thereof, such attorney's or officer's affidavit shall state that he has read the pleading and that he is informed and believes the matters therein to be true and on that ground alleges that the matters stated therein are true; provided that in such cases the pleadings shall not otherwise be considered as an affidavit or declaration establishing the facts therein alleged.

A person verifying a pleading need not swear to the truth or his belief in the truth of the matters stated therein but may, instead, assert the truth or his belief in the truth of such matters "under penalty of perjury."

Code of Civil Procedure #2015.5—*Certification or declaration under penalty of perjury.* Whenever, under any law of this state or under any rule, regulation, order or requirement made pursuant to law, any matter is required or permitted to be supported, evidenced, established, or proved by the sworn statement, declaration, verification, certificate, oath, or affidavit, in writing of the person making the same (other than a deposition, or an oath of office, or an oath required to be taken before a specified official other than a notary public), such matter may with like force and effect be supported, evidenced, established or proved by the unsworn statement, declaration, verification, or certificate, in writing of such person stating the date and place of execution within this state and which is subscribed by him and certified or declared by him to be true "under penalty of perjury," which certification or declaration may be in substantially the following form:

I certify (or declare) under penalty of perjury that the foregoing is true and correct.

P.C. 121—*Irregularity in administering oath.* It is no defense to a prosecution for perjury that the oath was administered or taken in an irregular manner, or that the person accused of perjury did not go before, or was not in the presence of, the officer purporting to administer the oath, if such accused caused or procured such officer to certify that the oath had been taken or administered.

P.C. 123—*Witness' knowledge of materiality of his testimony not necessary.* It is no defense to a prosecution for perjury that the accused did not know the materiality of the false statement made by him; or that it did not, in fact, affect the proceeding in or from which it was made. It is sufficient that it was material, and might have been used to affect such proceeding.

P.C. 124—*Deposition, when deemed to be complete.* The making of a deposition, affidavit or certificate is deemed to be complete, within the provisions of this chapter, from the time when it is delivered by the accused to any other person, with the intent that it be uttered or published as true.

P.C. 129—*False return under oath, whether oath is taken or not.* Every person who, being required by law to make any return, statement, or report, under oath, willfully makes and delivers any such return, statement, or report, purporting to be under oath, knowing the same to be false in any particular, is guilty of perjury, whether such oath was in fact taken or not.

P.C. 128—*Procuring the execution of innocent person.* Every person who, by willful perjury or subornation of perjury, procures the conviction and execution of any innocent person, is punishable by death.

P.C. 127—*Subornation of perjury.* Every person who willfully procures another person to commit perjury is guilty of subornation of perjury, and is punishable in the same manner as he would be if personally guilty of the perjury so procured.

P.C. 1103a—*Perjury, how proved.* Perjury must be proved by the testimony of two witnesses, or of one witness and corroborating circumstances.

LEGAL DISCUSSION

A criminal defendant who testifies falsely at his trial may be subject to prosecution for perjury notwithstanding his acquittal of his first offense. There are two distinct offenses presented on different issues, and neither the defense of former jeopardy nor of collateral estoppel is available to the defendant.

The corpus delicti of perjury consists of the following:

1. Taking an oath to testify truly before a competent tribunal officer or person;
2. That the oath was administered by an officer empowered to do so within the scope of his authority to act.
3. That willfully and contrary to the oath the defendant stated a material matter which he knew to be false.

The elements of the offense are:

1. An oath before a competent tribunal or person;
2. A false statement;
3. The intent to swear falsely and knowingly;
4. Materiality of the statement;
5. Corroboration.

The oath must be administered by a competent tribunal or person in a lawful proceeding. A clerk of court may not administer an oath except in court or where otherwise authorized by statute.[1] If a court of limited jurisdiction acts beyond its jurisdiction, the oath will not suffice.[2]

The oath must be authorized or required by a valid statute, a local ordinance, or an administrative regulation or rule validly adopted pursuant to statutory or ordinance authority. If the false statement is an affidavit, certificate, or deposition, perjury is not complete until the document is issued, uttered, or published.

The intent to swear falsely imparts that the witness knew his testimony was false. Testimony given rashly and inconsiderately but according to belief will not sustain perjury.[3] Where the witness testifies to opinion rather than to fact, he is similarly bound by his belief. He can commit perjury by testifying corruptly and falsely as to what his opinion is. Thus two directly opposed, inconsistent statements will not of themselves sustain conviction of perjury.

The testimony must be material. Its materiality must be alleged and proved; materiality cannot be inferred from its admission in evidence. Defendant's lack of knowledge of the materiality of his testimony and his incompetence to testify are not defenses. If the testimony tended to influence the decision, it is immaterial whether it did in fact so influence it.

There must be corroboration. The requirement of two witnesses or of corroborating circumstances is most important. This rule has been interpreted as also requiring that one of the witnesses be a direct witness.[4]

Corroborative evidence usually takes one of two forms: (1) Defendant's testimony including his demeanor and manner of testifying and inferences drawn therefrom;[5] (2) Extra-judicial acts or declarations of defendant amounting to express or implied admissions.

In connection with the foregoing statutes, note that perjury in connection with welfare applications is a felony except in connection with "Aid to Needy Children" where the perjury is a misdemeanor.

The elements of subornation of perjury are:

1. Perjury by the witness;
2. Inducement or procurement of perjury by the suborner;
3. Knowledge or belief by the suborner that the testimony was false.

The distinction between solicitation of perjury and subornation is the act of perjury itself. One who solicits perjury becomes a suborner when the perjury is committed.

Since subornation and perjury are distinct offenses, the suborner and the perjurer are not accomplices and either can be convicted on the uncorroborated testimony of the other except that by statute there must be two witnesses to convict the perjurer.

The witness must know and believe that he testifies falsely. If he believes that he tells the truth, there can be no perjury and a fortiori no subornation. If the witness knows and believes that he testifies falsely and the suborner believes that the witness testifies truly, there is no subornation. Accordingly, both witness and suborner must know and believe that the testimony is false.

We have looked at solicitation to perjury; now we ask what is *attempted subornation* of perjury. The case law on this is unclear.[6] It would appear that solicitation lies in the preparatory stages and is punishable under specific statutes, whereas attempt lies after the crime has progressed past the preparation stage under the general statute on attempts (see P.C. 663–664 in Chapter 2).

The oath includes an affirmation and a declaration. Irregularities in the taking of the oath are generally disregarded.

ENFORCEMENT ASPECTS

In general municipal police officers do not have many occasions to investigate or arrest violators of the perjury statutes. It is, however, important that they be familiar with the law of perjury as many violations are committed but go unprosecuted.

The most difficult elements for the officer to prove are:

1. Materiality—Often the judge or jurors must be contacted to ascertain whether the subject of the perjury was considered in their deliberations, or if considered would or could have influenced same.

2. Knowingly—This precludes misbelief or misconstruing of facts with resulting false testimony from being perjury. False testimony given by one who believes it to be true is not perjury.

3. Falsity—This is usually the easiest to prove; however, one must be able to do this with two witnesses or corroborating circumstances.

Usually this type of case is handled by the district attorney's office or the grand jury. Remember that "lying" is not necessarily perjury.

DISCUSSION QUESTIONS

1. What are the elements of perjury?
2. What are the elements of subornation of perjury?
3. What is the effect of materiality on perjury?
4. Does lying on the witness stand always constitute perjury?

NOTES

[1]People v. Barry, 153 CA 2d 193; 314 P 2d 531.
[2]People v. Howard, 111 C 655; 44 P 342.
[3]People v. Von Tiedeman, 120 C 128; 52 P 155.
[4]People v. DiGiacomo, 193 CA 2d 688; 14 CR 574.
[5]People v. Agnew, 77 CA 2d 748; 176 P 2d 724.
[6]People v. Gray, 52 CA 2d 620; 127 P 2d 72.

17
Bribery

APPLICABLE STATUTES—BRIBERY

P.C. 67—*Giving or offering bribes to executive officers.* Every person who gives or offers any bribe to an executive officer in this state, with intent to influence him in respect to any act, decision, vote, opinion, or other proceeding as such officer, is punishable by imprisonment in the state prison not less than one nor more than fourteen years, and is disqualified from holding any office in this state.

P.C. 68—*Asking or receiving bribes.* Every executive or ministerial officer, employee or appointee of the state of California, county or city therein or political subdivision thereof, who asks, receives, or agrees to receive, any bribe, upon any agreement or understanding that his vote, opinion, or action upon any matter then pending, or which may be brought before him in his official capacity, shall be influenced thereby, is punishable by imprisonment in the state prison not less than one nor more than fourteen years; and, in addition thereto, forfeits his office, and is forever disqualified from holding any office in this state.

P.C. 85—*Giving or offering bribes to members of the legislature.* Every person who gives or offers to give a bribe to any member of the legisla-

229

ture, or to another person for him, or attempts by menace, deceit, suppression of truth, or any corrupt means, to influence a member in giving or withholding his vote, or in not attending the House or any committee of which he is a member, is punishable by imprisonment in the state prison not less than one nor more than ten years.

P.C. 67½—*Offering bribe to state employee.* Every person who gives or offers as a bribe to any ministerial officer, employee, or appointee of the state of California, county, or city therein or political subdivision thereof, any thing the theft of which would be petty theft is guilty of a misdemeanor; if the theft of the thing so given or offered would be grand theft the offense is a felony.

California Constitution—Article IV #35—*Bribery of legislator, etc.* A person who seeks to influence the vote or action of a member of the legislature in his legislative capacity by bribery, promise of reward, intimidation, or other dishonest means, or a member of the legislature so influenced, is guilty of a felony.

P.C. 86—*Receiving bribes by members of the legislature.* Every member of either of the Houses composing the legislature of this state who asks, receives, or agrees to receive any bribe upon any understanding that his official vote, opinion, judgement, or action shall be influenced thereby, or shall be given in any particular manner, or upon any particular side of any question or matter, upon which he may be required to act in his official capacity, or gives, or offers, or promises to give any official vote in consideration that another member of the legislature shall give any such vote, either upon the same or another question is punishable by imprisonment in the state prison not less than one nor more than fourteen years, and upon conviction thereof shall, in addition to said punishment, forfeit his office, be disfranchised, and forever disqualified from holding any office or public trust.

P.C. 165—*Bribing councilmen, supervisors, etc.* Every person who gives or offers a bribe to any member of any common council, board of supervisors, or board of trustees of any county, city and county, city, or public corporation, with intent to corruptly influence such member in his action on any matter or subject pending before, or which is afterward to be considered by, the body of which he is a member, and every member of any of the bodies mentioned in this section who receives, or offers or agrees to receive any bribe upon any understanding that his official vote, opinion, judgement, or action shall be influenced thereby, or shall be given in any particular manner or upon any particular side of any question or matter, upon which he may be required to act in his official capacity, is punishable by imprisonment in the state prison not less than one nor more than fourteen years, and upon conviction thereof shall, in addition to said punishment, forfeit his office, and forever be disfranchised and disqualified from holding any public office or trust.

P.C. 92—*Giving bribes to judges, jurors, referees, etc.* Every person who gives or offers to give a bribe to any judicial officer, juror, referee, arbitrator, or umpire, or to any person who may be authorized by law to hear or determine any question or controversy, with intent to influence his vote, opinion, or decision upon any matter or question which is or may be brought before him for decision, is punishable by imprisonment in the state prison not less than one nor more than ten years.

P.C. 93—*Receiving bribes by judicial officers, jurors, etc.* Every judicial officer, juror, referee, arbitrator, or umpire, and every person authorized by law to hear or determine any question or controversy, who asks, receives, or agrees to receive, any bribe, upon any agreement or understanding that his vote, opinion, or decision upon any matter or question which is or may be brought before him for decision, shall be influenced thereby, is punishable by imprisonment in the state prison not less than one nor more than ten years.

P.C. 137—*Bribing witnesses.* Every person who gives or offers, or promises to give, to any witness, or person about to be called as a witness, any bribe, upon any understanding or agreement that the testimony of such witness shall be thereby influenced, or who attempts by any other means fraudulently to induce any person to give false or withhold true testimony, is guilty of a felony.

P.C. 133—*Deceiving a witness.* Every person who practices any fraud or deceit, or knowingly makes or exhibits any false statement, representation, token, or writing, to any witness or person about to be called as a witness upon any trial, proceeding, inquiry, or investigation whatever, authorized by law, with intent to affect the testimony of such witness, is guilty of a misdemeanor.

P.C. 136—*Preventing or dissuading witness from attending.* Every person who willfully prevents or dissuades any person who is or may become a witness, from attending upon any trial, proceeding, or inquiry, authorized by law, is guilty of a misdemeanor.

P.C. 138—*Witness receiving bribes.* Every person who is a witness, or is about to be called as such, who receives, or offers to receive, any bribe, upon any understanding that his testimony shall be influenced thereby, or that he will absent himself from the trial or proceeding upon which his testimony is required, is guilty of a felony.

Election Code #12000—*Receipt of bribes.* A person shall not directly or through any other person receive, agree, or contract for, before or during an election, any money, gift, loan, or other valuable consideration, office, place, or employment for himself or any other person for either:

(a) Voting or agreeing to vote.

(b) Coming or agreeing to come to the polls.

(c) Refraining or agreeing to refrain from voting.

(d) Voting or agreeing to vote for any particular person.

(e) Refraining or agreeing to refrain from voting for any particular person.

Election Code #12001—*Receipt of consideration for prior action.* A person shall not directly or through any other person receive any money or other valuable thing, during or after any election, because he or any other person:

(a) Voted or refrained from voting for any particular person.

(b) Came to the polls or remained away from the polls.

(c) Induced any other person to:
(1) Vote or refrain from voting.
(2) Vote or refrain from voting for any particular person.
(3) Come to or remain away from the polls.

Election Code #12002—*Receipt of bribe for vote or aid to candidate in securing nomination or endorsement.* A person shall not directly or through any other person receive any money or other valuable thing, before, during, or after an election, because he or any other person:

(a) Voted to secure the election or endorsement of any other person as the nominee or candidate of any convention, organized assemblage of delegates, or other body representing, or claiming to represent, a political party or principle, or any club, society, or association.

(b) Aided in securing the selection or endorsement of any other person as a nominee or candidate as provided in subdivision (a).

Election Code #12003—*Payment of bribe.* A person shall not directly or through any other person pay, lend, or contribute, or offer or promise to pay, lend, or contribute, any money or other valuable consideration to or for any voter or to or for any other person:

(a) Induce the voter to:
(1) Vote or refrain from voting at any election.
(2) Vote or refrain from voting at an election for any particular person.
(3) Come to the polls at an election.
(4) Remain away from the polls at an election.

    (b)   Reward the voter for having:
        (1)   Voted.
        (2)   Refrained from voting.
        (3)   Voted for any particular person.
        (4)   Refrained from voting for any particular person.
        (5)   Come to the polls at an election.
        (6)   Remained away from the polls at an election.

Election Code #12004—*Offer or promise of employment.* A person shall not directly or through another person give, offer, or promise any office, place, or employment, or promise to procure or endeavor to procure any office, place, or employment to or for any voter, or to or for any other person, in order to induce that voter at any election to:

    (a)   Vote.
    (b)   Refrain from voting.
    (c)   Vote for any particular person.
    (d)   Refrain from voting for any particular person.

Election Code #12005—*Gift or consideration to one to procure election or vote of another.* A person shall not directly or through any other person make any gift, loan, promise, offer, procurement, or agreement to, for, or with any person, in order to induce that person to procure or endeavor to procure the election of any person or the vote of any voter at any election.

Election Code #12006—*Procuring or promising to procure election or vote of another.* A person shall not directly or through any other person procure, engage, promise, or endeavor to procure, in consequence of any gift, loan, offer, promise, procurement, or agreement, the election of any person or the vote of any voter at an election.

Election Code #12007—*Payment of money for use as bribe.* A person shall not directly or through any other person advance or pay, or cause to be paid, any money or other valuable thing to or for the use of any other person, with the intent that it, or any part thereof, shall be used in bribery at any election; or knowingly pay or cause to be paid any money or other valuable thing to any person in discharge or repayment of any money, wholly or in part, expended in bribery at any election.

Election Code #12008—*Payment of consideration to establish residence of another.* A person shall not directly or through any other person advance or pay, or cause to be paid, any money or other valuable thing to or for the use of any other person, with the intent that it, or any part thereof, will be used for boarding, lodging, or maintaining a person at any place or domicile in any election precinct, ward, or district, with intent to secure the vote of that person or to induce that person to vote for any particular person.

Election Code #12009—*Payment of money for use in evading arrest.* A person shall not directly or through any other person advance or pay, or cause to be paid, any money or other valuable thing to or for the use of any other person, with the intent that it, or any part thereof, shall be used to aid or assist any person to evade arrest, who is charged with the commission of a felony against the elective franchise.

Election Code #12010—*Payment for obtaining nomination or endorsement.* A person shall not directly or through any other person advance or pay, or cause to be paid, any money or other valuable thing to or for the use of any other person in consideration of:

(a) Being selected or indorsed as the candidate of any convention, organized assemblage of delegates, or other body representing, or claiming to represent, a political party or principle, or any club, society, or association, for a public office.

(b) The selection or indorsement of any other person as a candidate for a public office.

(c) Any member of a convention, club, society, or association having voted to select or indorse any person as a candidate for a public office.

Election Code #12011—*Payment to obtain withdrawal of candidate.* A person shall not directly or through any other person advance or pay, or cause to be paid, any money or other valuable thing to or for the use of any other person, in consideration of a person withdrawing as a candidate for a public office.

Election Code #12012—*Penalties for violation.* Every person who commits any of the offenses mentioned in this article is punishable by imprisonment in the state prison for not less than one nor more than seven years.

Election Code #29160—*Giving or receiving bribes.* Every person is punishable by imprisonment in the state prison for not less than one nor more than seven years who:

(a) Gives or offers a bribe to any officer or member of any legislative caucus, political convention, committee, or political gathering of any kind, held for the purpose of nominating candidates for offices of honor, trust, or profit in this state, with intent to influence the person to whom the bribe is given or offered to be more favorable to one candidate than another.

(b) Being a member of any of the bodies mentioned in this section receives or offers to receive any such bribe.

P.C. 337b—*Bribery of a player.* Any person who gives, or offers or promises to give, or attempts to give or offer, any money, bribe, or thing of value, to any participant or player or to any prospective participant or player in any sporting event, contest, or exhibition of any kind whatsoever, except a wrestling exhibition as defined in section 18607 of the business and professions code, and specifically including, but without being limited to such sporting events, contests, and exhibitions as baseball, football, basketball, boxing, horse racing and wrestling matches, with the intention or understanding or agreement that such participant or player or such prospective participant or player shall not use his best efforts to win such sporting event, contest, or exhibition or shall so conduct himself in such sporting event, contest or exhibition that any other player, participant or team of players or participants shall thereby be assisted or enabled to win such sporting event, contest, or exhibition, or shall so conduct himself in such sporting event, contest or exhibition as to limit his or his team's margin of victory in such sporting event, contest or exhibition is guilty of a felony, and shall be punished by imprisonment in the state prison for a period not exceeding five years, or by a fine not exceeding five thousand dollars ($5,000), or by both fine and imprisonment.

P.C. 337c—*Acceptance of bribes by players.* Any person who accepts, or attempts to accept, or offers to accept, or agrees to accept any money, bribe or thing of value, with the intention or understanding or agreement that he will not use his best efforts to win any sporting event, contest, or exhibition of any kind whatsoever, except a wrestling exhibition as defined in section 18607 of the business and professions code, and specifically including but without being limited to, such sporting events, contests or exhibitions as baseball, football, basketball, boxing, horse racing, and wrestling matches, in which he is playing or participating or is about to play or participate in, or will so conduct himself in such sporting event, contest, or exhibition that any other player or participant or team of players or participants shall thereby be assisted or enabled to win such sporting event, contest or exhibition or will so conduct himself in such sporting event, contest, or exhibition as to limit his or his team's margin of victory in such sporting event, contest, or exhibition is guilty of a felony, and shall be punished by imprisonment in the state prison for a period not exceeding five years, or by a fine not exceeding five thousand dollars ($5,000), or by both such fine and imprisonment.

P.C. 337d—*Bribery of officials.* Any person who gives or offers to give, or promises to give, or attempts to give, any money, bribe, or thing of value to any person who is umpiring, managing, directing, refereeing, supervising, judging, presiding or officiating at, or who is about to umpire, manage, direct, referee, supervise, judge, preside or officiate at any sporting event, contest or exhibition of any kind whatsoever, and specifically including but without being limited to, such sporting events, contests and exhibitions as baseball, football, boxing, horse racing and wrestling matches, with the intention or agreement or understanding that such person shall corruptly or dishonestly umpire, manage, direct, referee, supervise, judge, preside or officiate at, any such sporting event, contest, or exhibition, or the players or participants thereof, with the intention or purpose that the result of the sporting event, contest or exhibition will be affected or influenced thereby, is guilty of a felony and shall be punished by imprisonment in the state prison for a period not exceeding five years, or by a fine not exceeding five thousand dollars ($5,000), or by both such fine and imprisonment.

P.C. 337e—*Penalty for accepting bribe.* Any person who as umpire, manager, director, referee, supervisor, judge, presiding officer or official receives or agrees to receive, or attempts to receive any money, bribe or thing of value, with the understanding or agreement that such umpire, manager, director, referee, supervisor, judge, presiding officer or official shall corruptly conduct himself or shall corruptly umpire, manage, direct, referee, supervise, judge, preside, or officiate at, any sporting event, contest, or exhibition of any kind whatsoever, and specifically including but without being limited to, such sporting events, contests and exhibitions as baseball, football, boxing, horse racing and wrestling matches; or any player or participant thereof, with the intention or purpose that the result of the sporting event, contest, exhibition will be affected or influenced thereby, is guilty of a felony and shall be punished by imprisonment in the state prison for a period not exceeding five years, or by a fine not exceeding five thousand dollars ($5,000), or by both such fine and imprisonment.

P.C. 7 (6)—The word "bribe" signifies anything of value or advantage, present or prospective, or any promise or undertaking to give any, asked, given, or accepted, with a corrupt intent to influence, unlawfully, the person to whom it is given, in his action, vote, or opinion, in any public or official capacity.

P.C. 70—*Acceptance of bribe by state employee.* Every executive or ministerial officer, employee or appointee of the state of California, county or city therein or political subdivision thereof, who knowingly asks, receives or agrees to receive any emolument, gratuity, or reward, or any promise thereof excepting such as may be authorized by law for doing an official act, is guilty of a misdemeanor.

LEGAL DISCUSSION

Bribery is distinguishable from extortion in that in extortion payment is made under threat whereas in bribery payment is offered without any action by the recipient. The elements of bribery are (1) the giving or receiving of something of value; (2) with a corrupt intent to influence unlawfully the action, vote, or opinion of the person to whom the payment is given; (3) in his public capacity.

The bribe is anything of present or prospective value or any promise or understanding to give or transfer same. It is not necessary that the value be definitely ascertainable.

Normally the giving calls for delivering to the officer or his agent. Where legislators are involved, the offerer can be guilty without delivery to the legislator or even without the legislator's knowledge. The giving includes the offer. Tender or production is not required,[1] and the language of the offer need not be explicit. A sufficiently strong inference can be drawn from suggestive language.

The intent is described as a "corrupt intent to influence unlawfully." The word "corrupt" implies the creation of a pecuniary advantage to some person not necessarily the offerer.

The object of the bribe as distinguished from the intent is to influence unlawfully the recipient's action, vote or opinion. The object must be within the scope of his duties or the offerer must believe the person capable of accomplishing the desired object. If the offerer knows that the object is unattainable, there can be no intent to influence.

Because of the secrecy of the crime of bribery, the county sanctions police activity in detecting and bringing the culprit to justice which would otherwise border on entrapment.[2]

Note that separate statutes proscribe the giving and the receiving. Accordingly, the giver and the receiver are not accomplices, and, therefore, the testimony of one against the other does not require corroboration. In fact, an offerer can be punished even though the receiver rejects the offer and reports same. Conversely, a person can ask for and agree to receive a bribe even though no offer is ever made.

The solicitation statute (P.C. 653f) covers a person who solicits the offer or acceptance of a bribe.

ENFORCEMENT ASPECTS

The crime of bribery is related specifically to an act with a specific intent to corruptly influence. The act may be one of giving, asking, or receiving.

There are a number of bribery statutes applicable to various categories of persons, so it is important to study all the facts and choose the appropriate statute.

The identification of the act should be considered next: determine whether it is an offer, a request (solicitation), or an acceptance; identify the parties making the offer (suspects) and the parties who are being approached (victims); and ascertain if the parties are any of those subject to a bribery by a particular code section.

It is extremely important in bribery investigations to secure ample corroboration. Accordingly, all witnesses to representations, payoffs, etc., must be located, identified, and interviewed.

The object or goal of the bribe is also an important investigative area. Is the bribe offered for performance of an official act or for its nonperformance, etc.? The subject of the bribe is important and is defined under P.C. 7(6).

DISCUSSION QUESTIONS

1. Define bribery.
2. List five categories of persons for which there are specific applicable bribery statutes.
3. What is meant by "corruptly influencing"?
4. Under the bookmaking sections P.C. 337 who are the persons who are subject to bribery?

NOTES

[1]People v. Ahfook, 62 C 493.
[2]People v. Bunkers, 2 CA 197; 84 P 364;
  People v. Finkelstein, 98 CA 2d 545; 220 P 2d 934.

18

Escape
and Rescue

APPLICABLE STATUTES—ESCAPE

P.C. 4530—*Escape from state prison.* (a) Every prisoner confined in a state prison who, by force or violence, escapes or attempts to escape therefrom and every prisoner committed to a state prison who, by force or violence, escapes or attempts to escape while being conveyed to or from such prison or any other state prison, or any prison road camp, prison forestry camp, or other prison camp or prison farm or any other place while under the custody of prison officials, officers or employees; or who, by force or violence, escapes or attempts to escape from any prison road camp, prison forestry camp, or other prison camp or prison farm or other place while under the custody of prison officials, officers or employees; or who, by force or violence, escapes or attempts to escape while at work outside or away from prison under custody of prison officials, officers, or employees, is punishable by imprisonment in a state prison for a term of not less than one year. The second term of imprisonment of a person convicted under this subdivision shall commence from the time he would otherwise have been discharged from said prison. No additional probation report shall be required with respect to such offense.

(b)   Every prisoner who commits an escape or attempts an escape as described in subdivision (a) without force or violence, is punishable by imprisonment in the state prison for a term of not less than six months nor more than five years. No additional probation report shall be required with respect to such offense.

P.C. 2042—*Escape from vocational institution.* Every person confined in any vocational institution under the control of the Youth Authority who escapes or attempts to escape therefrom is guilty of a crime and shall be imprisoned in a state prison for not exceeding five years or in the county jail for not exceeding one year.

P.C. 4532—*Escape, or attempted escape, from jail, prison, road camp industrial farm.* (a) Every prisoner arrested and booked for, charged with or convicted of a misdemeanor and every person committed under the terms of sections 5654, 5656, or 5677 of the Welfare and Institutions Code as an inebriate who is confined to any county or city jail or prison or industrial farm or industrial road camp or who is engaged on any county road or other county work or who is in the lawful custody of any officer or person, or who is employed or authorized to secure employment away from the place of confinement, pursuant to the work furlough rehabilitation law (section 1208), and who thereafter escapes or attempts to escape from such county or city jail, prison, industrial farm or industrial road camp or from the custody of the officer or person in charge of him while engaged on or going to or returning from such county work or from the custody of any officer or person in whose lawful custody he is, is guilty of a felony and, if such escape or attempt to escape was not by force or violence, is punishable by imprisonment in the state prison for not exceeding one year and one day, regardless of any prior convictions, or in the county jail not exceeding one year; provided, however, that if such escape or attempt to escape is by force or violence, such person is guilty of a felony and is punishable by imprisonment in the state prison not exceeding 10 years, or in the county jail not exceeding one year; provided, that when said second term of imprisonment is to be served in the county jail it shall commence from the time such prisoner would otherwise have been discharged from said jail.

The willful failure of a prisoner employed or authorized to secure employment pursuant to the work furlough rehabilitation law (section 1208) to return to the place of confinement not later than the expiration of a period during which, pursuant to that law, he is authorized to be away from such place of confinement, is an escape from such place of confinement punishable as provided in this subdivision.

A conviction of violation of this subdivision, not by force or violence, shall not be charged as a prior felony conviction in any subsequent prosecution for a public offense.

(b)   Every prisoner arrested and booked for, charged with or convicted of a felony who is confined in any county or city jail or prison or industrial farm or industrial road camp or who is engaged on any county road or other county work or who is in the lawful custody of any officer or person, who escapes or attempts to escape from such county or city jail, prison, industrial farm or industrial road camp or from the custody of the officer or person in charge of him while engaged on or going to or returning from such county work or from the custody of any officer or person in whose lawful custody he is, is guilty of a felony and, if such escape or attempt to escape was not by force or violence, is punishable by imprisonment in the state prison for not less than six months or more than five years or in the county jail not exceeding one year, provided, that if such escape or attempt to escape is by force or violence, such person is guilty of a felony and is punishable by imprisonment in the state prison not exceeding 10 years, or in the county jail not exceeding one year; provided, that when said second term of imprisonment is to be served in the county jail it shall commence from the time such prisoner would otherwise have been discharged from said jail.

P.C. 4600—*Destruction of, or injury to, jail; felony.* Every person who willfully and intentionally breaks down, pulls down, or otherwise destroys or injures any jail or prison, is punishable by fine not exceeding ten thousand dollars ($10,000), and by imprisonment in the state prison not exceeding five years, except that where the damage or injury to any city, city and county or county jail property is determined to be two hundred dollars ($200) or less, he is guilty of a misdemeanor.

P.C. 107—*Punishment for escape.* Every prisoner charged with or convicted of a felony who is an inmate of any public training school or reformatory or county hospital who escapes or attempts to escape from such public training school or reformatory or county hospital is guilty of a felony and is punishable by imprisonment in the state prison not exceeding ten years, or by a fine not exceeding ten thousand dollars ($10,000), or by both such fine and imprisonment.

P.C. 4011.5—*Removal of prisoner to hospital.* Whenever it appears to a sheriff or jailer that a prisoner in a county jail or a city jail under his charge is in need of immediate medical or hospital care, and that the health and welfare of the prisoner will be injuriously affected unless he is forthwith removed to a hospital, the sheriff or jailer may authorize the immediate removal of the prisoner under guard to a hospital, without first obtaining a court order as provided in section 4011. In any such case, however, if the condition of the prisoner prevents his return to the jail within 48 hours from the time of his removal, the sheriff or jailer shall apply to a judge of the superior court for an order authorizing the continued absence of the prisoner from the jail in the manner provided in section 4011. The provisions of section 4011 governing the cost of medical and hospital care of prisoners and the liability therefor, shall apply to the cost of, and the liability for, medical or hospital care of prisoners removed from jail pursuant to this section.

P.C. 3064—*Deemed fugitive.* From and after the suspension or revocation of the parole of any prisoner and until his return to custody he shall be deemed an escapee and fugitive from justice and no part of the time during which he is an escapee and fugitive from justice shall be part of his term.

P.C. 3080—*Parolee leaving county without permission.* If any paroled prisoner leaves the county in which he is imprisoned without permission from the board granting his parole, he shall be arrested as an escaped prisoner and held as such.

Welfare and Institutions Code 1768.7—*Escape; misdemeanor.* Any person committed to the youth authority who escapes or attempts to escape from the institution or county in which he is confined is guilty of a misdemeanor.

Welfare and Institutions Code 6330—*Escape or attempt, punishment.* Every person ordered placed in a county facility or state hospital temporarily for observation pursuant to this article or committed for an indeterminate period to a state hospital or state institution as a mentally disordered sex offender, who escapes or attempts to escape therefrom, or who escapes or attempts to escape while being conveyed to or from such county facility, state hospital or state institution, is punishable by imprisonment in the state prison not to exceed five years or in the county jail not to exceed one year.

LEGAL DISCUSSION

Escape is the unauthorized departure of a person from legal custody. California law has no general statute covering escape but has several specific statutes governing the crime and prosecution. The elements of the crime are (1) lawful custody and (2) unauthorized departure.

Lawful custody does not exist where the confinement is wholly without legal authority as under false imprisonment. Escape from such custody is not a crime.[1] Where there is a mere defect in arrest, charge or trial which could be raised on appeal or habeas corpus, a person must seek release by legal means. He has no right to escape.[2]

To be unauthorized, departure need be only a few feet from the limits of confinement or for only a few moments. But if the prisoner thinks he is leaving the limits of confinement with the permission of his jailer, the required intent is negated and there is no unauthorized departure.

The departure can be from reasonable work limits by a parolee or trusty or from a hospital as above.

APPLICABLE STATUTES—RESCUE

P.C. 4550—*Attempting to or aiding rescue; punishment.* Every person who rescues or attempts to rescue, or aids another person in rescuing or attempting to rescue, any prisoner from any prison, or prison road camp, or any jail or county road camp, or from any officer or person having him in lawful custody, is punishable as follows:

1. If such prisoner was in custody upon a conviction of a felony punishable with death: by imprisonment in the state prison not less than one nor more than 14 years;
2. If such prisoner was in custody otherwise than as specified in subsection 1 hereof: by imprisonment in the state prison not to exceed five years, or by imprisonment in the county jail not to exceed one year.

P.C. 4533—*Officer assisting prisoner to escape.* Every keeper of a prison, sheriff, deputy sheriff, constable, or jailor, or person employed as a guard, who fraudulently contrives, procures, aids, connives at, or voluntarily permits the escape of any prisoner in custody, is punishable by imprisonment in the state prison not exceeding 10 years, and fine not exceeding ten thousand dollars ($10,000).

P.C. 4534—*Aiders and abettors, punishment.* Any person who willfully assists any paroled prisoner whose parole has been revoked, any escape, any prisoner confined in any prison or jail, or any person in the lawful custody of any officer or person, to escape, or in an attempt to escape from such prison, or jail, or custody, is punishable as provided in section 4533 of the Penal Code.

P.C. 4004—*Committed persons to be actually confined.* A prisoner committed to the county jail for examination, or upon conviction for a public offense, must be actually confined in the jail until he is legally discharged; and if he is permitted to go at large out of the jail, except by virtue of a legal order or process, it is an escape; provided, however, that during the pendency of a criminal proceeding, the superior court or any inferior court, as the case may be, before which said proceeding is pending may make a legal order, good cause appearing therefor, for the removal of the prisoner from the county jail in custody of the sheriff: and provided further, that the superior court of the county may make a legal order, good cause appearing therefor, for the removal of prisoners confined in the county jail, after conviction, in the custody of the sheriff.

P.C. 109—*Assisting prisoners to escape.* Any person who willfully assists any inmate of any public training school or reformatory to escape, or in an attempt to escape from such public training school or reformatory is punishable by imprisonment in the state prison not exceeding 10 years, and fine not exceeding ten thousand dollars ($10,000).

Welfare and Institutions Code 7325—*Arrest of escaped mental patients; peace officer.* When any judicially committed patient has escaped from any state hospital or from any hospital or facility operated by or under the Veterans' Administration of the United States Government, or when a judicially committed patient's return from leave of absence has been authorized or ordered by the department of mental hygiene or the facility of the veterans' administration, any peace officer, upon written request of a state hospital or veterans' facility, shall without the necessity of a warrant or court order, or any officer or employee of the department of mental hygiene designated to perform such duties may, apprehend, take into custody and deliver him to a state hospital or to a facility of the veterans' administration, or to any person or place authorized by the department of mental hygiene, or by the veterans' administration, as the case may be, to receive him. Every officer or employee of the department designated to apprehend or return such patients shall have the powers and privileges of peace officers so far as necessary to enforce the provisions of this section.

As used in this section "any peace officer" means any sheriff, undersheriff, deputy sheriff, constable of a township, chief of police or policeman of a city or town, who is regularly employed and paid as such by a county, township, city or town.

Welfare and Institutions Code 7326—*Assisting escape; offense.* Any person who willfully assists any judicially committed patient of a state hospital to escape, or to attempt to escape therefrom or to resist being returned from a leave of absence, is guilty of a misdemeanor.

P.C. 110—*Carrying things into training school to aid in escape.* Every person who carries or sends into a public training school, or reformatory, anything useful to aid a prisoner or inmate in making his escape, with intent thereby to facilitate the escape of any prisoner or inmate confined therein, is guilty of a felony and shall be imprisoned in the state prison not less than one year.

P.C. 4574—*Bringing firearms, deadly weapons or explosives into prison.* Except when otherwise authorized by law, or when authorized by the person in charge of the prison or other institution referred to in this section or by an officer of the institution empowered by the person in charge of the institution to give such authorization, any person, who knowingly brings or sends into, or knowingly assists in bringing into, or sending into, any state prison or prison road camp or prison farm or any other place where prisoners of the state prison are located under the custody of prison officials, officers or employees, or any jail or any county road camp in this state, or within the grounds belonging or adjacent to any such institution, any firearms, deadly weapons or explosives, and any person who, while lawfully confined in a jail or county road camp possesses therein any firearms, deadly weapon, or explosive, is guilty of a felony and punishable by imprisonment in the state prison for not less than one year.

ENFORCEMENT ASPECTS

Most of the sections relate to actual escape from correctional institutions. The police officer is more concerned with the field arrest and consequent escape. The crime of escape states that the suspect must be *formally charged* or *booked*. To be formally charged, the defendant would have been brought before the court for arraignment, plea, or setting of bail prior to being chargeable with escape. This is very rare. The booking process usually takes place in a custodial setting; i.e., county or city jail. If the suspect escapes from jail, we undoubtedly have the crime of escape. The booking process may not have been completed, but as long as it has been started an escape becomes chargeable.

In the field when an officer takes a person into custody, he may be handcuffed and placed in the patrol unit. If this prisoner flees and he was arrested as a misdemeanant, no felony crime of escape is being committed; hence, deadly force could never be justified. The most serious added crime being committed at this point might be petty theft—handcuffs.

A few police agencies are starting to use a field booking process. If a field booking had actually started, it is possible that an escape at this point could amount to the crime of escape. There is little case law in point and too few agencies using field booking to be able to be specific in this area, but it is worth mentioning.

APPLICABLE STATUTES

P.C. 405a—*Lynching*. The taking by means of a riot of any person from the lawful custody of any peace officer is a lynching.

P.C. 405b—*Punishment*. Every person who participates in any lynching is punishable by imprisonment in the state prison for not more than twenty years.

P.C. 150—*Posse comitatus.* Every male person above eighteen years of age who neglects or refuses to join the posse comitatus or power of the county, by neglecting or refusing to aid and assist in taking or arresting any person against whom there may be issued any process, or by neglecting to aid and assist in retaking any person who, after being arrested or confined, may have escaped from such arrest or imprisonment, or by neglecting or refusing to aid and assist in preventing any breach of the peace, or the commission of any criminal offense, being thereto lawfully required by any uniformed peace officer or by any judge, is punishable by fine of not less than fifty dollars ($50) nor more than one thousand dollars ($1,000).

LEGAL DISCUSSION

It should be noted that in P.C. section 405a the elements are:

1. the taking of a person in custody
2. from the lawful custody of a peace officer, and
3. by means of riot, which in turn requires two or more persons threatening force with the ability to perform and admit to disturbance of the peace.

The posse comitatus section does not apply to females. It does, however, include every male person over the age of 18. There is no requirement for citizenship, hence a foreigner would be subject to the statute.

ENFORCEMENT ASPECTS

The felonious crime of lynching is encountered by law officers with increasing frequency. The riots in Watts and other areas have all seen violations of this section.

The posse comitatus section requires males over eighteen to aid officers. The Good Samaritan Law (P.C. 13600 et seq.) permits reimbursement of a person other than a peace officer who sustains injury or damage as a direct consequence of preventing the commission of a crime against the person or property of another, or of apprehending a criminal or of materially assisting a peace officer in the prevention of a crime or apprehension of a criminal. The private citizen or law enforcement agency acting on such person's behalf may file a claim with the State Board of Control for indemnification for such injury or damage; the claim must be accompanied by a corroborating statement and recommendation from the appropriate state or local law enforcement agency.

DISCUSSION QUESTIONS

1. Would a suspect serving time for a felony who attempts to escape from a reformatory or public training school be guilty of a felony or a misdemeanor?
2. What are the elements of the crime of escape?
3. Explain rescue.
4. Is it a misdemeanor or a felony to bring firearms into a jail?
5. What are the elements of the crime of lynching?
6. Is it a misdemeanor for a twenty-two-year-old girl to refuse to aid a policeman when such aid is requested?

NOTES

[1]People v. Ahtung, 92 C 425, 28 P 577;
 People v. Clark, 69 CA 520, 231 P 590.
[2]People v. Ganger, 97 CA 211, 217 P 241.

19

Deadly Weapons Control Law

APPLICABLE STATUTES—DEADLY WEAPONS

P.C. 12000—This chapter shall be known and may be cited as "the dangerous weapons control law."

P.C. 12001—*Pistol; revolver; firearm capable of being concealed upon the person.* "Pistol," "revolver," and "firearm capable of being concealed upon the person," as used in this chapter apply to and include any device, designed to be used as a weapon, from which is expelled a projectile by the force of any explosion, or other form of combustion, and which has a barrel less than 12 inches in length.

P.C. 12001.5—*Chapter as not authorizing manufacture, importation, possession, etc., of sawed-off shotguns.* Limitation on what may be construed. Nothing in this chapter shall be construed as authorizing the manufacture, importation into the state, keeping for sale, offering for sale, or giving, lending, or possession of any sawed-off shotgun, as defined in section 12020.

P.C. 12002—*Exceptions.* Nothing in this chapter prohibits police officers, special police officers, peace officers, or law enforcement officers from carrying any wooden club, baton, or any equipment authorized for the enforcement of law or ordinance in any city or county.

P.C. 12020—*Manufacture, sale, possession of certain weapons prohibited.* Any person in this state who manufactures or causes to be manufactured, imports into this state, keeps for sale, or offers or exposes for sale, or who gives, lends or possesses any instrument or weapon of the kind commonly known as a blackjack, slung shot, sandclub, sandbag, sawed-off shotgun, or metal knuckles, or who carries concealed upon his person any explosive substance, other than fixed ammunition or who carries concealed upon his person any dirk or dagger, is guilty of a felony, and upon conviction shall be punishable by imprisonment in the county jail not exceeding one year or in a state prison for not less than one year nor more than five years.

As used in this section a "sawed-off shotgun" means a shotgun having a barrel or barrels of less than 18 inches in length, or a rifle having a barrel or barrels of less than 16 inches in length, or any weapon made from a rifle or shotgun (whether by alteration, modification, or otherwise) if such weapon as modified has an overall length of less than 26 inches.

P.C. 12021—*Aliens, narcotic addicts, forbidden possession of firearms.* Any person who is not a citizen of the United States and any person who has been convicted of a felony under the laws of the United States, of the state of California, or any other state, government, or country, or who is addicted to the use of any narcotic drug, who owns or has in his possession or under his custody or control any pistol, revolver, or other firearm capable of being concealed upon the person is guilty of a public offense, and shall be punishable by imprisonment in the state prison not exceeding 15 years, or in a county jail not exceeding one year or by a fine not exceeding five hundred dollars ($500), or by both.

P.C. 12021.5—*Possession of concealed firearm by minor.* A minor may not possess a concealable firearm unless he has the written permission of his parent or guardian to have such firearm or is accompanied by his parent or guardian while he has such firearm in his possession.

P.C. 12022—*Concealed weapons.* Provides for additional sentences to be imposed where a defendant is convicted of committing or attempting to commit any felony while armed with any of the deadly weapons described in subdivision (f) of Section 3024, (blackjack, sling shot, billy . . . . pistol, revolver, or any other firearm . . .).

P.C. 12023—*Prima facie evidence.* In the trial of a person charged with committing or attempting to commit a felony against the person of another while armed with any of the weapons mentioned in section 12020, or while armed with any pistol, revolver, or other firearm capable of being concealed upon the person, without having a license or permit to carry such firearm as provided by this chapter, the fact that he was so armed shall be prima facie evidence of his intent to commit the felony if such weapon was used in the commission of the offense.

P.C. 12025—*Carrying certain firearms without a license.* Except as otherwise provided in this chapter, any person who carries concealed upon his person or concealed within any vehicle which is under his control or direction any pistol, revolver, or other firearm capable of being concealed upon the person without having a license to carry such firearm as provided in this chapter is guilty of a misdemeanor, and if he has been convicted previously of any felony or of any crime made punishable by this chapter, is guilty of a felony.

Firearms carried openly in belt holsters are not concealed within the meaning of this section, nor are knives which are carried openly in sheaths suspended from the waist of the wearer.

P.C. 12026—*Exceptions.* Section 12025 shall not be construed to prohibit any citizen of the United States over the age of 18 years who resides or is temporarily within this state, and who is not within the excepted classes prescribed by section 12021, from owning, possessing, or keeping within his place of residence or place of business any pistol, revolver, or other firearm capable of being concealed upon the person, and no permit or license to purchase, own, possess, or keep any such firearm at his place of residence or place of business shall be required of him.

P.C. 12027—*Sheriffs, constables, policemen, etc.* Section 12025 does not apply to or affect any of the following:

(a)   Peace officers listed in section 830.1 or 830.2, whether active or honorably retired, other duly appointed peace officers, full-time paid peace officers of other states and the federal government who are carrying out official duties while in California, or any person summoned by any such officers to assist in making arrests or preserving the peace while he is actually engaged in assisting such officer.

(b)   The possession or transportation by any merchant of unloaded firearms as merchandise.

(c)   Members of the Army, Navy, or Marine Corps of the United States, or the National Guard, when on duty, or organizations which are by law authorized to purchase or receive such weapons from the United States or this state.

(d)   Duly authorized military or civil organizations while parading, or the members thereof when going to and from the places of meeting of their respective organizations.

(e) Guards or messengers of common carriers, banks, and other financial institutions while actually employed in and about the shipment, transportation, or delivery of any money, treasure, bullion, bonds or other thing of value within this state.

(f) Members of any club or organization organized for the purpose of practicing shooting at targets upon established target ranges, whether public or private, while such members are using any of the firearms referred to in this chapter upon such target ranges, or while going to and from such ranges.

(g) Licensed hunters or fishermen while engaged in hunting or fishing, or while going to or returning from such hunting or fishing expedition.

(h) Members of any club or organization organized for the purpose of collecting and displaying antique or historical pistols, revolvers or other firearms, while such members are displaying such weapons at meetings of such clubs or organizations or while going to and from such meetings, or individuals who collect such firearms not designed to fire, or incapable of firing fixed cartridges or fixed shot shells, or other firearms of obsolete ignition type for which ammunition is not readily available and which are generally recognized as collector's items, provided such firearm is kept in the trunk. If the vehicle is not equipped with a trunk, such firearm shall be kept in a locked container in an area of the vehicle other than the utility or glove compartment.

P.C. 12028—*Destruction of weapons as nuisances.* (a) The unlawful concealed carrying upon the person or within the vehicle of the carrier of any of the weapons mentioned in section 653k, 12020, or 12025 is a nuisance.

(b) A firearm of any nature used in the commission of a felony, or any attempt to commit a felony, is, upon a conviction of the defendant, a nuisance.

(c) Whenever a felony charge is reduced to a misdemeanor charge and a conviction is obtained based upon the unlawful use of a firearm, the weapon is a nuisance and shall be subject to destruction as provided in this section.

(d) Any weapon described in subdivision (a), or, upon conviction of defendant, any weapon described in subdivision (b), shall be surrendered to the magistrate before whom the person is taken, except that in any city or county the weapons shall be surrendered to the head of the police or sheriff's department. The officers to whom the weapons are surrendered, except upon the certificate of a judge of a court of record, or of the district attorney of the county, that the preservation thereof is necessary or proper to the ends of justice, shall annually, between the 1st and 10th days of July, in each year, destroy the weapons or cause them to be destroyed to such extent that they shall be wholly and entirely ineffective and useless for the purpose for which they were manufactured. If any weapon has been stolen and is thereafter recovered from the thief or his transferee, it shall not be destroyed but shall be restored to the lawful owner, as soon as its use as evidence has been served, upon his identification of the weapon and proof of ownership.

P.C. 12031—*Carrying of loaded firearms misdemeanor; exceptions.* (a) Except as provided in subdivision (b), every person who carries a loaded firearm on his person or in a vehicle while in any public place or on any public street in an incorporated city or in any public place or on any public street in a prohibited area of unincorporated territory is guilty of a misdemeanor.

(b)   Subdivision (a) shall not apply to any of following:

(1) Peace officers listed in Section 830.1 or 830.2, or sub-division (a) of Section 830.3, whether active or honorably retired, other duly appointed peace officers, full-time paid peace officers of other states who are carrying out official duties while in California, or any person summoned by any such officers to assist in making arrests or preserving the peace who reasonably believes that it is or will be necessary to make or attempt to make a lawful arrest and that the carrying of a loaded firearm is necessary to make such arrest in assisting such officer, or full-time paid peace officers of the federal government, whether on active duty or honorably retired.

(2) Guards or messengers of common carriers, banks, and other financial institutions while actually employed in and about the shipment, transportation, or delivery of any money, treasure, bullion, bonds, or other thing of value within this state, or while traveling by means of a reasonably direct and uninterrupted route between their respective places of work and their homes.

(3) Members of the military forces of this state or of the United States engaged in the performance of their duties.

(4) Persons who are using target ranges for the purpose of practice shooting with a firearm, or who are members of shooting clubs while hunting on the premises of such clubs.

(5) Patrol special police officers appointed by the police commission of any city, county, or city and county under the express terms of its charter who also under the express terms of the charter (i) are subject to suspension or dismissal after a hearing on charges duly filed with the commission after a fair and impartial trial, (ii) must possess physical qualifications prescribed by the commission, and (iii) are designated by the police commission as the owners of a certain beat or territory as may be fixed from time to time by the police commission.

(6) The carrying of weapons, not otherwise prohibited by law, by persons who are authorized to carry such weapons pursuant to Article 3 (commencing with Section 12050) of Chapter 1 of Title 2 of Part 4 of the Penal Code.

(7) Private investigators, private patrol operators, building guards or night watchmen, and operators of a private patrol service who are

licensed or employed by persons licensed pursuant to Chapter 11 (commencing with Section 7500) of Division 3 of the Business and Professions Code, while acting within the course and scope of their employment, or while traveling by means of a reasonably direct and uninterrupted route between their respective places of work and their homes.

(8) The carrying of weapons by persons who are authorized to carry such weapons pursuant to Section 607f of the Civil Code, while actually engaged in the performance of their duties pursuant to such section.

(9) Harbor policemen designated pursuant to Section 663.5 of the Harbors and Navigation Code.

(10) Building guards or night watchmen employed by any public agency, while acting within the scope and in the course of their employment.

(c)   In order to determine whether or not a firearm is loaded for the purpose of enforcing this section, peace officers are authorized to examine any firearm carried by anyone on his person or in a vehicle while in any public place or on any public street in an incorporated city or prohibited, area of an unincorporated territory. Refusal to allow a peace officer to inspect a firearm pursuant to the provisions of this section is a misdemeanor.

(d)   As used in this section "prohibited area" means any place where it is unlawful to discharge a weapon.

(e)   A firearm shall be deemed to be loaded for the purposes of this section when there is an unexpended cartridge or shell, consisting of a case which holds a charge of powder and a bullet or shot, in, or attached in any manner to, the firearm, including, but not limited to, in the firing chamber, magazine, or clip thereof attached to the firearm; except that a muzzleloader firearm shall be deemed to be loaded when it is capped or primed and has a powder charge and ball or shot in the barrel or cylinder. The mere presence in a vehicle of a firearm and unexpended ammunition capable of being discharged from such firearm, without such ammunition being in, or attached in any manner to, the firearm, shall not be enough to consider a firearm to be loaded.

(f)   Nothing in this section shall prevent any person engaged in any lawful business, including a nonprofit organization, or any officer, employee, or agent authorized by such person for lawful purposes connected with such business, from having a loaded firearm within such person's place of business, or any person in lawful possession of private property from having a loaded firearm on such property.

(g)   Nothing in this section shall prevent any person from carrying a loaded firearm in an area within an incorporated city while engaged in hunting, during such time and in such area as the hunting is not prohibited by the city council.

(h)   Nothing in this section is intended to preclude the carrying of any loaded firearm, under circumstances where it would otherwise be lawful, by a person who reasonably believes that the person or property of himself or another, at a particular time or place, is or will be in immediate danger and that the carrying of such weapon is presently necessary for the preservation of such person or property.

(i) Nothing in this section is intended to preclude the carrying of a loaded firearm by any person who (1) is engaged in the act of making or attempting to make a lawful arrest, or (2) reasonably believes that it is or will be necessary to make or attempt to make a lawful arrest and that the carrying of such weapon is presently necessary to make such arrest.

(j) Nothing in this section shall prevent any person from having a loaded weapon, if it is otherwise lawful, at his place of residence, including any temporary residence or campsite.

P.C. 12302—Nothing in this chapter shall prohibit the sale to, purchase by, possession of, or use of destructive devices by:

(a) Any peace officer listed in Section 830.1 or 830.2, or any peace officer in the Department of Justice authorized by the Attorney General, while on duty and acting within the scope and course of his employment.

(b) Any member of the Army, Navy, Air Force, or Marine Corps of the United States, or the National Guard, while on duty and acting within the scope and course of his employment.

Nothing in this chapter shall prohibit the sale to, purchase by, possession by, or use by any person who is regularly employed and paid officer, employee or member of a fire department or fire protection or firefighting agency of the federal government, the State of California, a city, county, city and county, district, or other public or municipal corporation or political subdivision of this state, while on duty and acting within the scope and course of his employment, of any equipment used by such department or agency in the course of fire suppression.

P.C. 12501—Nothing in this chapter shall prohibit any peace officer listed in Section 830.1, or the military or naval forces of this state or of the United States from possessing silencers for official use in the discharge of their duties.

P.C. 3024f—*The words "deadly weapon" as used in this section are hereby defined to include* any instrument or weapon of the kind commonly known as a blackjack, slung shot, billy, sandclub, sandbag, metal knuckles, any dirk, dagger, pistol, revolver, or any other firearm, any knife having a blade longer than five inches, any razor with an unguarded blade and any metal pipe or bar used or intended to be used as a club.

LEGAL DISCUSSION

The Constitutional guarantee to bear arms is most important to Americans. This long-prevailing right has been affected by state and national legislation. In New York the Sullivan Gun Control Law completely prohibits citizens from bearing certain firearms. In California the Deadly Weapons Act was passed in 1923. In 1947 the name was changed to the Dangerous Weapons Control Law and its provisions were added to the Penal Code in 1953.

The basic philosophy is to lessen the danger to the public from acts of violence which arise because of easy access to firearms and dangerous weapons. It is hoped that the law will deter the possession and use of weapons and instruments used primarily for criminal purposes.

The act has been held not to violate Article I, Section 21 of the United States Constitution.[1] The second amendment states: "A well regulated militia, being necessary to the security of a free State, the right of the people to keep and bear arms, shall not be infringed." Actually, this does not grant citizens the right to bear arms but states that the right shall not be infringed upon. The individual states may legislate their own restrictions and regulations.[2] Local ordinances, of course, are usually invalid owing to state preemption.

The terms "pistol" and "revolver" as well as other firearms are defined as having a barrel length of less than 12 inches. A *shotgun* whose barrel length is less than 18 inches or whose overall length is less than 26 inches is a violation.

Altered rifles are also regulated. Any rifle whose overall length is less than 26 inches or whose barrel length is less than 16 inches is illegal.

A *blackjack* is a small club or bludgeon usually weighted at one end with an elastic shaft. It is frequently covered with leather or other material, but this is not a necessary element.[3]

A *slungshot* is a hard mass such as stone, metal, etc., on the end of a strap, wire or rope. This mass is "slung" around in much the same way as the knights of old used the mace.

A *billy* is a club or bludgeon. It differs from the blackjack as it usually has a tapering stiff shaft. This could be a cue stick, tire iron, pipe or other similar item.

A *sandbag* or *sandclub* is any bag or container filled with sand and used as a mace. A sock filled with sand is a violation, but a suspect, approached by an officer, need only grab the toe and empty the sand. The net result is a dirty sock, making prosecution difficult under this section.[4]

A *dirk* is a type of *dagger* usually honed on both sides. Both instruments are commonly used for stabbing. A stiletto is a dagger, but an ice pick would not qualify as such. All are fixed bladed instruments.

Metal knuckles are a device used over the hand, usually of metal or hard substance. A common name is "brass knuckles."

An *explosive substance*, which it is felonious to carry concealed, is anything that is capable of being exploded. Fixed ammunition is an exception. Nitroglycerin, dynamite, primer cord, and hand grenades are common examples of the violation.

Note the term "concealed"; the weapon must actually be hidden. A gun in a holster strapped on to a person's waist in plain view is legal. A jacket that still shows the holster or gun handle does not violate the section. A fishing knife in a holster would be judged similarly.

ENFORCEMENT ASPECTS

Police officers who thoroughly understand and apply the provisions of P.C. 12021 oftentimes will conduct a lawful search of a premises which will reveal a firearm. If the suspect who resides on the premises is an ex-convict, narcotic addict, or alien, a felony has been committed. This is so even if the weapon belongs to the suspect's wife or to some other occupant of the premises. No firearm is permitted to be within the custody or control of a person in any one of the classifications enumerated in the section.

The definition of alien is clear-cut: any person who is not a United States citizen. Frequently, officers are prone to treat with friendliness certain foreigners—e.g., Canadians, Mexicans, Cubans—and not specifically categorize them as aliens. While this is an understandable outgrowth of daily contacts, any such discriminatory treatment is legally a violation.

APPLICABLE STATUTES

P.C. 12050—*License to carry firearms*. The sheriff of a county, and the Board of Police Commissioners, Chief of Police, City Marshal, Town Marshal, or other head of the Police Department of any city or county, upon proof that the person applying is of good moral character, and that good cause exists for the issuance may issue to such person a license to carry concealed a pistol, revolver, or other firearm for a period of one year from the date of the license.

P.C. 12072—*Restrictions on transfer of certain firearms; misdemeanor*. No person, corporation or dealer shall sell, deliver, or otherwise transfer any pistol, revolver, or other firearm capable of being concealed upon the person to any person whom he has cause to believe to be within any of the classes prohibited by Section 12021 from owning or possessing such firearms, nor to any minor under the age of 18 years. In no event shall any such firearm be delivered to the purchaser within 5 days of the application for the purchase thereof, and when delivered such firearm shall be securely wrapped and shall be unloaded. Where neither party to the transaction holds a dealer's license, no person shall sell or otherwise transfer any such firearm to any other person within this state who is not personally known to the vendor. Any violation of the provisions of this section is a misdemeanor.

P.C. 12200—*Machinegun; definition.* The term "machinegun" as used in this chapter means any weapon which shoots, or is designed to shoot, automatically, more than one shot, without manual reloading, by a single function of the trigger, and includes any frame or receiver which can only be used with such weapon.

P.C. 12251—*Possession of machinegun as constituting nuisance: surrender and destruction of weapon.* It shall be a public nuisance to possess any machinegun in violation of this chapter and the attorney general, any district attorney or any city attorney may bring an action before the Superior court to enjoin the possession of any such machinegun.

Any such machinegun found to be in violation of this chapter shall be surrendered to the Bureau of Criminal Identification and Investigation, and the bureau shall destroy such machinegun so as to render it unusable and unrepairable as a machinegun, except upon the filing of a certificate with the bureau by a judge or district attorney stating that the preservation of such machinegun is necessary to serve the ends of justice.

P.C. 12301—*Destructive device.* The term "destructive device," as used in this chapter, shall include the following weapons:

(1) Any projectile containing any explosive or incendiary material or any other chemical substance;

(2) Any bomb, grenade, missile, or similar device or any launching device therefor;

(3) Any weapon of a caliber greater than .60 caliber which fires fixed ammunition, or any ammunition therefor, other than a shotgun or shotgun ammunition.

(4) Any rocket, rocket-propelled projectile, or similar device of a diameter greater than .60 inch, or any launching device therefor, and any rocket, rocket-propelled projectile, or similar device containing any explosive or incendiary material or any other chemical substance, other than the propellant for such device, except such devices as are designed primarily for emergency or distress signaling purposes.

P.C. 12401—*Tear gas defined.* "Tear gas" as used in this chapter shall apply to and include all liquid, gaseous or solid substances intended to produce temporary physical discomfort or permanent injury through being vaporized or otherwise dispersed in the air, but does not apply to, and shall not include, pesticides, dog repellents and other substances not intended to be used to produce discomfort or injury to human beings.

P.C. 12500—*"Silencer" defined.* The term "silencer" as used in this chapter shall apply to and include all devices or attachments of any kind designed, used or intended for use in silencing the report of a firearm.

P.C. 12501—*Exceptions.* Nothing in this chapter shall prohibit any city or county, state or federal officer, or the military or naval forces of this State or of the United States from possessing silencers for official use in the discharge of their duties.

P.C. 12520—*Possession unlawful.* Any person, firm or corporation who within this State possesses any device of the kind commonly known as a silencer for firearms is guilty of a felony and upon conviction thereof shall be punished by imprisonment in the state prison not to exceed three years or by a fine not to exceed five thousand dollars ($5,000), or by both.

P.C. 12550—*Sale of firearms to minor.* No person shall sell any firearm to any minor who is at least 16 years of age but not over the age of 18 years without the written consent of a parent or legal guardian of the minor.

P.C. 12551—*Sale of firearms to minor; misdemeanor.* Every person who sells to a minor under the age of 18 years any firearm, air gun, or gas-operated gun, designed to fire a bullet, pellet or metal projectile, is guilty of a misdemeanor.

P.C. 12552—*Furnishing weapon to minor.* Every person who furnishes any firearm, air gun, or gas-operated gun, designed to fire a bullet, pellet or metal projectile, to any minor under the age of 18 years, without the express or implied permission of the parent or legal guardian of the minor, is guilty of a misdemeanor.

P.C. 653k—*Sales or possession of switch-blade knives.* Every person who carries upon his person, and every person who sells, offers for sale, exposes for sale, loans, transfers, or gives to any other person a switch-blade knife having a blade over *two inches* in length is guilty of a misdemeanor.

For the purposes of this section a "switch-blade knife" is a knife having the appearance of a pocketknife, and shall include a spring-blade knife, snap blade knife, gravity knife or any other similar type knife; the blade or blades of which are two or more inches long and which can be released automatically by a flick of a button, pressure on the handle, flip of the wrists or other mechanical device, or is released by the weight of the blade or by any type of mechanism whatsoever.

P.C. 4502—*Possession of weapon.* Every person confined in a state prison or who while being conveyed to or from any state prison by vehicle at any prison road camp, prison forestry camp, or other prison camps or prison farms or while being conveyed to or from any such place or while under the custody of prison officials, officers or employees, possesses or carries upon his person or has under his custody or control any instrument or weapon of the kind commonly known as a blackjack, sling-shot, billy, sandclub, sandbag, or metal knuckles or any explosive substance or any dirk or dagger or sharp instrument, or any pistol, revolver or other firearm, is guilty of a felony and shall be punishable by imprisonment in a state prison for a term not less than three years.

Welfare Code 5152—*Confiscation and custody of firearms.* Whenever a person who has been detained or apprehended for examination of his mental condition, or who is a mental patient in any hospital or institution or who is on leave of absence from such hospital or institution, is found to own, have in his possession or under his control, any firearm whatsoever, said firearm shall be confiscated by any law enforcement agency or peace officer, who shall retain custody of said firearm until the release without commitment of the person or the restoration to capacity of the person, or until the appointment of a guardian for the person, or shall make such other disposition of the firearm as ordered by the court.

Welfare Code 5153—*Possession of firearms prohibited; exception; issuance of certificate; violation; misdemeanor.* No person who has been involuntarily committed after October 1, 1955, to any public or private mental hospital or sanitarium for a period of thirty (30) days or more shall have in his possession or under his custody or control any firearm unless there has been issued to such person a certificate as hereafter described in this section and such person has not, subsequent to the issuance of such certificate, again been involuntarily committed for a period of 30 days or more in any such hospital or sanitarium.

A certificate meeting the requirements of this section must be a written statement that is either part of a broader certificate of competency or a separate document and that is issued, on application of the person who was committed, either at the time of release or at a later date, by the superintendent of any California state hospital, stating that in the opinion of the persons issuing the certificate, based either on his own knowledge or on the opinions of members of his staff or on records of the institution, the applicant is a person who may possess a firearm without endangering others. If a person applies to a superintendent of a California state hospital for such a certificate and the applicant has not been committed to that hospital, or if the superintendent believes that a current mental examination is necessary to enable him to determine whether or not such a certificate shall be issued, the superintendent shall cause such person to be examined by a member of the staff of the hospital and may otherwise investigate the case. The superintendent may charge a reasonable fee for such examination and investigation.

Refusal of a superintendent to issue a certificate of competency or separate document as described in the preceding provisions of this section is reviewable by mandamus in the Superior court of the county of which the applicant is a resident or the county in which the hospital or sanitarium of which the superintendent is head. Upon a showing to the satisfaction of the court of abuse of discretion by the superintendent the court shall issue its writ directing the superintendent to issue its certificate or document.

Every person who possesses or has under his custody or control any firearm in violation of this section is guilty of a misdemeanor.

LEGAL DISCUSSION

It is proper to convict of the substantive crime (robbery) and to impose in addition to the penalties there involved the additional penalties of the Dangerous Weapons Control Law.[5] But in the case of assault with a deadly weapon the additional penalties may not be awarded.[6] The distinction seems to lie in the fact that robbery can be committed without a deadly weapon whereas assault with a deadly weapon would be a different crime if such weapon were not used.

When several persons are accomplices in the commission of a crime and only one is armed, the additional penalties apply to all accomplices whether or not they knew their accomplice was armed.[7]

The crime of burglary involves a difference in degree when the burglar is armed.[8]

ENFORCEMENT ASPECTS

As an aftermath of the violence in the United States which marked the assassinations of John F. Kennedy, the Reverend Martin Luther King, and Robert F. Kennedy, the control of firearms is being tightened throughout the nation. Police officers must use every possible caution in apprehending dangerous suspects. They should realize that pursuant to P.C. 12022 additional punishment is stipulated when a person is found guilty of other crimes and is armed at the time. Second convictions increase the penalty from five to ten years in the state prison. Third convictions increase the penalty from ten to fifteen years, and ultimately from twenty-five years to life. Suspects who are serving this type of sentence will not hesitate to shoot police officers or other persons in attempting to flee.

As with any other area of enforcement, the police officer must use discretion in enforcing violations of the Deadly Weapons Control Law. Thus, at 3 o'clock in the morning in a business district it would be most unusual for a licensed hunter to go hunting. However, an antique gun collector who is returning home from a display of his collection at 3 o'clock in the morning would call for a different approach.

WEAPON	MERE POSSESSION	CONCEALED ON PERSON OR IN VEHICLE	CARRIED OPENLY OR VISIBLY
Blackjack, slungshot, billy, sandbag, sandclub, metal knuckles	Felony to possess, offer for sale or keep for sale. (12020 P.C.)	Mere possession a felony. (12020 P.C.)	Mere possession a felony. (12020 P.C.)
Machine guns	Felony or misdemeanor to possess. (12020 P.C.)	Mere possession a felony or misdemeanor. (12220 P.C.)	Mere possession a felony or misdemeanor. (12220 P.C.)
Firearm silencers	Felony to possess. (12520 P.C.)	Felony to possess. Does not have to be concealed. (12520 P.C.)	Mere possession a felony. (12520 P.C.)

Handguns (concealable weapons)	Felony or misdemeanor if person is not a U.S. citizen, has previously been convicted of a felony or is addicted to narcotic drugs. (12021 P.C.) Misdemeanor if possessed by minor not accompanied by parent or guardian or without written permission of parent or guardian. (12021.5 P.C.)	Misdemeanor to carry concealed on the person or concealed in any vehicle under person's direction or control without license or permit to carry concealed. (12025 P.C.)* *See exceptions to 12025 P.C. in 12027 P.C.	Misdemeanor to carry loaded on person or in vehicle while in public place, public street within incorporated city, or public place or public street in an unincorporated area where it would be unlawful to discharge a weapon. Defines a "loaded" firearm for purposes of enforcement as that which has an unexpected cartridge or shell in, or attached in any manner to the firearm, including, but not limited to, the firing chamber, magazine or clip thereof attached to the firearm. (12031 P.C.)*
Rifles	Felony to possess only if barrel is less than 16" in length or if overall length is less than 26". (12020 P.C.)	Misdemeanor if cartridge is in chamber when the rifle is in a vehicle on any public highway or other way open to the public. (2006 Fish and Game Code)	Felony to carry loaded on person or in vehicle within the state capitol and other legislative offices, or upon the grounds of or within any residence of the governor or any state legislator, or upon the grounds of or within any public school. Defines a firearm as being "loaded" for purposes of enforcement whenever both the firearm and unexpended ammunition are in the possession of the same person. (171c, 171d and 171e P.C.)*
Shotguns	Felony to possess only if barrel is less than 18" in length or if overall length is less than 26". (12020 P.C.)	Misdemeanor if cartridge is in chamber when the shotgun is in a vehicle on any public highway or other way open to the public. (2006 Fish and Game Code)	Peace Officers are authorized to examine any such weapon for the purpose of determining if a violation exists. Refusal to allow such examination constitutes probable cause to arrest. *See exceptions in text of law(s).

DISCUSSION QUESTIONS

1. List the categories of persons who are exempt from the Deadly Weapons Control Law.
2. List the items which it is felonious for any private person to possess.
3. List the three types of persons who commit felonies when they own or possess a firearm.
4. Describe the switch-blade knife. When is it a misdemeanor to carry?
5. How short can a rifle barrel be and not fall in the unlawful category?

NOTES

[1]People v. Cruz, 113 CA 519; 298 P 556.
[2]U.S. v. Crinkshank, 92 US 542.
[3]People v. Odegard, 203 CA 2d 427; 21 CR 515.
[4]P.C. 12020.
[5]People v. Warren, 16 C 2d 103; 104 P 2d 1024.
[6]Ex Parte Shull, 23 C 2d 745; 146 P 2d 417;
  O'Donnell ex rel Rodgers, 121 CA 370; 9 P 2d 223.
[7]People v. Stevens, 32 CA 2d 666; 90 P 2d 595.
[8]P.C. 460(1).

20

Public Conduct
and Liquor Control

APPLICABLE STATUTES—DISORDERLY CONDUCT

P.C. 647—*Acts defined as disorderly conduct: a misdemeanor.* Every person who commits any of the following acts shall be guilty of disorderly conduct, a misdemeanor:

(a) Who solicits anyone to engage in or who engages in lewd or dissolute conduct in any public place or in any place open to the public or exposed to public view.

(b) Who solicits or who engages in any act of prostitution. As used in this subdivision, "prostitution" includes any lewd act between persons of the same sex for money or other consideration.

(c) Who accosts other persons in any public place or any place open to the public for the purpose of begging or soliciting alms.

(d) Who loiters in or about any toilet open to the public for the purpose of engaging in or soliciting any lewd or lascivious or any unlawful act.

(e) Who loiters or wanders upon the streets or from place to place without apparent reason or business and who refuses to identify himself and to account for his presence when requested by any peace officer so to do, if the surrounding circumstances are such as to indicate to a reasonable man that the public safety demands such identification.

(f)   Who is found in any public place under the influence of intoxicating liquor, or any drug, or the influence of toluene or any substance defined as a poison in schedule D of Section 4160 of the Business and Professions Code, or under the influence of any combination of any intoxicating liquor, drug, toluene or any such poison in such a condition that he is unable to exercise care for his own safety or the safety of others, or by reason of his being under the influence of intoxicating liquor, or any drug, or the influence of toluene or any substance defined as a poison in Schedule D of Section 4160 of the Business and Professions Code, or under the influence of any combination of any intoxicating liquor, drug, toluene or any such poison interferes with or obstructs or prevents the free use of any street, sidewalk or other public way.

(g)   Who loiters, prowls or wanders upon the private property of another, in the nighttime, without visible or lawful business with the owner or occupant thereof: or who, while loitering, prowling or wandering upon the private property of another, in the nighttime, peeks in the door or window of any inhabited building or structure located thereon, without visible or lawful business with the owner or occupant thereof.

(h)   Who lodges in any building, structure or place, whether public or private, without the permission of the owner or person entitled to the possession or in control thereof.

P.C. 647a—*Vagrancy—annoying or molesting children under 18.* [Quoted in Chapter 15.]

P.C. 647b—*Loitering prohibited about school where adults are in attendance.* Every person who loiters about any school in which adults are in attendance at courses established pursuant to Chapter 5.5 (commencing with Section 5701) of Division 6 of the Education Code, and who annoys or molests any person in attendance therein shall be punished by a fine of not exceeding five hundred dollars ($500) or by imprisonment in the county jail for not exceeding six months, or by both such fine and imprisonment.

P.C. 647c—*Willful and malicious obstruction of thoroughfares and other public places*: Effect of section on powers of local bodies to regulate conduct. Every person who, willfully and maliciously, obstructs the free movement of any person on any street, sidewalk, or other public place or on or in any place open to the public is guilty of a misdemeanor.

Nothing in this section affects the power of a county or a city to regulate conduct upon a street, sidewalk, or other public place or on or in a place open to the public.

P.C. 653g—*Loitering about schools or other places attended by children.* Every person who loiters about any school or public place at or near which children attend or normally congregate is a vagrant, and is punishable by a fine of not exceeding five hundred dollars ($500) or by imprisonment in the county jail for not exceeding six months, or by both such fine and imprisonment.

LEGAL DISCUSSION

Within recent years the State Legislature has made several changes in the Vagrancy Laws. While accomplishing these changes, they have seemingly duplicated numbers of the Penal Code. Prior to 1961, all 647 sections of the Penal Code were referred to as the Vagrant Sections but in that year the original twelve subsections were changed from number headings to eight letter headings while the 1929 additions to the Vagrancy Sections were not changed. These original subsections were redesignated as the Disorderly Conduct Sections and are written as:

P.C. 647(a) Disorderly Conduct—lewd or dissolute conduct
as opposed to:
P.C. 647a Vagrancy—annoying or molesting child under 18.

This is a classic example of the continuation of "Bills of Attainder" into modern law. It has been successively reduced by judicial interpretation to impotence. The law created the crime of status or condition because one wasn't punished for willfully, intentionally or negligently doing something but merely for "being" something or for "not being something." It sentenced a class of people not for their transgressions but for their failure to conform.[1]

In subsection (a) of P.C. 647 "solicit" means any use of words, actions or other device by which a person is requested, urged, advised, counseled, tempted, commanded, or otherwise enticed to engage in lewd or dissolute conduct. The words "lewd" and "dissolute" in this statute are used interchangeably. Each applies to the unlawful indulgence in lust. *Lewd* is defined to mean: lustful, lascivious, unchaste; that form of immorality which has relation to sexual impurity. *Dissolute* means: a person who is loose in his or her morals and conduct.

This statute has set out two separate acts, and the commission of either act independently of the other constitutes a crime. These two crimes are: (1) To solicit a person to engage in lewd or dissolute conduct; (2) To engage in lewd or dissolute conduct regardless of solicitation. As used in subsection (b) of P.C. 647 "prostitution" refers to any lewd act between persons of the same sex for money or other consideration. In its most general sense, the word "prostitution" means the selling of one's self. In the more restricted sense "prostitution" is the indiscriminate, illicit sexual intercourse of a woman with men. Two separate acts are set forth in this subdivision, the commission of either of which constitutes a violation: (1) To *solicit* a person to engage in any act of prostitution; (2) To actually *engage* in any act of prostitution.

Section 318 of the Penal Code prohibits encouraging a person to visit a place of prostitution and may also be used to augment this subdivision.

Subsection (c) provides that any solicitation must be done either in a public place or in any place open to the public. This condition was placed in the section in the 1961 Legislature changes. Apparently, if a person solicits alms or begs in a private place or in a place not open to the public, then any prosecution must be done under one of the subdivisions of section 602 of the Penal Code (Trespassing).

The term "loiter," used in subsection (d), has a long-recognized meaning: *to linger idly by the way, to idle.* The words "lewd" and "lascivious" in this statute are used interchangeably. Each applies to the unlawful indulgence in lust. They are defined to mean libidinous, lustful, unchaste; that form of immorality which has relation to sexual impurity.

It appears that the legislative intent dealing with that part of the section which reads "or any unlawful act" has reference to any lewd or lascivious act and *not* just *any* unlawful act. This is indicated by the fact that this subdivision has been made a registration offense under section 290 of the Penal Code which requires registration for certain sex offenders. Therefore, this subdivision should not be used to effect arrests for such acts as loitering for the purpose of theft, selling lottery tickets, etc.

Subdivision (e) has many restrictions within itself and often an arrest under this section constitutes grounds for a suspicion arrest for a felony. This section is often misinterpreted to mean that a person must have some identifying papers or other device on his person. Verbal identification, however, is enough to meet the requirements.

In subsection (f), note the phrase "any public place." The fact of merely being under the influence of any substance as described in subsection (f) does not constitute grounds for an arrest. Do not associate this with section 23102 of the Vehicle Code. The keys in this subdivision are: (1) Unable to exercise care for his safety or the safety of others; (2) Interferes with or obstructs or prevents the free use of any street, sidewalk or other public way.

This section is also very restrictive since it preempts the field of intoxication; thus the many municipal and county ordinances which prohibit drunkenness on private property to the annoyance of others have been invalidated.

The provision of being under the influence of toluene or poisons as defined in Schedule D of Section 4160 of the Business and Professions Code was added in the 1967 Legislature, which also added section 381 of the Penal Code making it a misdemeanor to willfully ingest, inhale or breathe the fumes.

Subsection (g) specifies "nighttime," which is defined by the Penal Code in Section 7, subdivision 13, as that time between sunset and sunrise. This subdivision sets out two separate acts. The first deals with "prowlers" and the second with "peeping toms." Although the elements are the same in both cases, the "peeping tom" must be peeking into an inhabited building.

Subsection (h) is closely related to P.C. 602 (1).

APPLICABLE STATUTES—DISTURBING THE PEACE

P.C. 415—*Disturbing the peace.* Every person who maliciously and willfully disturbs the peace or quiet of any neighborhood or person, by loud or unusual noise, or by tumultuous or offensive conduct, or threatening, traducing, quarreling, challenging to fight, or fighting, or who, on the public streets of any unincorporated town, or upon the public highways in such unincorporated town, runs any horse race, either for a wager or for amusement, or fires any gun or pistol in such unincorporated town, or use any vulgar, profane, or indecent language within the presence or hearing of women or children, in a loud and boisterous manner, is guilty of a misdemeanor, and upon conviction by any court of competent jurisdiction, shall be punished by fine not exceeding two hundred dollars, or by imprisonment in the county jail for not more than ninety days, or by both fine and imprisonment, or either, at the discretion of the court.

P.C. 417—*Drawing or exhibiting firearm or other deadly weapon.* Every person who, except in self-defense, in the presence of any other person, draws or exhibits any firearm, whether loaded or unloaded, or any other deadly weapon whatsoever, in a rude, angry or threatening manner, or who in any manner, unlawfully uses the same in any fight or quarrel is guilty of a misdemeanor.

LEGAL DISCUSSION

In this area of public conduct the reader should also keep in mind P.C. 650½, quoted in Chapter 11; the above statutes, by contrast, punish conduct which amounts to a breach of the peace.

In contrast to P.C. 647 this section punishes offensive acts rather than offensive status.

As a definitive portion of breach of the peace we have specific acts: prize fights illegally conducted (P.C. 412, 413, 414 and 414a) and affrays or duels (P.C. 415, 225, 227, 228, 229, and 230).

ENFORCEMENT ASPECTS

Generally speaking, the law enforcement officer will use section 415 under one of the following areas:

1. *Loud and unusual noise*—Keep in mind that this noise must be willful and malicious. Therefore, it is important that the person who is making the noise or the person who is in charge of the premises be notified prior to the police action. This warning and subsequent noncomplaint will usually suffice for the establishing of a prima facie case. It is practically impossible for a police officer's peace to be disturbed; accordingly, it is imperative when exercising this section that the officer have a complaining witness or victim. Persons making citizen arrests must be able to testify to the elements of a crime and are limited to arresting only those persons causing the disturbance.

2. *Offensive conduct*—The area of offensive conduct relates to the public being "shocked and offended." Offenses under this section may overlap with P.C. 650½ and frequently with P.C. 647a (lewd act). Examples may include: urinating in public, nudity in public, and other acts which are normally considered offensive.

3. *Quarreling or fighting*—Possibly the most frequent use of this section is when persons are challenging others to fight or engage in mutual combat; all parties are equally guilty. Whenever there is a victim, the proper charge would more likely be battery or felonious assault. From an enforcement standpoint, it is most advisable, after breaking up a fight, to determine the physical condition of the parties concerned. As long as there are no apparent injuries and the parties are not desirous of further prosecution, the officer should use discretion and send them on their way without further legal action.

4. *Vulgar, profane or indecent language*—Such language used in the presence of women or children must be heard by them. It is essential that the woman or the child testify to the hearing of the offensive language. Normally the women or children should be disinterested persons. The determination of whether or not the language used is vulgar is a question for the trial court to decide, taking into consideration contemporary usage.

Basically P.C. 417 requires the proving of the following specific elements:

1. That a firearm (loaded or unloaded) or other deadly weapon be drawn or exhibited;

2. That it be drawn in a rude, angry or threatening manner;

3. That it be used in a fight or quarrel.

This offense is not necessarily included within the purview of Section 245 "Assault with a Deadly Weapon."

APPLICABLE STATUTES—LIQUOR CONTROL

P.C. 367d—*Drunk driving motor vehicle while under the influence of liquor or drugs.* Any person driving a motor vehicle who is under the influence of intoxicating liquor, or under the combined influence of intoxicating liquor and any drug, shall be guilty of a misdemeanor.

P.C. 397—*Selling or furnishing liquor to drunkards forbidden.* Every person who sells or furnishes or causes to be sold or furnished, intoxicating liquors to any habitual or common drunkard, or to any person who has been adjudged legally incompetent or insane by any court of this State and has not been restored to legal capacity, knowing such person to have been so adjudged, is guilty of a misdemeanor.

V.C. 23101—*Drunk driving.* Any person who, while under the influence of intoxicating liquor, or under the combined influence of intoxicating liquor and any drug, drives a vehicle and when so driving does any act forbidden by law or neglects any duty imposed by law in the driving of such vehicle, which act or neglect proximately causes bodily injury to any person other than himself is guilty of a felony and upon conviction thereof shall be punished by imprisonment in the state prison for not less than one year nor more than five years or in the county jail for not less than 90 days nor more than one year and by fine of not less than two hundred fifty dollars ($250) nor more than five thousand dollars ($5,000).

V.C. 23102—*Drunk driving.* It is unlawful for any person who is under the influence of intoxicating liquor, or under the combined influence of intoxicating liquor and any drug, to drive a vehicle upon any highway. Any person convicted under this section shall be punished upon a first conviction by imprisonment in the county jail for not less than 30 days nor more than six months or by fine of not less than two hundred fifty dollars ($250) nor more than five hundred dollars or by both such fine and imprisonment and upon a second or any subsequent conviction, within seven years of a prior conviction, by imprisonment in the county jail for not less than five days nor more than one year and by a fine of not less than two hundred fifty dollars ($250) nor more than one thousand dollars ($1,000). A conviction under this section shall be deemed a second conviction if the person has previously been convicted of a violation of Section 23101 of this code.

V.C. 23121—*Drinking in motor vehicle.* No person shall drink any alcoholic beverage in any motor vehicle when such vehicle is upon any highway. As used in this chapter, alcoholic beverage shall have the same meaning as in Section 23004 of the Business and Professions Code.

V.C. 23122—*Possession of opened container.* No person shall have in his possession on his person, while in a privately owned motor vehicle upon a highway, any bottle, can, or other receptacle, containing any alcoholic beverage which has been opened, or a seal broken, or the contents of which have been partially removed.

V.C. 23123—*Storage of opened container.* It is unlawful for the registered owner of any privately owned motor vehicle or the driver, if the registered owner is not then present in the vehicle, to keep in a motor vehicle, when such vehicle is upon any highway, any bottle, can, or other receptacle containing any alcoholic beverage which has been opened, or a seal broken, or the contents of which have been partially removed, unless such bottle, can, or other receptacle is kept in the trunk of the vehicle, if such vehicle is equipped with a trunk, or kept in some other area of the vehicle not normally occupied by the driver or passengers, if the vehicle is not equipped with a trunk. A utility compartment or glove compartment shall be deemed to be within the area occupied by the driver and passengers.

V.C. 23124—*Motor vehicle; except common carrier.* As used in Sections 23121, 23122, and 23123 of this Chapter, "Motor Vehicle" shall not include those motor vehicles operated by a common carrier or a publicly owned transit system.

V.C. 23125—*Possession of alcoholic beverage; exceptions.* The provisions of Sections 23121, 23122, and 23123 shall not apply to any person who, upon the recommendation of a doctor, carries alcoholic beverages in his motor vehicle for medicinal purposes. Such sections shall also not apply to any clergyman who carries alcoholic beverages in his motor vehicle for religious purposes.

LEGAL DISCUSSION

For crimes involving liquor in connection with the operation of motor vehicles, refer to V.C. 23101 and V.C. 23102. Aside from such crimes there are misdemeanors and felonies arising from the possession, sale, use, and effects of alcoholic beverages.

In general the Vehicle Code defines crimes in terms which describe the use of alcoholic beverages to such extent that "one is under the influence of liquor and does or fails to do something he should or should not have done" or is under the influence of liquor to such extent that he is unable to function normally. In the first example we couple a condition with (a) an action or (b) a failure to act whereas in the second we do not punish the act which created the condition but we punish the condition itself. Offenses therefore arise from the combined operation of (a) alcohol or (b) alcohol and drug and (c) a vehicle, resulting in (d) no damage or (e) personal injury or death.

The manufacture and sale of liquor is controlled. The provisions of the Alcoholic Beverage Control Act duplicate and overlap provisions of the Penal Code. The parallel provisions in the Penal Code impose restrictions on the place of sale[3] and the time when sales can be made,[4] the solicitation of sales,[5] the advertising,[6] the packaging and labeling,[7] and the conditions of sale.[8]

ENFORCEMENT ASPECTS

Law enforcement officers have several investigative techniques and problems which are germane to drunken driving cases. One of the first problems is to establish the identity of the driver. It is always required that the suspect be "placed behind the wheel." While it may appear obvious that the suspect is the driver, all efforts should be made to secure a witness who can actually testify that the suspect was the driver of the vehicle.

In both of the Vehicle Code sections involving driving under the influence of alcohol, it is always necessary to prove that the defendant's accident was caused by a violation of the law. For example, if a driver under the influence of alcohol was legally stopped by a traffic light and his car was struck in the rear, these facts would not constitute a violation. The driving of a vehicle under the influence of alcohol or drugs is not per se an unlawful act. There must also be a violation. Ascertaining whether a person is under the influence of alcohol or actually intoxicated requires the administering of chemical tests or field sobriety tests.[9] These tests are extremely important.

DISCUSSION QUESTIONS

1. What is the corpus delicti of disorderly conduct (P.C. 647)?
2. What are the elements of disturbing the peace?
3. What dangerous drug is referred to in disorderly conduct (P.C. 647f)?
4. Identify three sections applicable to the control of alcohol or intoxicated driving in motor vehicles.
5. Explain the term "under the influence."

NOTES

[1]*Unemployment*
People v. Wilson, 145 CA 2d 1; 301 P 2d 974.
Loitering
In re Cregler, 56 C 2d 308; 14 CR 289; 36 P 2d 305.
Common Drunk
In re Newlern, 53 C 2d 786; 3 CR 364; 350 P 2d 116.
In General
Thompson v. Louisville, 362 US 199; 80 SCY 624; 4 LEd 2d 654.

[2]People v. Gossman, 95 CA 2d 293; 212 P 2d 585.

[3]P.C. 172(a), (b), (d) and (e).

[4]B. & P. C. §25630; 25632; 25631; and P.C. 398.

[5]B. & P. C. §25657; P.C. 303.

[6]B. & P. C. §25611; 25611.1; 25612; 25644.

[7]B. & P. C. §25170; 25177; 25178; 25179; 25180; 25205; 25206; 25207; 25613; 25236; 25237; 25609; 25614;
H. & S. C. §26517.

[8]B. & P. C. §24750; 25500; 25600; 25601; 25610; 25615.

[9]George T. Payton, Patrol Procedure (Los Angeles, Calif.: Legal Book Store, 1966), pp. 285–296.

21

Gambling and Bookmaking

APPLICABLE STATUTES—LOTTERY

P.C. 319—*Lottery defined.* A lottery is any scheme for the disposal or distribution of property by chance, among persons who have paid or promised to pay any valuable consideration for the chance of obtaining such property, upon any agreement, understanding, or expectation that it is to be distributed, or disposed of by lot or chance, whether called a lottery, raffle, or gift enterprise, or by whatever name the same may be known.

P.C. 320—*Punishment for drawing lottery.* Every person who contrives, prepares, sets up, proposes, or draws any lottery, is guilty of a misdemeanor.

P.C. 321—*Punishment for selling lottery tickets.* Every person who sells, gives, or in any manner whatever, furnishes or transfers to or for any other person any ticket, chance, share, or interest, or any paper, certificate, or instrument purporting or understood to be or to represent any ticket, chance, share, or interest in or depending upon the event of any lottery, is guilty of a misdemeanor.

P.C. 322—*Aiding lotteries.* Every person who aids or assists either by printing, writing, advertising, publishing, or otherwise in setting up, managing, or drawing any lottery, or in selling or disposing of any ticket, chance, or share therein, is guilty of a misdemeanor.

P.C. 323—*Lottery offices.* Advertising lottery offices. Every person who opens, sets up, or keeps,' by himself or by any other person, any office or other place for the sale of, or for registering the number of any ticket in any lottery, or who, by printing, writing, or otherwise, advertises or publishes the setting up, opening, or using of such office, is guilty of a misdemeanor.

P.C. 324—*Insuring lottery tickets: publishing offers to insure.* Every person who insures or receives any consideration for insuring for or against the drawing of any ticket in any lottery whatever, whether drawn or to be drawn within this state or not, or who receives any valuable consideration upon any agreement to repay any sum, or deliver the same, or any other property, if any lottery ticket or number of any ticket in any lottery shall prove fortunate or unfortunate, or shall be drawn or not be drawn, at any particular time or in any particular order, or who promises or agrees to pay any sum of money, or to deliver any goods, things in action, or property, or to forbear to do any thing for the benefit of any person, with or without consideration, upon any event or contingency dependent on the drawing of any ticket in any lottery, or who publishes any notice or proposal of any of the purposes aforesaid, is guilty of a misdemeanor.

P.C. 326—*Letting building for lottery purposes.* Every person who lets, or permits to be used, any building or vessel, or any portion thereof, knowing that it is to be used for setting up, managing, or drawing any lottery, or for the purpose of selling or disposing of lottery tickets, is guilty of a misdemeanor.

LEGAL DISCUSSION

A lottery is not removed from the proscribed area unless the element of skill added thereto is the predominant factor so long as the basic elements of consideration for the privilege of playing, the element of chance, and the recouping of a prize of property value are involved.[1]

If the prize or property is transferred as a result of chance without the requirement of a consideration for the privilege of playing as in an *advertising* contest, there is no lottery.[2]

APPLICABLE STATUTES—GAMING

P.C. 330—*Gaming a misdemeanor; penalty.* Every person who deals, plays, or carries on, opens, or causes to be opened, or who conducts, either as owner or employe, whether for hire or not, any game of faro, monte, roulette, lansquenet, rouge et noire, rondon, tan, fan-tan, stud-horse poker, seven-and-a-half, twenty-one, hokey-pokey, or any banking or percentage game played with cards, dice, or any device, for money, checks, credit, or other representative of value, and every person who plays or bets at or against any of said prohibited games, is guilty of a misdemeanor, and shall be punishable by a fine not less than one hundred dollars nor more than five hundred dollars, or by imprisonment in the county jail not exceeding six months, or by both such fine and imprisonment.

P.C. 330a—*Gambling by use of slot machines prohibited: dice having more than six faces.* Every person, who has in his possession or under his control either as owner, lessee, agent, employee, mortgagee, or otherwise, or who permits to be placed, maintained or kept, in any room, space, enclosure or building owned, leased or occupied by him, or under his management or control, any slot or card machine, contrivance, appliance or mechanical device, upon the result of action of which money or other valuable thing is staked or hazarded, and which is operated, or played, by placing or depositing therein any coins, checks, slugs, balls, or other articles or device, or in any other manner and by means whereof, or as a result of the operation of which any merchandise, money, representative or articles of value, checks, or tokens, redeemable in, or exchangeable for money or any other thing of value, is won or lost, or taken from or obtained from such machine, when the result of action or operation of such machine, contrivance, appliance, or mechanical device is dependent upon hazard or chance, and every person, who has in his possession or under his control, either as owner, lessee, agent, employee, mortgagee, or otherwise, or who permits to be placed, maintained or kept, in any room, space, enclosure or building, owned, leased or occupied by him, or under his management or control, any card dice, or any dice having more than six faces or bases each, upon the result of action of which any money or other valuable thing is staked or hazarded, or as a result of the operation of which any merchandise, money, representative or article of value, check or token, redeemable in or exchangeable for money or any other thing of value, is won or lost or taken, when the result of action or operation of such dice is dependent upon hazard or chance, is guilty of a misdemeanor, and shall be punishable by a fine not less than one hundred dollars nor more than five hundred dollars, or by imprisonment in the county jail not exceeding six months, or by both such fine and imprisonment.

P.C. 330b—*Slot machines prohibited; defined. Possession or keeping a slot machine or device.* (1) It is unlawful for any person to manufacture, repair, own, store, possess, sell, rent, lease, let on shares, lend or give away, transport, or expose for sale or lease, or to offer to repair, sell, rent, lease, let on shares, lend or give away or to permit the operation of, or for any person to permit to be placed, maintained or kept in any place, room, space or building owned, leased or occupied by him or under his management or control, any slot machine or device as hereinafter defined, or to make or to permit to be made with any person any agreement with reference to any slot machine or device, as hereinafter defined, pursuant to which the user thereof, as a result of any hazard or chance or other outcome unpredictable by him, may become entitled to receive any money, credit, allowance, or thing of value or additional chance or right to use such slot machine or device, or to receive any check, slug, token or memorandum entitling the holder to receive any money, credit, allowance or thing of value; provided, however, that this section, insofar as it relates to owning, storing, possessing, or transporting any slot machine or device as hereinafter defined, shall not apply to any slot machine or device as hereinafter defined, located upon or being transported by any vessel regularly operated and engaged in interstate or foreign commerce, so long as such slot machine or device is located in a locked compartment of the vessel, is not accessible for use and is not used or operated within the territorial jurisdiction of this state.

(2)   Any machine, apparatus or device is a slot machine or device within the provisions of this section if it is one that is adapted, or may readily be converted into one that is adapted, for use in such a way that, as a result of the insertion of any piece of money or coin or other object, or by any other means, such machine or device is caused to operate or may be operated and by reason of any element of hazard or chance or of other outcome of such operation unpredictable by him, the user may receive or become entitled to receive any piece of money, credit, allowance or thing of value or additional chance or right to use such slot machine or device, or any check, slug, token or memorandum, whether of value or otherwise, which may be exchanged for any money, credit, allowance or thing of value, or which may be given in trade, irrespective of whether it may, apart from any element of hazard or chance or unpredictable outcome of such operation, also sell, deliver or present some merchandise, indication of weight, entertainment or other thing of value.

(3)   Every person who violates this section is guilty of a misdemeanor.

(4)   It is expressly provided that with respect to the provisions of Section 330b only of this code, pin ball, and other amusement machines or devices which are predominantly games of skill, whether affording the opportunity of additional chances or free plays or not, are not intended to be and are not included within the term slot machine or device as defined in said Section 330b of this code.

P.C. 330.1—*Slot machines forbidden; defined.* Every person who manufactures, owns, stores, keeps, possesses, sells, rents, leases, lets on share, lends or gives away, transports or exposes for sale or lease or offers to sell, rent, lease, let on shares, lend or give away or who permits the operation of, or permits to be placed, maintained, used or kept in any room, space or building owned, leased or occupied by him or under his management or control, any slot machine or device as hereinafter defined, and every person who makes or permits to be made with any person any agreement with reference to any slot machine or device as hereinafter defined, pursuant to which agreement the user thereof, as a result of any element of hazard or chance, may become entitled to receive any thing of value or additional chance or right to use such slot machine or device, or to receive any check, slug, token or memorandum, whether of value or otherwise, entitling the holder to receive any thing of value, is guilty of a misdemeanor and shall be punishable by a fine of not more than five hundred dollars ($500) or by imprisonment in the county jail not exceeding six months or by both such fine and imprisonment. A slot machine or device within the meaning of Section 330.1 to 330.5, inclusive, of this code is one that is, or may be, used or operated in such a way that, as a result of the insertion of any piece of money or coin or other object such machine or device is caused to operate or may be operated or played, mechanically, electrically, automatically, or manually, and by reason of any element of hazard or chance, the user may receive or become entitled to receive any thing of value or any check, slug, token or memorandum, whether of value or otherwise, which may be given in trade, or the user may secure additional chances of rights to use such machine or device, irrespective of whether it may, apart from any element of hazard or chance also sell, deliver or present some merchandise, indication of weight, entertainment or other thing of value. If any provision of this act or the application thereof to any person or circumstance is held invalid such invalidity shall not affect other provisions or applications of the act which can be given effect without the invalid provision or application, and to this end the provisions of this act are declared to be severable.

P.C. 330.2—*Thing of value defined.* As used in Sections 330.1 to 330.5, inclusive, of this code a "thing of value" is defined to be any money, coin, currency, check, chip, allowance, token, credit, merchandise, property, or any representative of value.

P.C. 330.3—*May be seized and disposed of.* In addition to any other remedy provided by law any slot machine or device may be seized by any of the officers designated by Sections 335 and 335a of the Penal Code, and in such cases shall be disposed of, together with any and all money seized in or in connection with such machine or device, as provided in Section 335a of the Penal Code.

P.C. 330.4—*Mere possession prohibited.* It is specifically declared that the mere possession or control, either as owner, lessee, agent, employee, mortgagor, or otherwise of any slot machine or device, as defined in Section 330.1 of this code, is prohibited and penalized by the provisions of Sections 330.1 to 330.5, inclusive, of this code.

It is specifically declared that every person who permits to be placed, maintained or kept in any room, space, enclosure, or building owned, leased or occupied by him, or under his management or control, whether for use or operation or for storage, bailment, safekeeping or deposit only, any slot machine or device, as defined in Section 330.1 of this code, is guilty of a misdemeanor and punishable as provided in Section 330.1 of this code.

It is further declared that the provisions of this Section specifically render any slot machine or device as defined in Section 330.1 of this code subject to confiscation as provided in Section 335a of this code.

P.C. 330.5—*Certain machines not banned.* It is further expressly provided that Sections 330.1 to 330.4, inclusive, of this code shall not apply to music machines, weighing machines and machines which vend cigarettes, candy, ice cream, food, confections or other merchandise, in which there is deposited an exact consideration and from which in every case the customer obtains that which he purchases; and it is further expressly provided that with respect to the provisions of Sections 330.1 to 330.4, inclusive, only, of this code, pin ball, and other amusement machines or devices which are predominantly games of skill, whether affording the opportunity of additional chances or free plays or not, are not intended to be and are not included within the term slot machine or device as defined within Sections 330.1 to 330.4, inclusive, of this code.

P.C. 331—*Gambling in houses owned or rented.* Every person who knowingly permits any of the games mentioned in Section Three Hundred Thirty and Section Three Hundred Thirty A of this code to be played, conducted, or dealt in any house owned or rented by such person, in whole or in part, is punishable as provided in the preceding sections.

P.C. 336—*Allowing minors to play, etc.* Every owner, lessee, or keeper of any house used in whole, or in part, as a saloon or drinking place, who knowingly permits any person under twenty-one years of age to play at any game of chance therein, is guilty of a misdemeanor.

P.C. 318—*Prevailing upon person to visit a place kept for gambling or prostitution.* Refer to Chapter 15.

LEGAL DISCUSSION

Note that "draw poker" is not included in the above,[3] but it may be prohibited by local ordinance.[4] Maintaining a place for gambling, permitting same, or inducing persons to visit or transporting people to a place of gaming are crimes. Draw poker is not gaming, but prevailing on a person to visit a place where draw poker is played is a crime under P.C. 318 supra.[5]

APPLICABLE STATUTES—BOOKMAKING

P.C. 337a—*Pool-selling, bookmaking, bets and wagers; penalty.* Every person:

1. Who engages in pool-selling or bookmaking, with or without writing, at any time or place; or

2. Who, whether for gain, hire, reward, or gratuitously or otherwise, keeps or occupies, for any period of time whatsoever, any room, shed, tenement, tent, booth, building, float, vessel, place, stand or enclosure, of any kind, or any part thereof, with a book or books, paper or papers, apparatus, device or paraphernalia, for the purpose of recording or registering any bet or bets, or any purported bet or bets, or wager or wagers, or any purported wager or wagers, or of selling pools, or purported pools, upon the result, or purported result, of any trial, or purported trial, or contest, or purported contest, of skill, speed or power of endurance of man or beast, or between men, beasts, or mechanical apparatus, or upon the result, or purported result, of any lot, chance, casualty, unknown or contingent event whatsoever; or

3. Who, whether for gain, hire, reward, or gratuitously, or otherwise, receives, holds, or forwards, or purports or pretends to receive, hold, or forward, in any manner whatsoever, any money, thing or consideration of value, or the equivalent or memorandum thereof, staked, pledged, bet or wagered, or to be staked, pledged, bet or wagered, or offered for the purpose of being staked, pledged, bet or wagered, upon the result, or purported result, of any trial, or purported trial, or contest, or purported contest, of skill, speed or power of endurance of man or beast, or between men, beasts, or mechanical apparatus, or upon the result, or purported result, of any lot, chance, casualty, unknown or contingent event whatsoever; or

4. Who, whether for gain, hire, reward, or gratuitously, or otherwise, at any time or place, records, or registers any bet or bets, wager or wagers, upon the result, or purported result, of any trial, or purported trial, or contest, or purported contest, of skill, speed or power of endurance of man or beast, or between men, beasts, or mechanical apparatus, or upon the result, or purported result, or any lot, chance, casualty, unknown or contingent event whatsoever; or

5. Who, being the owner, lessee or occupant of any room, shed, tenement, tent, booth, building, float, vessel, place, stand, enclosure or grounds, or any part thereof, whether for gain, hire, reward, or gratuitously, or otherwise, permits the same to be used or occupied for any purpose, or in any manner prohibited by subdivisions one, two, three or four of this section; or

6. Who lays, makes, offers or accepts any bet or bets, or wager or wagers, upon the result, or purported result, of any trial, or purported trial, or contest, or purported contest, of skill, speed or power of endurance of man or beast, or between men, beasts, or mechanical apparatus, is punishable by imprisonment in a county jail for not more than a year or two years in the state prison.

This section shall apply, not only to persons who may commit any of the acts designated in subdivisions one to six inclusive of this section, as a business or occupation, but shall also apply to every person or persons who may do in a single instance any one of the acts specified in said subdivisions one to six inclusive.

P.C. 337f—*Penalty for fixing horse race.* Any person:

(a) Who influences, or induces, or conspires with, any owner, jockey, groom or other person associated with or interested in any stable, horse, or race in which a horse participates, to affect the result of such race by stimulating or depressing a horse through the administration of any drug to such horse, or by the use of any electrical device or any electrical equipment or by any mechanical or other device not generally accepted as regulation racing equipment, or

(b) Who so stimulates or depresses a horse, or

(c) Who knowingly enters any horse in any race within a period of 24 hours after any drug has been administered to such horse for the purpose of increasing or retarding the speed of such horse, is punishable by a fine not exceeding five thousand dollars ($5,000), by imprisonment in the state prison not exceeding two years or in a county jail not exceeding one year, or by both such fine and imprisonment, or

(d) Who willfully or unjustifiably enters or races any horse in any running or trotting race under any name or designation other than the name or designation assigned to such horse by and registered with the Jockey Club or the United States Trotting Association or who willfully sets on foot, instigates, engages in or in any way furthers any act by which any horse is entered or raced in any running or trotting race under any name or designation other than the name or designation duly assigned by and registered with the Jockey Club or the United States Trotting Association is guilty of a felony and punishable by imprisonment in the state prison for a period not exceeding five years or by a fine not exceeding five thousand dollars ($5,000) or by both fine and imprisonment.

The term "drug" includes all substances recognized as having the power of stimulating or depressing the central nervous system, respiration, or blood pressure of an animal, such as narcotics, hypnotics, benzedrine or its derivatives, but shall not include recognized vitamins or supplemental feeds approved by the veterinarian representing the California Racing Board.

P.C. 337g—*Drugs within race track.* The possession, transport or use of any local anaesthetic of the cocaine group, including but not limited to natural or synthetic drugs of this group, such as Allocaine, Apothesine, Alypine, Benzyl Carbinol, Butyn, Procaine, Nupercaine, Betaeucain, Novol or Anestubes, within the racing inclosure is prohibited, except upon a bona fide veterinarian's prescription with complete statement of uses and purposes of same on the container. A copy of such prescription shall be filed with the stewards, and such substances may be used only with approval of the stewards and under the supervision of the veterinarian representing the board.

P.C. 337h—*Drugs, administered to animals.* Any person who, except for medicinal purposes, administers any poison, drug, medicine, or other noxious substance, to any horse, stud, mule, ass, mare, horned cattle, neat cattle, gelding, colt, filly, dog, animals, or other livestock, entered or about to be entered in any race or upon any race course, or entered or about to be entered at or with any agricultural park, or association, race course, or corporation, or other exhibition for competition for prize, reward, purse, premium, stake, sweepstakes, or other reward, or who exposes any poison, drug, medicine, or noxious substance, with intent that it shall be taken, inhaled, swallowed, or otherwise received by any of these animals or other livestock, with intent to impede or affect its speed, endurance, sense, health, physical condition, or other character or quality, or who causes to be taken by or placed upon or in the body of any of these animals or other livestock, entered or about to be entered in any race or competition described in this section any sponge, wood, or foreign substance of any kind, with intent to impede or affect its speed, endurance, sense, health, or physical condition, is guilty of a misdemeanor.

LEGAL DISCUSSION

Each subdivision of 337 creates a separate offense.[6] Bookmaking and pool-selling are the prohibited acts most frequently encountered. Bookmaking is defined as the making of a betting book, a procedure that involves the taking and receiving of bets or wagers upon the results or purported results of a real or purported contest of skill, speed or power of endurance of horses, and the recording or registering of such bets or wagers whether real or purported. The term may also mean the keeping or occupying of any room, building or automobile wherein books or papers or devices or paraphernalia are kept for the above purposes.

The word "engages," as used in the law just stated, does not require an extended or continuous participation in the forbidden activity. One instance of pool-selling or bookmaking, done with criminal intent, is a crime.

Pool-selling and bookmaking are both procedures by which betting is facilitated and the winners of the bets are or may be paid off. In pool-selling, a wagering pool is created, and shares or chances in or against that pool are sold or distributed. In bookmaking, as the term is used in the accusatory pleading, a person called a bookmaker receives bets or wagers made upon the results or purported results of a race, contest, trial or other contingency, and records or registers such bets either in a book of bets or on papers, cards, or other devices, his real or purported purpose in so doing being to facilitate the distribution of moneys to the winners of the bets.

Related offenses are keeping a place for bookmaking,[7] and keeping books or equipment.[8] The item of intent in these related offenses is contained in the words "the purpose" for which the plan or equipment is maintained. The defendant must definitely be connected with the place or equipment.[9] There is no need to show that a bet was placed on a race run.[10] The purpose can be shown by the utterance of words, the exchange of money, the finding of markers, attempts to destroy or conceal evidence, altered and unauthorized telephones, and failure to explain otherwise incriminating circumstances.[11]

The bookmaker confronts the betting public, but the "lay off man" and the operator of a "relay spot" are guilty of aiding and abetting the crime of bookmaking.[12] Parties who "make or accept a bet," "pretend to receive a bet," "receive a bet," "hold a bet," or "forward a bet" or a memorandum thereof violate P.C. 337a, subsections 3, 4, and 6.

APPLICABLE STATUTES—TOUTING

P.C. 337.1—*Tout; definition; guilt.* Any person, who knowingly and designedly by false representation attempts to, or does persuade, procure or cause another person to wager on a horse in race to be run in this state or elsewhere, and upon which money is wagered in this state, and who asks or demands compensation as a reward for information or purported information given in such case is a tout and is guilty of touting.

P.C. 337.2—*Punishment.* Any person who is a tout, or who attempts or conspires to commit touting, is guilty of a misdemeanor and is punishable by a fine of not more than five hundred dollars ($500) or by imprisonment in the county jail for not more than six months, or by both such fine and imprisonment. For a second offense in this state, he shall be imprisoned.

P.C. 337.3—*False use of name of official, etc.; felony.* Any person who in the commission of touting falsely uses the name of any official of the California Horse Racing Board, its inspectors or attaches, or of any official of any race track association, or the names of any owner, trainer, jockey or other person licensed by the California Horse Racing Board as the source of any information or purported information is guilty of a felony and is punishable by a fine of not more than five thousand dollars ($5,000) or by imprisonment in the state prison for a term of not less than one nor more than five years, or by both such fine and imprisonment.

P.C. 337.4—*Tout obtaining more than $200.* Any person who in the commission of touting obtains money in excess of two hundred dollars ($200) may, in addition to being prosecuted for the violation of any provision of this chapter, be prosecuted for the violation of Section 487 of this code.

P.C. 337.5—*Exclusion from race track.* Any person who has been convicted of touting, and the record of whose conviction on such charge is on file in the office of the California Horse Racing Board or in the State Bureau of Criminal Identification and Investigation of the Federal Bureau of Investigation, or any person who has been ejected from any race track of this or any other state for touting or practices inimical to the public interest shall be excluded from all race tracks in this state. Any such person who refuses to leave such track when ordered to do so by inspectors of the California Horse Racing Board, or by any peace officer, or by an accredited attache of a race track or association is guilty of a misdemeanor.

P.C. 337.6—*Credentials, when may be revoked.* Any credential or license issued by the California Horse Racing Board to licensees, if used by the holder thereof for a purpose other than identification and in the performance of legitimate duties on a race track, shall be automatically revoked whether so used on or off a race track.

LEGAL DISCUSSION

Particular attention is directed to P.C. 337.7 and P.C. 337.8 (quoted previously in Chapter 9) involving the use of another person's Horse Racing Board Credential or license, or a forged credential or license for the purpose of touting. This is a felony, not a felony-misdemeanor; furthermore, if a person has previously been convicted of touting, the sentence involves mandatory "imprisonment."

ENFORCEMENT ASPECTS AND GENERAL SUMMARY

The investigation of gambling laws and bookmaking operations is usually done by a specialized police detail. There are certain departmental policies with which the police officer must be familiar. For example, a group of "little old ladies" who usually get together to play bridge for a few cents are technically in violation of the law. The church-sponsored bingo games and the fund-raising games played in private groups also are violations. Vice enforcement must be under the direction of the Chief of Police, and police officers must act accordingly.

One of the finest organizations that can assist an officer on horse racing operations is the Thoroughbred Racing Protective Bureau (T.R.P.B.). This private agency operates at all the large racetracks in the country and maintains affiliations in foreign countries; e.g., Tijuana, Mexico. Licensing of horse racing employees is done through the California Horse Racing Board, but national records on these employees are also maintained by T.R.P.B. All investigations that take place on a race track should be done with the assistance of this organization.

In off-track investigations the most frequent arrests occur in bookmaking operations. Most bookmakers operate from an "office." Depending on the size of the operation, this could be a shoe-shine stand, a coin-operated laundromat, or a rented room used for telephone calls. The most necessary evidence to be secured are the "betting markers." Betting marks are usually on paper, but many experienced bookmakers use chalk boards, magic slates, and grease pencils on smooth surfaces so that the incriminating information may be easily erased. A radio tuned in to a station which broadcasts race results, the telephone instrument as well as recording devices constitute possible evidence and are subject to seizure.

DISCUSSION QUESTIONS

1. What is a lottery?
2. Are card games a lottery?
3. Define a "thing of value."
4. Can slot machines be confiscated and destroyed?
5. Are pinball machines included under the slot machine prohibitive statutes?
6. Explain "touting."
7. Explain the elements of bookmaking (P.C. 337a).

NOTES

1People v. Rehm, 13 CA Supp 755; 57 P 2d 238.
  People v. Settles, 29 CA 2d Supp 781; 78 P 2d 274.
2People v. Cardas, 137 CA 2d Supp 788; 28 P 2d 99;
  People v. Carpenter, 141 CA 2d 884; 297 P 2d 498.

3People v. Phillin, 50 CA 2d 859; 123 P 2d 159.

4Reimer v. Munic. Court, 90 CA 2d 854; 204 P 2d 92.

5People v. Phillin, supra.

6People v. Plath, 166 C 227; 135 P 954;
People v. Smith, 113 CA 2d 416; 248 P 2d 444;
People v. Allen, 115 CA 2d 745; 252 P 2d 968;
People v. Cahn, 126 CA 2d 785; 273 P 2d 64;
People v. Cuda, 178 CA 2d 397; 3 CR 86.

7People v. Reche, 68 CA 2d 665; 157 P 2d 440;
People v. Goldstein, 139 CA 2d 146; 293 P 2d 495.

8People v. Smith, 35 CA 2d 73; 94 P 2d 633;
People v. Watkins, 126 CA 2d 199; 271 P 2d 641.

9People v. Rahalete, 28 CA 2d 480; 82 P 2d 707;
People v. Simon, 66 CA 2d 860; 153 P 2d 420;
People v. Foreman, 112 CA 2d 616; 246 P 2d 979.

10People v. Warrich, 86 CA 2d 900; 195 P 2d 552.

11See cases in footnotes #8 to 10, inclusive.

12People v. Oreck, 74 CA 2d 215; 168 P 2d 186;
People v. Allen, 113 CA 2d 593; 248 P 2d 474.

22

Civil Disorder

APPLICABLE STATUTES

P.C. 402—*Sightseeing at scene of disaster; impeding activities; disaster defined.* Every person who goes to the scene of a disaster, or stops at the scene of a disaster, for the purpose of viewing the scene or the activities of policemen, firemen, other emergency personnel, or military personnel coping with the disaster in the course of their duties during the time it is necessary for emergency vehicles or such personnel to be at the scene of the disaster or to be moving to or from the scene of the disaster for the purpose of protecting lives or property, unless it is part of the duties of such person's employment to view such scene or activities, and thereby impedes such policemen, firemen, emergency personnel or military personnel in the performance of their duties in coping with the disaster, is guilty of a misdemeanor.

P.C. 403—*Disturbance of public meetings, other than religious or political.* Every person who, without authority of law, willfully disturbs or breaks up any assembly or meeting, not unlawful in its character, is guilty of a misdemeanor.

288

P.C. 407—*Unlawful assembly.* Whenever two or more persons assemble together to do an unlawful act, and separate without doing or advancing toward it, or do a lawful act in a violent, boisterous, or tumultuous manner, such assembly is an unlawful assembly.

P.C. 409—Every person remaining present at the place of any riot, rout, or unlawful assembly, after the same has been lawfully warned to disperse, except public officers and persons assisting them in attempting to disperse the same, is guilty of a misdemeanor.

P.C. 727—*Arrest for failure to disperse.* If the persons assembled do not immediately disperse, such magistrates and officers must arrest them, and to that end may command the aid of all persons present or within the county.

P.C. 416—*Refusing to disperse upon lawful command.* If two or more persons assemble for the purpose of disturbing the public peace, or committing any unlawful act, and do not disperse on being desired or commanded so to do by a public officer, the persons so offending are severally guilty of a misdemeanor.

LEGAL DISCUSSION AND ENFORCEMENT ASPECTS

Section P.C. 403 safeguards religious meetings from harassment. Political meetings are likewise protected. This section empowers police action to protect Constitutional guarantes of freedom of religion and speech. The meeting must not be unlawful, and there must be a specific intent to disrupt the meeting. These two elements should be given police attention to assure proper presentation of the case.

It is interesting to note that "unlawful assembly" is in and of itself punishable. This also becomes an important vehicle for law enforcement action. The declaration regarding unlawful assembly is set forth as follows:

> Where any number of persons whether armed or not, are unlawfully or riotously assembled, the sheriff of the county and his deputies, the officials governing the town or city, or the judges of the justice courts and constables thereof, or any of them, must go among the persons assembled, or as near to them as possible, and command them in the name of the people of the State, immediately to disperse.[1]

It must be emphasized that prior to violation a formal dispersal order must have been given.

This law does not require that a formal command be given. The elements, however, require:

1. An assembly of two or more persons;

2. A purpose (specific intent) to disturb the public peace or commit an unlawful act;

3. A request or order to disperse that was not complied with.

Those liable for arrest under this section are only the *participants* in the unlawful assembly. The acts must be *unlawful* and do not include lawful acts done in a violent manner.

The authority of law enforcement officers to close an area is clear.

> Whenever a menace to the public health or safety is created by a calamity such as flood, storm, fire, earthquake, explosion, accident or other disaster, officers of the California Highway Patrol, police departments or sheriff's office may close the area where the menace exists for the duration thereof by means of ropes, markers or guards to any and all persons not authorized by such officer to enter or remain within the closed area. If such a calamity creates an immediate menace to the public health, the local health officers may close the area where the menace exists pursuant to the conditions which are set forth above in this section. Any person not authorized willfully entering the area or willfully remaining within the area after notice to evacuate shall be guilty of a misdemeanor.[2]

It should be noted that this section exempts authorized members of the press, radio, and television pursuant to Constitutional guarantees.

Before an arresting violation occurs, the dispersal order must be given. The form may be very general as long as it is a command to disperse, declares the assembly to be unlawful, and is made in the name of the people of the State.[3] An example of a dispersal order follows:

> I am officer (or Lt., etc.) John Doe of the (Local City) Police Department, a peace officer of the State of _____. I hereby declare this an unlawful assembly and, in the name of the people of the State of _____ command you to immediately disperse.

Thinking ahead to prosecution the diligent officer will repeat this command several times (usually three). He should make the command through a loudspeaker. In order to provide courtroom testimony an officer or tape recorder should be at the rear of the crowd. This evidence will prove that those arrested could reasonably be expected to have heard the dispersal order.

Under these conditions it then becomes the duty of citizens to disperse without further challenge to the authority of the peace officer.[4]

APPLICABLE STATUTES—ROUT

> P.C. 406—*"Rout" defined.* Whenever two or more persons, assembled and acting together, make any attempt or advance toward the commission

of an act which would be a riot if actually committed, such assembly is a rout. (In effect this is also definable as an attempted riot.)

P.C. 408—*Punishment of rout and unlawful assembly.* Every person who participates in any rout or unlawful assembly is guilty of a misdemeanor.

P.C. 404—*"Riot" defined.* Any use of force or violence, disturbing the public peace, or any threat to use such force or violence, if accompanied by immediate power of execution, by two or more persons acting together, and without authority of law, is a riot.

P.C. 404.6—Every person who with the intent to cause a riot does an act or engages in conduct which urges a riot, or urges others to commit acts of force or violence, or the burning or destroying of property, and at a time and place and under circumstances which produce a clear and present and immediate danger of acts of force or violence or the burning or destroying of property, is guilty of a misdemeanor.

P.C. 454—*Violation of arson statutes during and within area of state of insurrection, state of disaster or extreme emergency.* Every person who violates the provisions of Sections 447a, 449a, 449b, 449c or 450a during and within the area of a state of insurrection, a state of disaster or a state of extreme emergency as proclaimed by the Governor pursuant to Sections 143, 1575 or 1580, respectively, of the Military and Veterans Code, provided that such state of disaster or extreme emergency is proclaimed because of riot, is punishable by imprisonment in the state prison for not less than five years.

LEGAL DISCUSSION

Riot is punishable by a fine not exceeding one thousand dollars, or by imprisonment in a county jail not exceeding one year, or both (P.C. 405). The elements of riot require:

1. *Concerted action* (two or more persons)—There may be a plan for the action; however, there need not be previous agreement. As long as there is cooperative action for the unlawful purpose of using force or violence to disturb the peace, there is sufficient evidence for this element. Mere presence is not sufficient. Support, encouragement, or incitement should be shown.
2. *Force, violence or threats of*—To support this element actual physical force should be shown, i.e., clubs, stones and other potential weapons. Threats must have the apparent ability to be carried out, but they need not be completed or attempted to constitute the crime.
3. *Disturbance of the peace*—There must be sufficient proof of this

violation. Two persons who assault a third in a remote area would not be sufficient to term the violation prosecutable, although strictly it might be a legal violation.[5]

P.C. 404.6 prohibits any person (it does not require two or more) from exhorting others to riot, commit acts of violence, or burn or destroy property. If there is no open violence, no group assembled to attempt violence or some other unlawful act, and no group doing a lawful act violently, but there is conduct by one person urging resort to violence, this section may be applicable.

1. *Intent*: The intent of the actor is always a question of fact. There must be evidence of statements made or acts done for the purpose of causing a riot.

2. *Urging a Riot*: The conduct must be undertaken by one who acts by himself or with others to incite a riot, do violence, burn or destroy property. This conduct can be verbal, physical or a combination thereof. If the conduct is verbal alone, whether oral or written, the Constitutional freedom to speak freely, or to assemble freely, may be involved.

3. *Clear and Present Danger*: If the suspect engages in acts or conduct as described above, it must be done at a time and place that will indicate the clear and present danger of an act of force and violence, or the burning or destruction of property. If a speaker urges the use of force and violence, there must be a clear and present danger that force and violence will occur. Free speech and assembly are given considerable protection by the courts, and great latitude is allowed to speakers and writers to air their opinions, however distasteful.

ENFORCEMENT ASPECTS

A riot does not suddenly occur. It is usually the culmination of tension that has been developing in the community. It is essential that the police be trained to spot early manifestations of this tension so that appropriate remedial action may be taken in time. The only way for law enforcement personnel to handle a riot is to prevent it.

Once a riot has started, quick and effective action must be taken. This includes planning, mobilization and deployment of sufficient manpower, and procurement of equipment for the "show of force." Positive further action, when necessary, must be taken by trained and effective law enforcement personnel.

The variety of speech and conduct likely to be encountered by law enforcement officers is infinite. If time is available, we suggest that legal advice be obtained from the respective city or county prosecutors.

APPLICABLE STATUTES—RESISTING

P.C. 69—*Resisting executive officer.* Every person who attempts, by means of any threat or violence, to deter or prevent any executive officer from performing any duty imposed upon such officer by law, or who knowingly resists, by the use of force or violence, such officer, in the performance of his duty, is punishable by fine not exceeding five thousand dollars, or by imprisonment in the state prison not exceeding five years, or in a county jail not exceeding one year or by both such fine and imprisonment.

P.C. 148—*Resisting.* Every person who willfully resists, delays, or obstructs any public officer, in the discharge or attempt to discharge any duty of his office, when no other punishment is prescribed, is punishable by fine not exceeding one thousand dollars, or by imprisonment in a county jail not exceeding one year, or by both such fine and imprisonment.

LEGAL DISCUSSION AND ENFORCEMENT ASPECTS

The person arrested is not entitled to resist even if the arrest is unlawful. In fact:

If a person has knowledge, or by the exercise of reasonable care, should have knowledge, that he is being arrested by a peace officer, it is the duty of such person to refrain from using force or any weapon to resist such arrest.[6]

Law enforcement officers are included in both of these laws. For a felony, some type of force, violence, or serious threat is required. Under the misdemeanor section the degree of force or violence may be considerably less. It is discretionary in many cases and is ultimately decided by the prosecutor.

APPLICABLE STATUTES

P.C. 418—*Forcible entry and detainer.* Every person using or procuring, encouraging or assisting another to use, any force or violence in entering upon or detaining any lands or other possessions of another, except in the cases and in the manner allowed by law, is guilty of a misdemeanor.

P.C. 594—*Definition malicious mischief in general.* [Quoted in Chapter 11.]

V.C. 10853—*Malicious mischief to vehicle.* No person shall with intent to commit any malicious mischief, injury, or other crime, climb into or upon a vehicle whether it is in motion or at rest, nor shall any person attempt to manipulate any of the levers, starting mechanism, brakes, or other mechanism or device of a vehicle while the same is at rest and unattended.

P.C. 602—*Trespasses upon land enumerated: misdemeanor.* [Refer to Chapter 11.]

P.C. 602.5—*Unauthorized entry of property.* Every person other than a public officer or employee acting within the course and scope of his employment in performance of a duty imposed by law, who enters or remains in any noncommercial dwelling house, apartment, or other such place without consent of the owner, his agent, or the person in lawful possession thereof, is guilty of a misdemeanor.

P.C. 603—*Vandalism.* Every person other than a peace officer engaged in the performance of his duties as such who forcibly and without the consent of the owner, representative of the owner, lessee or representative of the lessee thereof, enters a dwelling house, cabin, or other building occupied or constructed for occupation by humans, and who damages, injures, or destroys any property of value in, around or appertaining to such dwelling house, cabin or other building, is guilty of a misdemeanor.

P.C. 650½—*Injuring person or property of another.* [Refer to Chapter 11.]

LEGAL DISCUSSION

P.C. 418 refers primarily to the forcible entry upon lands.

P.C. 602 and 602.5 cover a nonforcible entry. It is important, therefore, to show that there is no implied consent. In fact, the person should have been expressly notified that there was no consent. This also would cover "party crashers."

P.C. 603 refers to the forcible entry and damage to buildings and other private properties. This section differs from malicious mischief as that provision covers all types of property whereas 603 requires an entry of a building.

P.C. 650½ is often used as a "compromise plea" in the interests of justice by prosecuting and defense attorneys. A disturbance of the peace or possibly disorderly conduct may be "broken down."

Recent court interpretation has decreed that the phrase "outrage of public decency" as in P.C. 650½ violates the due process clause of the

Fourteenth Amendment in that it is unconstitutionally vague. The court held that the words "outrages public decency" taken together or individually did not, in the light of contemporary experience and by all judicial test, inform the defendants with sufficient particularity what kind of behavior is prohibited or required by the statute.[7]

All other portions of the statute besides the words "outrages public decency" are still valid and may be charged.

These statutes safeguard property. For successful prosecution it is advisable to have a victim. Frequently private citizen arrests are made by the victims.

The elements of intent and maliciousness, when applicable, should be noted. Property damaged or injured should be examined for conditions which might reflect on the corpus delicti.

The difference between the unlawful firing of a weapon in P.C. 415 (Disturbing the Peace) and 602k is that the act done on private property is covered in the latter section.

GENERAL POLICE ASPECTS AND CONSIDERATIONS

Many violations of these laws may be committed during civil demonstration, disorders, and mob actions. The enforcement of these requires great patience and tact on the part of law enforcement officers. Too often they have been "baited" into action. It must be kept in mind that the ends of justice and the good of society are of great concern to law enforcement.

If a group of persons are creating a violation of law at high noon outside a building, some officers will zealously proceed with arrests. However, police experiences have shown that the broiling hot sun and mere supervision of the group will serve society and justice. Demonstrators who do not get arrested and do not get publicity and attention soon grow physically and mentally weary of their role. As long as there is no danger to persons nor excessive damage to property, containment and control are more practical police methodology than is legal action.

For mass arrests to be made, no matter how legal and lawful, police techniques must be considered. In many recent instances mass arrests have created complete frustration and unworkability in our agencies and courts. Arresting teams must be used to avoid the necessity for many members of a police force to appear in court. The riots in the Watts area of Los Angeles in 1965 placed a great strain and subsequent case load on the court structure. Often the cost of prosecution is completely out of relation to the punishment imposed.

A protest march was recently announced by a group of students who planned to go from one area to another. Their line of march was through several small cities, two of which were Baldwin Park and El Monte. These cities required parade permits which had not even been sought. The law clearly was being violated. Strict interpretation and enforcement, however, was not the best answer. When the demonstrators reached the city limits, they were told that they were in violation of local ordinances but would be allowed to proceed providing there were no disturbances. The group marched on. The plans had been made to repeat the march each week; however, after the first march less than twenty persons appeared to participate in the second. All of this was due to the lack of interest and notoriety. As might be supposed, the marchers expected to be "arrested" or at least "stopped" or dispersed. All they had to show for their twenty-mile walk were tired feet. This physical and emotional discouragement did much to prevent future demonstrations of this nature. The police handling prevented manpower loss for arrest, booking and prosecution. The courts were not cluttered with relatively insignificant cases. Above all, justice was served, painlessly and effectively.

Therefore, it is strongly recommended that officers use discretion, common sense, and knowledge of the laws in determining the most suitable police action to initiate and follow.

DISCUSSION QUESTIONS

1. Explain the corpus delicti of unlawful assembly.
2. How is an assembly declared unlawful?
3. Explain the difference between rout and riot.
4. Give an example of a disaster.
5. Discuss the problems involved for law enforcement officers in handling civil disorders.
6. What violation is committed by a person who secretes himself in a garage without the homeowner's consent?

NOTES

[1]P.C. 726.
[2]P.C. 409.5.
[3]People v. Sklar, 111 CA 776; 292 P 1068.
[4]People v. Yuen, 32 CA 2d 151; 89 P 2d 438.
[5]Connel v. Clark, 88 CA 2d 941; 200 P 2d 26.
[6]P.C. 8342.
[7]In re Davis, 242 ACA 760.

23

Public Health

APPLICABLE STATUTES—NARCOTICS

H. & S. 11500. Except as otherwise provided in this division, every person who possesses any narcotic other than marijuana except upon the written prescription of a physician, dentist, podiatrist, or veterinarian licensed to practice in this State, shall be punished by imprisonment in the state prison for not less than two years nor more than 10 years, and shall not be eligible for release upon completion of sentence, or on parole, or on any other basis until he has served not less than two years in prison.

If such a person has been previously convicted once of any felony offense described in this division or has been previously convicted once of any offense under the laws of any other state or of the United States which if committed in this State would have been punishable as a felony offense described in this division, the previous conviction shall be charged in the indictment or information and if found to be true by the jury, upon a jury trial, or if found to be true by the court, upon a court trial, or is admitted by the defendant, he shall be imprisoned in the state prison for not less than five years nor more than 20 years, and shall not be eligible for release upon completion of sentence, or on parole, or on any other basis until he has served not less than five years in prison.

If such a person has been previously convicted two or more times of any felony offense described in this division or has been previously convicted two or more times of any offense under the laws of any other state or of the United States which if committed in this State would have been punishable as a felony offense described in this division, the previous convictions shall be charged in the indictment or information and if found to be true the jury, upon a jury trial, or if found to be true by the court, upon a court trial, or are admitted by the defendant, he shall be imprisoned in the state prison from 15 years to life, and shall not be eligible for release upon completion of sentence, or on parole, or on any other basis until he has served not less than 15 years in prison.

H. & S. 11500.5. Except as otherwise provided in this division, every person who possesses for sale any narcotic other than marijuana shall be punished by imprisonment in the state prison for not less than five years nor more than 15 years, and shall not be eligible for release upon completion of sentence, or on parole, or on any other basis until he has served not less than 2½ years in prison.

If such person has been previously once convicted of any felony offense described in this division or has been previously once convicted of any offense under the laws of any other state of the United States which if committed in this State would have been punishable as a felony offense described in this division, the previous conviction shall be charged in the indictment or information and if found to be true by the jury, upon a jury trial, or if found to be true by the court, upon a court trial, or is admitted by the defendant, he shall be imprisoned in the state prison for not less than 10 years, and shall not be eligible for release upon completion of sentence, or parole, or on any other basis until he has served not less than six years in prison.

If such a person has been previously two or more times convicted of any felony offense described in this division or has been previously two or more times convicted of any offense under the laws of any other state or of the United States which if committed in this State would have been punishable as a felony offense described in this division, the previous convictions shall be charged in the indictment or information and if found to be true by the jury, upon a jury trial, or if found to be true by the court, upon a court trial, or are admitted by the defendant, he shall be imprisoned in the state prison for not less than 15 years, and shall not be eligible for release upon completion of sentence, or on parole, or on any other basis until he has served not less than 15 years in prison.

H. & S. 11501. Except as otherwise provided in this division, every person who transports, imports into this State, sells, furnishes, administers or gives away, or offers to transport, import into this State, sell, furnish, administer, or give away, or attempts to import into this State, or transport any narcotic other than marijuana except upon the written prescription of a physician, dentist, podiatrist, or veterinarian licensed to practice in this

State shall be punished by imprisonment in the state prison from five years to life, and shall not be eligible for release upon completion of sentence, or on parole, or on any other basis until he has served not less than three years in prison.

If such a person has been previously convicted once of any felony offense described in this division, or has been previously convicted once of any offense under the laws of any other state or of the United States which if committed in this State would have been punishable as a felony offense described in this division, the previous conviction shall be charged in the indictment or information and if found to be true by the jury, upon a jury trial, or if found to be true by the court, upon a court trial, or is admitted by the defendant, he shall be imprisoned in a state prison from 10 years to life, and shall not be eligible for release upon completion of sentence, or on parole, or on any other basis until he has served not less than 10 years in prison.

If such a person has been previously convicted two or more times of any felony offense described in this division or has been previously convicted two or more times of any offense under the laws of any other state or of the United States which if committed in this State would have been punishable as a felony offense described in this division, the previous convictions shall be charged in the indictment or information and if found to be true by the jury, upon a jury trial, or if found to be true by the court, upon a court trial, or are admitted by the defendant, he shall be imprisoned in the state prison from 15 years to life, and shall not be eligible for release upon completion of sentence, or on any other basis until he has served not less than 15 years in prison.

H. & S. 11502. Every person of the age of 21 years or over who in any voluntary manner solicits, induces, encourages, or intimidates any minor with the intent that said minor shall knowingly violate, with respect to a narcotic other than marijuana, any provision of this chapter or Section 11721, or who hires, employs, or uses a minor to knowingly and unlawfully transport, carry, sell, give away, prepare for sale, or peddle any narcotic other than marijuana or who unlawfully sells, furnishes, administers, gives, or offers to sell, furnish, administer or give, any narcotic other than marijuana to a minor shall be punished by imprisonment in the state prison from 10 years to life, and shall not be eligible for release upon completion of sentence, or on parole, or on any other basis until he has served not less than five years in prison.

If such a person has been previously convicted once of any felony offense described in this division or has been previously convicted once of any offense under the laws of any other state or of the United States which if committed in this State would have been punishable as a felony offense described in this division, the previous conviction shall be charged in the indictment or information and if found to be true by the jury, upon a jury trial, or if found to be true by the court, upon a court trial, or is admitted by the defendant, he shall be imprisoned in the state prison from 10 years to life, and shall not be eligible for release upon completion of sentence, or on parole, or on any other basis until he has served not less than 10 years in prison.

If such a person has been previously convicted two or more times of any felony offense described in this division or has been previously convicted two or more times of any offense under the laws of any other state or of the United States which if committed in this State would have been punishable as a felony offense described in this division, the previous convictions shall be charged in the indictment or information and if found to be true by the jury, upon a jury trial, or if found to be true by the court, upon a court trial, or are admitted by the defendant, he shall be imprisoned in the state prison from 15 years to life and shall not be eligible for release upon completion of sentence, or on parole, or on any other basis until he has served not less than 15 years in prison.

H. & S. 11502.1. Every person under the age of 21 years who in any voluntary manner solicits, induces, encourages, or intimidates any minor with the intent that said minor shall knowingly violate any provision of this chapter or Section 11721, or who hires, employs, or uses a minor to knowingly and unlawfully transport, carry, sell, give away, prepare for sale or peddle any narcotic other than marijuana or who unlawfully sells, furnishes, administers, gives, or offers to sell, furnish, administer, or give, any narcotic other than marijuana to a minor shall be punished by imprisonment in the state prison not less than five years.

If such a person has been previously convicted of any felony offense described in this division or has been previously convicted of any offense under the laws of any state or of the United States which if committed in this State would have been punishable as a felony offense described in this division, the previous conviction shall be charged in the indictment or information and if found to be true by the jury, upon a jury trial, or if found to be true by the court, upon a court trial, or is admitted by the defendant, he shall be imprisoned in the state prison for not less than 10 years.

(This section is not intended to affect the jurisdiction of the juvenile court.)

H. & S. 11503. Every person who agrees, consents, or in any manner offers to unlawfully sell, furnish, transport, administer, or give any narcotic to any person, or offers, arranges, or negotiates to have any narcotic unlawfully sold, delivered, transported, furnished, administered, or given to any person and then sells, delivers, furnishes, transports, administers, or gives, or offers, arranges, or negotiates to have sold, delivered, transported, furnished, administered, or given to any person any other liquid, substance, or material in lieu of any narcotic shall be punished by imprisonment in the county jail for not more than one year, or in the state prison for not more than 10 years.

H. & S. 11504. As used in this article "felony offense" and offense "punishable as a felony" refer to an offense for which the law prescribes imprisonment in the state prison as either an alternative or the sole penalty, regardless of the sentence the particular defendant received.

LEGAL DISCUSSION

What is a narcotic? Although fundamental to this discussion, the answer is frequently unclear. The most specific definition for the law enforcement officer is found in Article 1, Section 11001 of the California Health and Safety Code. To qualify as a narcotic the substance must be enumerated thereunder. Without going into the technical, chemical definitions the following are narcotics:

1. Opium and its derivatives including:
   a. Morphine
   b. Heroin
   c. Codeine
2. Cocaine and cocoa derivatives
3. Marihuana (*cannabis sativa*)
4. Lophophora (peyote or mescal)

It should be pointed out that the Health and Safety Code increases the penalty for violations involving persons under 21 years of age and also the penalties for prior offenders.

As regards narcotic prescriptions the burden of proving the authorized possession of a narcotic is upon the defendant. In absence of proof that the defendant had a lawful prescription for the narcotics, it is a fair assumption that he had none.[1]

> "Sale," as used in this division, includes barter, exchange, or gift, or offer thereof, and each such transaction made by any person, whether as principal, proprietor, agent, servant, or employee.[2]
> "Transport," as used in this division, with reference to narcotics, includes "Conceal," "Convey," or "Carry."[3]
> The word "Induce" means to lead on; to influence; to prevail on; to move by persuasion or influence. The word "Encourage" means to give courage to; to inspire with courage, spirit or hope; to raise the confidence of; to animate; hearten.[4]

An essential element of the crime of offering to sell a narcotic is specific intent. The crime is complete when the defendant expresses his intent to sell a narcotic. No overt act is required for the crime of attempt; in fact, delivery is not an essential element.[5] Arrest and conviction are possible even if the substance is not a narcotic but is represented to be one.

Specific intent for possession, however, is not required. The corpus may be proven by circumstantial evidence. A person is "in possession" when a narcotic is under his dominion and control. This includes carrying the narcotic on his person or even in his presence and custody as long as it is easily and immediately accessible to the defendant. Of course, possession must be knowingly committed. In this regard the attempts to conceal a narcotic may be sufficient to prove the knowledge of the illegal nature of the contraband. Prior convictions may also be used to prove guilty knowledge.

Lawful possession may become unlawful under certain circumstances. Narcotics in the possession of medical personnel or by persons who have valid medical prescription are exempt. However, narcotics which are not used or authorized in connection with medical treatment would be unlawfully possessed as would possession by a third party of someone else's prescribed narcotics.[6]

APPLICABLE STATUTES—Marihuana

H. & S. 11530—*Marihuana.* Every person who plants, cultivates, harvests, dries, or processes any marijuana, or any part thereof, or who possesses any marijuana, except as otherwise provided by law, shall be punished by imprisonment in the county jail for not exceeding one year or imprisonment in the state prison for not less than one year nor more than 10 years.

If such person has been previously convicted once of any felony offense described in this division or has been previously convicted once of any offense under the laws of any other state or of the United States which if committed in this State would have been punishable as a felony offense described in this division, the previous conviction shall be charged in the indictment or information and if found to be true by the jury, upon a jury trial, or if found to be true by the court, upon a court trial, or is admitted by the defendant, he shall be imprisoned in the state prison for not less than two years nor more than 20 years, and shall not be eligible for release upon completion of sentence, or on parole, or on any other basis until he has served not less than two years in prison.

If such person has been previously convicted two or more times of any felony offense described in this division or has been previously convicted two or more times of any offense under the laws of any other state or of the United States which if committed in this State would have been punishable as a felony offense described in this division, the previous convictions shall be charged in the indictment or information and if found to be true by the jury, upon a jury trial, or if found to be true by the court, upon a court trial, or are admitted by the defendant, he shall be imprisoned in the state prison for five years to life and shall not be eligible for release upon completion of sentence, or on parole or on any other basis until he has served not less than five years in prison.

H. & S. 11530.5. Every person who possesses for sale any marijuana except as otherwise provided by law shall be punished by imprisonment in the state prison for not less than two years nor more than 10 years, and shall not be eligible for release upon completion of sentence, or on parole, or on any other basis until he has served not less than two years in prison.

If such a person has been previously once convicted of any felony offense described in this division or has been previously once convicted of any offense under the laws of any other state or of the United States which if committed in this State would have been punishable as a felony offense described in this division, the previous conviction shall be charged in the indictment or information and if found to be true by the jury, upon a jury trial, or if found to be true by the court, upon a court trial, or is admitted by the defendant, he shall be imprisoned in the state prison for not less than five years nor more than 15 years, and shall not be eligible for release upon completion of sentence, or parole, or any other basis until he has served not less than three years in prison.

If such a person has been previously two or more times convicted of any felony offense described in this division or has been previously two or more times convicted of any offense under the laws of any other state or of the United States which if committed in this State would have been punishable as a felony offense described in this division, the previous convictions shall be charged in the indictment or information and if found to be true by the jury, upon a jury trial, or if found to be true by the court, upon a court trial, or are admitted by the defendant, he shall be imprisoned in the state prison from 10 years to life, and shall not be eligible for release upon completion of sentence, or on parole, or on any other basis until he has served not less than six years in prison.

H. & S. 11531. Every person who transports, imports into this State, sells, furnishes, administers or gives away, or offers to transport, import into this State, sell, furnish, administer, or give away, or attempts to import into the State or transport any marijuana shall be punished by imprisonment in the state prison from five years to life and shall not be eligible for release upon completion of sentence, or on parole, or on any other basis until he has served not less than three years.

If such a person has been previously convicted once of any felony offense described in this division or has been previously convicted once of any offense under the laws of any other state or of the United States which if committed in this State would have been punishable as a felony offense described in this division, the previous conviction shall be charged in the indictment or information and if found to be true by the jury, upon a jury trial, or if found to be true by the court, upon a court trial, or is admitted by the defendant, he shall be imprisoned in a state prison from five years to life, and shall not be eligible for release upon completion of sentence, or on parole, or on any other basis until he has served not less than five years in prison.

If such a person has been previously convicted two or more times of any felony offense described in this division or has been previously convicted two or more times of any offense under the laws of any other state or of the United States which if committed in this State would have been punishable as a felony offense described in this division, the previous convictions shall be charged in the indictment or information and if found to be true by the jury, upon a jury trial, or if found to be true by the court, upon a court trial, or are admitted by the defendant, he shall be imprisoned in a state prison from 10 years to life and shall not be eligible for release upon completion of sentence, or on parole, or on any other basis until he has served not less than 10 years in prison.

H. & S. 11532. Every person of the age of 21 years or over who hires, employs, or uses a minor in unlawfully transporting, carrying, selling, giving away, preparing for sale or peddling any marijuana, or who unlawfully sells, furnishes, administers, gives, or offers to sell, furnish, administer, or give, any marijuana to a minor, or who induces a minor to use marijuana in violation of law, is guilty of a felony punishable by imprisonment in the state prison from 10 years to life and shall not be eligible for release upon completion of sentence, or on parole, or on any other basis until he has served not less than five years in prison.

If such a person has been previously convicted once of any felony offense described in this division or has been previously convicted once of any offense under the laws of any other state or of the United States which if committed in this State would have been punishable as a felony offense described in this division, the previous conviction shall be charged in the indictment or information and if found to be true by the jury, upon a jury trial, or if found to be true by the court, upon a court trial, or is admitted by the defendant, he shall be imprisoned in the state prison from 10 years to life, and shall not be eligible for release upon completion of sentence, or on parole, or on any other basis until he has served not less than 10 years in prison.

If such a person has been previously convicted two or more times of any felony offense described in this division or has been previously convicted two or more times of any offense under the laws of any other state or of the United States which if committed in this State would have been punishable as a felony offense described in this division, the previous convictions shall be charged in the indictment or information and if found to be true by the jury, upon a jury trial, or if found to be true by the court, upon a court trial, or are admitted by the defendant, he shall be imprisoned in the state prison from 15 years to life and shall not be eligible for release upon completion of sentence, or on parole, or on any other basis until he has served not less than 15 years in prison.

H. & S. 11533. As used in this article "felony offense" and offense "punishable as a felony" refer to an offense for which the law prescribes imprisonment in the state prison as either an alternative or the sole penalty, regardless of the sentence the particular defendant received.

H. & S. 11540—*Lophophora.* Every person who plants, cultivates, harvests, dries, or processes any plant of the genus Lophophora, also known as peyote, or any part thereof shall be punished by imprisonment in the county jail for not more than one year, or in the state prison for not more than 10 years.

If such a person has been previously convicted of any offense described in this division or has been previously convicted of any offense under the laws of any other state or of the United States which if committed in this State would have been punishable as an offense described in this division, the previous conviction shall be charged in the indictment or information and if found to be true by the jury, upon a jury trial, or if found to be true by the court, upon a court trial, or is admitted by the defendant, he shall be imprisoned in the state prison for not less than two years nor more than 20 years.

H. & S. 11555—*Narcotic pipes and resorts.* It is unlawful to possess an opium pipe or any device, contrivance, instrument or paraphernalia used for unlawfully injecting or smoking a narcotic.

H. & S. 11556. It is unlawful to visit or to be in any room or place where any narcotics are being unlawfully smoked or used with knowledge that such activity is occurring.

H. & S. 11557. Every person who opens or maintains any place for the purpose of unlawfully selling, giving away or using any narcotic shall be punished by imprisonment in the county jail for not more than one year or in the state prison for not more than 10 years.

LEGAL DISCUSSION

Legislators will be receiving more and more pressure from certain social groups who advocate the legalization of marihuana. There are many arguments as to how injurious to health the smoking of marihuana is. The American Medical Association has publicly announced its findings against the legalization of marihuana and further indicates that it is injurious to health.

One of the legal arguments involves the fact that many jurists would not sentence a marihuana smoker to state prison. Accordingly, even if penalties were increased, it is felt the courts would probably place more defendants on probation instead of giving them a more severe sentence.

Voluntary commitment for narcotic addicts is legally possible. However, it should be noted that the number of voluntary commitments is very small.

APPLICABLE STATUTES—DANGEROUS DRUGS

H. & S. 11170.

    1. No person shall obtain or attempt to obtain narcotics, or procure

or attempt to procure the administration of or prescription for narcotics, (a) by fraud, deceit, misrepresentation, or subterfuge; or (b) by concealment of a material fact.

2. No person shall make a false statement in any prescription, order, report or record required by this division.

3. No person shall, for the purpose of obtaining narcotics, falsely assume the title of, or represent himself to be, a manufacturer, wholesaler, pharmacist, physician, dentist, veterinarian or other authorized person.

4. No person shall affix any false or forged label to a package or receptacle containing narcotics.

H. & S. 11170.5. No person shall, in connection with the prescribing, furnishing, administering or dispensing of a narcotic, give a false name or address.

H. & S. 11170.7. A violation of sections 11170 and 11170.5 is punishable by imprisonment in a county jail for not less than six months or in the state prison for not more than six years.

H. & S. 11710—*Immunity of peace officers.* All duly authorized peace officers, while investigating violations of this division in performance of their official duties, and any person working under their immediate direction, supervision or instruction, are immune from prosecution under this division.

H. & S. 11715—*Forgeries.* Every person who forges or alters a prescription or who issues or utters an altered prescription, or who issues or utters a prescription bearing a forged or fictitious signature for any narcotic, or who obtains any narcotic by any forged, fictitious, or altered prescription, or who has in possession any narcotic secured by such forged, fictitious, or altered prescription, shall for the first offense be punished by imprisonment in the county jail for not less than six months nor more than one year, or in the state prison for not more than six years, and for each subsequent offense shall be imprisoned in the state prison for not more than 10 years.

H. & S. 23105—*Narcotics.* It is unlawful for any person who is addicted to the use, or under the influence of narcotic drugs or amphetamine or any derivative thereof to drive a vehicle upon any highway. Any person convicted under this section is guilty of a felony and upon conviction thereof shall be punished by imprisonment in the state prison for not less than one year nor more than five years or in the county jail for not less than 90 days nor more than one year or by a fine of not less than two hundred dollars ($200) nor more than five thousand dollars ($5,000) or by both such fine and imprisonment.

H. & S. 23106—*Non-narcotic drugs.* It is unlawful for any person under the influence of any drug, other than a narcotic or amphetamine or any derivative thereof, to a degree which renders him incapable of safely driving a vehicle, to drive a vehicle upon any highway. Any person convicted under this section is guilty of a misdemeanor and shall be punished by imprisonment in the county jail not to exceed one year or by a fine of not to exceed five hundred dollars ($500) or both.

P.C. 222. Every person guilty of administering to another any chloroform, ether, laudanum, narcotic, anaesthetic, or intoxicating agent, with intent thereby to enable or assist himself or any other person to commit a felony, is guilty of a felony.

V.C. 23101—*Driving under influence of drugs—felony.* Refer to Chapter 20.

V.C. 23102—*Driving under influence of drugs—misdemeanor.* Refer to Chapter 20.

LEGAL DISCUSSION

Under section 11901 restricted dangerous drugs are defined as:

1. Hypnotic drugs (barbiturates)
2. Amphetamines (stimulants)
3. Lysergic acid (LSD)

Possession of dangerous drugs by anyone except a licensed physician, dentist, podiatrist, veterinarian, or pharmacist is a felony.

Selling, furnishing, administering, giving, offering, or transporting of dangerous drugs to anyone is a felony but may be deemed a misdemeanor by sentence.[7]

In a case involving minors the crime is and must remain a felony.

The term "intoxicating agent" includes any drug, substance or compound which, when introduced into the human system, produces a serious disturbance of the physical and mental equilibrium by causing sleep, stupor, unconsciousness or semi-consciousness together with impairment of the power of self-control.[8]

ENFORCEMENT ASPECTS

Narcotic officers have a most difficult task of gathering legally significant evidence which will lead to convictions. Hence, it is mandatory that officers working these assignments be well schooled in search and seizure; entrapment; self-incrimination; and laws granting immunity. Generally these investigations are performed by specialists.

The most frequent areas involving narcotics and drugs that police officers come in contact with routinely also involve automobiles as a rule.

An important difference between forgery (P.C. 470) and the narcotic prescription law is the issue of specific intent. This is required for forgery but not for the narcotic violation. Not only is it not necessary to prove the intent to defraud but knowledge on the part of the defendant that the prescription was forged, fictitious or altered need not be shown. This differentiates it from the act of uttering in straight forgery crimes.

In addition to the foregoing, remember that P.C. 381 makes it a misdemeanor for any person to willfully ingest, inhale, or breathe the fumes of toluene and similar substances with intent to become intoxicated. "Glue sniffing" under section 647 (Disorderly Conduct) also allows for arrest of persons under the influence of toluene or other drugs.

ENFORCEMENT ASPECTS AND GENERAL SUMMARY

The police officer must realize that many crimes are reported and prosecuted that involve narcotics, and yet the charge is usually some other crime, e.g., burglary. Narcotic addicts commit many crimes against property and sometimes persons in order to secure sufficient money to support their habit. The narcotic craving is such that the suspect will commit many major crimes which then go on the police blotter as the substantive offense rather than a narcotic offense.

Usually narcotic enforcement officers are specialized by assignments and require additional training. In California very close liaison should be maintained with the California Department of Justice, the Bureau of Narcotic Enforcement, and the Federal Narcotic Enforcement Bureau. Pharmacists and lab technicians are available through the state agency. The federal agency is usually concerned with entry of narcotics into the country or over state boundaries.

Inasmuch as there are in narcotics, as in vice, no "victims," a great deal of undercover work is usually required. Much information may be obtained through intelligence units within law enforcement agencies. Frequently there is an overlapping of activities among organized crime, vice, and narcotics. Violations of this type usually are not restricted to one law enforcement agency's jurisdiction but extend to many jurisdictions.

DISCUSSION QUESTIONS

1. What is a narcotic?
2. Is the gift of narcotics an illegal act?

3. List three narcotic derivatives of opium.

4. Explain the differences between misdemeanor and felony in marihuana violations.

5. Dangerous drugs are in three categories; name them.

6. Discuss the sections applicable to glue sniffing.

7. Why are the "Drunk Driving" sections under the California Vehicle Code referred to in this chapter?

NOTES

[1] People v. Bill, 140 CA 389; 35 P 2d 645.
[2] P.C. 11008.
[3] H. & S. Sec. 11012.
[4] People v. Drake, 151 CA 2d 28; 310 P 2d 997.
[5] People v. Blake, 179 CA 2d 246; 3 CR 749.
[6] People v. Ard, 25 CA 2d 630; 78 P 2d 254.
[7] P.C. 11910.
[8] People v. Cline, 138 CA 184; 31 P 2d 1095.

Subject Index

Index of Codes